TABLE OF CONTENTS

FOREWORD by PH Mark Ivy

INTRODUCTION

1 ETHICS OF HUNTING
THE ANTI-HUNTING ATTITUDE — 1/1
WHY I HUNT, AND MUST — 1/3
    Rules of Fair Chase — 1/5

2 THE GOLDEN AGE
LORD RANDOLPH CHURCHILL, 1892 — 2/1
THEODORE ROOSEVELT, 1909 — 2/1

3 PLANNING & PRICING
a few terms to know — 3/1
choosing your game and hunting area — 3/5
SOUTH AFRICA or TANZANIA? — 3/7
    South Africa — 3/7
    Tanzania — 3/9
    go to a hunters' convention — 3/12
IMPORTANT QUESTIONS TO ASK — 3/13
    questions for the agent — 3/13
    questions for the outfitter — 3/14
VARIOUS TIPS — 3/15
PRICE NEGOTIATIONS — 3/15
    what is *not* included — 3/16
THE SAFARI CONTRACT — 3/17
GET INTO *SHAPE!* — 3/18
    typical American hunter shortcomings — 3/18
DOCUMENTS — 3/19
BUFFALO HUNT COST OVERVIEW — 3/21
PLAINS GAME HUNT COST — 3/22

4 INSURANCE & HEALTH

trip/baggage insurance	4/1
health insurance	4/2
HEALTH	4/3
get a dental check-up before you go!	4/3
vaccinations	4/3
malaria	4/4
trypanosomiasis (sleeping sickness, *tyrps*)	4/5
yellow fever	4/5
schistosomiasis (bilharzia, schisto)	4/5
diarrhea	4/5
dysentery (diarrhea with blood/mucus in it)	4/6
get this $6 book!	4/6
final comments on prescription drugs	4/7
prescription eyeglasses/contacts	4/7
GSW blood clot powder (www.quikclot.com)	4/7
DISCLAIMER	4/7

5 TRANSPORTATION

BOOKING YOUR FLIGHT	5/1
Economy, Business, or First Class?	5/1
don't rely on your airline miles for Africa!	5/2
Internet vs. a travel agent	5/2
FLYING TO SOUTH AFRICA	5/3
European layover in comfort	5/6
FLYING TO TANZANIA	5/7
PRE-FLIGHT GOVT. PAPERWORK	5/8
the US Customs 4457 gun form	5/8
Dutch transit license for your rifles	5/8
visas	5/9
TRAVEL DOCUMENT FOLDER	5/10
AT THE AIRPORT	5/11
security tips	5/12
tips for comfort in Economy Class	5/12
are your checked bags *onboard*?	5/14
MY AFRICAN TRAVEL EXPERIENCES	5/15
Tanzania	5/15
South Africa	5/17
GROUND TRANSPORTATION	5/18
South Africa	5/18
Tanzania	5/19
GOING HOME	5/20
packing for the airport	5/20

SAFARI DREAMS

A Practical Guide To Your Hunt In Africa

by

Kenneth W. Royce

Published by

JAVELIN PRESS
c/o P.O. Box 31D, Ignacio, Colorado. (81137-0031)
(Without any 4 USC §§ 105-110 *"Federal area"* or *"State."*)
www.javelinpress.com

Safari Dreams **by Kenneth W. Royce**
Common Law Copyright 2005-2007 by Javelin Press.
With explicit reservation of all Common Law Rights without prejudice.
Sold for academic study and informational purposes only.

Read the following disclaimer very carefully and thoroughly!

Firearms are potentially dangerous and must be handled responsibly by individual trainees and shooters alike. The technical information presented herein on firearms use and alteration, ammunition handloading and loading, training, and shooting inevitably reflects the Author's beliefs and experience with particular firearms and training techniques under specific circumstances that the reader (hereafter "You") cannot duplicate exactly. This book is not intended to serve as a replacement for professional gunsmithing by or instruction under experienced, competent, qualified personnel. All information herein is presumed accurate, typos aside.

All the loads listed in this book were safe in the particular firearms that they were tried with the unique lot of components that were used and under unique conditions that existed at the exact instant they were fired. Every load must be carefully and systematically worked up by the shooter using his or her own firearm. The Author, Publisher, and anybody else connected with this book (hereafter "We") disclaim ALL liability for your handloads and firearms handling.

Some of the products (or combination thereof) discussed in this book may not currently (or in the future) be legal for possession, sale, or interstate transportation in certain jurisdictions. Therefore, You have the responsibility to consult with local law enforcement. We do not encourage or endorse You to break any laws or experiment with any activities of a criminal nature.

This book's information is presented *for academic study only* and should be approached with great caution. **We disclaim ALL liability, injuries, or damages from the use or misuse, directly or indirectly, of any information herein.**

No part of this book may be reproduced or transmitted in any form or by any means, electronic, mechanical, or yet to be invented, including, but not limited to, photocopying, recording, or by any information storage and retrieval system, without express written permission from the Publisher.

The sole exception to this Copyright limitation is the privilege, hereby granted by the Publisher, to incorporate brief quotations of no more than 1,000 words in critical articles, so long as these two conditions are met: ❶ A copy of the work in which *Safari Dreams* is quoted is sent to the Publisher within 30 days of its publication, and ❷ The following reference is given (in at least eight point type) at the bottom of the first page in which said privileged quotation begins:

From *Safari Dreams* by Kenneth W. Royce (Common Law Copyright 2005-2007, Javelin Press. www.javelinpress.com).

Sale of this book without a front cover may be unauthorized. If stripped, it may have been reported to the Publisher as *"unsold or destroyed"* and neither the Author nor the Publisher may have received payment for it.

Safari Dreams January, 2008

**Printed in the united states of America,
without any 4 USC §§ 105-110 *"Federal area"* or *"State."***

10 9 8 7 6 5 4 3 2 1   /   15 14 13 12 11 10 09 08

ISBN 1-888766-10-7

ACKNOWLEDGMENTS

Many people advised and encouraged me on my first African safari, such as Rich Wyatt and Tom Russell. Thanks also to you regular attendees of the Theodore Roosevelt Reunion weekend at the NRA Whittington Center in Raton, New Mexico. Two years of hearing your African stories finally spurred me into action!

I wrote much of *Safari Dreams* during several road trips, and am very grateful to my hosts Mark & Beverly, and Jared for their friendship and untiring hospitality.

Brian Sheetz of the NRA's *American Rifleman* did a fantastic job in proofing, and was most helpful with his many suggestions. *Safari Dreams* is a much better book for it.

Great thanks are due to all the great folks at Zuka Safaris. PH Craig Lang and camp manager Jackson were superb, as was the entire staff at Mahenge South. I couldn't have asked for better service from them all for my first safari.

Finally, my deep gratitude to PH Mark Ivy and his family, and staff of Ivy Safaris for my 40 excellent days of plains game hunting in South Africa, and for graciously contributing his Foreword and numerous comments. I learned a lot about hunting and Africa from Mark, which I hope shines through.

DEDICATION

John "Jeff" Dean Cooper
1920—2006
Lt. Colonel USMC, Ret.
Founder, American Pistol Institute (Gunsite)
Author of numerous books and articles

Colonel Cooper passed away in September 2006, after a long and debilitating affliction. His contributions to defensive shooting and ethical hunting are legion. His decades of essays and comments about Africa not only "set the hook" for me, but regularly tugged on the line. Without his influence (beginning with a personal correspondence in 1987), I certainly wouldn't have hunted Africa as soon as I did, and maybe never at all.

Thank you, Jeff.

by Kenneth Royce (Boston T. Party)

You & The Police!   (revised for 2005)

The definitive guide to your rights and tactics during police confrontations. When can you *refuse* to answer questions or consent to searches?   Don't lose your liberty through ignorance! This 2005 edition covers the *USA PATRIOT Act* and much more.
  168 pp. softcover (2005) $16 + $5 s&h (cash, please)

Bulletproof Privacy
How to Live Hidden, Happy, and Free!

Explains precisely how to lay low and be left alone by the snoops, government agents and bureaucrats. Boston shares many of his own unique methods. Now in its 10th printing!
  160 pp. softcover (1997) $16 + $5 s&h (cash, please)

Hologram of Liberty
The Constitution's Shocking Alliance with Big Government

The Convention of 1787 was the most brilliant and subtle *coup d'état* in history. The nationalist framers *designed* a strong government, guaranteed through purposely ambiguous verbiage. Many readers say this is Boston's best book. A jaw-dropper.
  262 pp. softcover (1997) $20 + $5 s&h (cash, please)

Boston on Surviving Y2K
And Other Lovely Disasters

Even though Y2K was Y2¿Qué? this title remains highly useful for all preparedness planning. **Now on sale for 50% off!**   (It's the same book as The Military Book Club's *Surviving Doomsday*.)
  352 pp. softcover (1998) only $11 + $5 s&h (cash, please)

Boston's Gun Bible   (new text for 2006)

A rousing how-to/*why*-to on our modern gun ownership. Firearms are *"liberty's teeth"* and it's time we remembered it. No other general gun book is more thorough or useful! Indispensable!
  848 pp. softcover (2002-2006) $33 + $6 s&h (cash, please)

Molôn Labé!   (a novel)

If you liked *Unintended Consequences* by John Ross and Ayn Rand's *Atlas Shrugged*, then Boston's novel will be a favorite. It dramatically outlines an innovative recipe for Liberty which could actually work! A thinking book for people of action; an action book for people of thought. It's getting people moving to Wyoming!
  454 pp. softcover (2004) $27 + $6 s&h (cash, please)
  limited edition hardcover $44 + $6 (while supplies last)

Safari Dreams   (new for 2008!)
A Practical Guide To Your Hunt In Africa

Possibly the most useful "one book" for making your first safari. Thoroughly covers: rifles, calibers, bullets, insurance, health, packing and planning, trip prep, airlines, choosing your PH, shot placement, and being in the bush. Don't go to Africa without it!
  352 pp. softcover, 100 color photos (Jan 2008) $30 + $5

www.javelinpress.com
www.freestatewyoming.org

6	**2x1 HUNTS**	
	HUNT ALONE OR WITH OTHERS?	6/1
7	**PACKING**	
	MONEY	7/1
	PACKING FOR AIR TRAVEL	7/3
	check-through bags	7/3
	carry-on luggage and gear	7/5
	CLOTHES	7/7
	footwear (three pairs are all you need)	7/7
	field clothes	7/8
	town outfit and something for the pool/beach	7/9
	PACKING FOR THE FIELD	7/10
	misc. stuff to take for the field	7/10
	misc. on-person field gear	7/13
	on your belt	7/13
	backpack left in truck	7/17
	MISC. CAMP STUFF	7/18
	gifts	7/18
	GOING HOME	7/19
8	**PLAINS GAME CALIBERS & RIFLES**	
	BULLETS	8/1
	Bullet Behavior Classification (BBC)	8/4
	7mm (.284)	8/6
	7-08 and 7x57 Mauser (140gr/2900fps)	8/7
	.280 Remington (160gr/2800fps)	8/7
	.284 Winchester (160gr/2850fps)	8/7
	7mm Rem, WSM, SAUM mags (160gr/2950fps)	8/7
	.30	8/8
	.308 (200gr/2450fps) or .30-06 (200gr/2600fps)	8/8
	.30-06 Ackley Improved (200gr/2700fps)	8/8
	.300 WSM and SAUM (200gr/2800fps)	8/9
	.300 H&H Mag (200gr/2850fps)	8/10
	.300 Win Mag (180gr/3120fps, 220/2750)	8/10
	.308 Norma Mag (180gr/3120fps, 220/2800)	8/10
	.300 Weatherby Mag (200gr/3100fps, 220/2900)	8/10
	thoughts on .30 *über* mags	8/10
	8mm (.323)	8/11
	8x57S (170/2600fps, 220gr/2300fps)	8/11
	8mm-06 (220gr/2500fps)	8/11

8x68S (220gr/2800fps)	8/11
.325 WSM (180/3050, 200/2950, 220/2800)	8/12
8mm Rem Mag (220gr/2900fps)	8/13
.338	8/13
.338 Federal (210gr/2500fps)	8/14
.338-06 (200gr/2700fps, 250/2500)	8/14
.338 Win (225gr/2850fps, 250/2700, 275/2450)	8/15
.340 Weatherby (250gr/2850fps)	8/15
.330 Dakota (250gr/2900fps)	8/15
.338 Lapua (250gr/3150fps)	8/15
.338 RUM (250gr/3150fps)	8/15
.338 Excalibur (250gr/3200fps)	8/15
.358 (9mm)	8/16
.358 Win (200/2500, 225/2500, 250/2400)	8/17
.35 Whelen (180/2800, 225/2610, 250/2500)	8/17
.350 Rem Mag (200/2675, 250/2475)	8/18
.358 Norma (125/3200, 225/3000, 275/2700)	8/18
.358 STA (225/3100, 275/2850)	8/18
9.3mm (.366)	8/19
9.3x62 (286gr/2400fps from 22", 300/2375)	8/19
9.3x64 (286/2650fps, 300/2550)	8/20
9.3x66 SAKO (286/2750fps, 300/2650)	8/21
.375 H&H (270gr/2700fps, 300gr/2550fps)	8/21
.45-70 Marlin (325gr/2050fps, 350gr/1900fps)	8/21
BUT HOW TO COMPARE?	8/23
calculating RoyceKoV (plains game) index	8/24
the 100-400yd RoyceKoV Plains Game table	8/27
The Winners..	8/28
RELIABLE CALIBER MINIMUMS	8/29
200yd and 300yd winners for *all* plains game	8/30
African hunting reflections on the...	8/33
Royce wildcats	8/34
PLAINS GAME RIFLES	8/35
bolt actions	8/35
lever actions	8/35
pumps	8/36
scopes	8/36
rifle misc.	8/38

9   BUFFALO BULLETS, CALIBERS, RIFLES

CALIBER vs. CALIBER	9/1
.375 H&H vs. .416 (Rigby and Remington)	9/3
.416 vs. .458	9/5

what's the deal with belted cases?	9/6
.375 calibers	9/7
.416 calibers	9/9
.458 calibers	9/12
.475 calibers	9/16
.500 calibers (.505 and .510)	9/17
the RoyceKoV (dangerous game)	9/18
PROPER BULLETS	9/20
solids	9/21
soft-nose	9/22
OTHER THAN BOLT-ACTIONS	9/26
BOLT-ACTION BUFFALO RIFLES	9/27
your viable choices of DG rifles	9/28
recoil	9/30
barrel length (22"-24")	9/31
iron sights	9/32
scopes	9/32
stocks	9/32
trigger	9/32
SO, WHAT *DID* I TAKE TO AFRICA?	9/33
my M70's modifications	9/34
scoping the Win M70 Classic Super Express	9/35
AT THE RANGE	9/39
A Few Words about Cast Steel Rifle Receivers	9/42
(by Kevin McClung, Senior Engineer, MD Labs)	

10 SAFE GUN HANDLING

THE FOUR BASIC SAFETY RULES	10/1
GUN SAFETY AND CHILDREN	10/3
CONDITION OF WEAPON	10/4
MALFUNCTIONS	10/5

11 SOUTH AFRICA PEOPLE & CUSTOMS

understanding South African English	11/1
South African races	11/3
South African etiquette	11/3
food	11/6
prices	11/6
communication	11/7
political hot potatoes	11/7
OUTLOOK FOR SOUTH AFRICA	11/10
METRIC CONVERSIONS	11/10

12 ANIMALS

names for the sexes ("buck" and "doe" not used)	12/1
female animals without/with horns; species herding?	12/1
savanna/woodland diet of animals	12/2
pachyderms	12/2
buffalo	12/3
carnivores	12/4
spiral horned antelope	12/7
ringed horned antelope	12/9
gnu (wildebeest)	12/13
hartebeest	12/13
misc. antelopes	12/14
pig	12/15
misc. mammals	12/16
birds	12/19
venomous bushveld snakes	12/20

13 CAMP LIFE

SOUTH AFRICAN GAME RANCH	13/1
TANZANIAN TENT CAMP	13/5
OTHER PHs & RANCHES	13/8
TAKE YOUR RIFLE *EVERYWHERE!*	13/9
YOU & THE CAMP STAFF	13/10
EATING WHAT YOU KILL	13/11
DRINKING	13/12
THE SOUNDS OF AFRICA	13/12
READING	13/13
YOUR ATTITUDE	13/13

14 HUNTING

PRACTICING	14/1
YOU'VE ARRIVED IN CAMP!	14/4
THE CRAFT OF HUNTING	14/7
seeing game	14/8
hunting Cape buffalo	14/8
hunting plains game	14/9
stalking	14/9
target angles (be *choosy*)	14/11
"*Should I take this animal, or wait?*"	14/15
taking aim	14/18
the shot	14/18

the kill	14/25
photographing your animal	14/25
SKINNING	14/28

15 TIPPING

16 HOTELS & SHOPPING

HOTELS	16/1
SHOPPING	16/2
shopping in Dar	16/2
shopping in Zanzibar	16/4
HAGGLING WITH THE LOCALS	16/5

17 TROPHY COSTS

GETTING YOUR TROPHIES HOME	17/1
TAXIDERMY	17/2
in the USA	17/2
taxidermy in South Africa	17/3

18 PLANNING TIMELINE

19 PACKING CHECKLIST

20 FOR WOMEN ONLY

CLOTHING	20/1
CALIBERS & RIFLES	20/2
MISC. GEAR	20/4
MISC. CONSIDERATIONS	20/4

21 RESOURCES

BOOKS & VIDEOS	21/1

FOREWORD
by PH Mark Ivy

There are many ways of looking at hunting and the calibres, bullets, rifles, etc. needed for a successful hunting trip. Depending on one's past exposure and the experiences one has had as a hunter, the answer to the question *"What hunting gear is right for this safari?"* will differ from one hunter to another. One should carefully consider the experienced advice of others, especially when traveling to Africa to hunt for the first time.

What Royce has done in *Safari Dreams* is to draw on his own experiences along with information garnered from many different sources. He combines these with numerous, interesting scientific facts and by so doing gives one an alternative insight into how to make calculated choices. The options come in many forms and each person can choose what is to be hunted and match the tools to do the job. The term "tools" encompasses the gun, bullet, scope, etc. — *i.e.*, all the items used for a successful safari. What works for one hunting area or for a particular animal species is not always suitable for another.

Common ballistics descriptors such as sectional density, muzzle energy, and BC do not clearly indicate the preferred calibre and bullet for a particular quarry. So, Royce very cleverly developed his own Knockout Value index to simplify the fairly complicated ballistics tables. His unique RoyceKoV is very helpful in choosing between, for example, .308 or .30-06 or .300 Win Mag — as well as their various bullet weights — regarding any African plains game animal out to 300 yards. (Buffalo calibres appropriately have their own RoyceKov table.)

From my many years of hunting in Africa, a few facts, which Royce clearly illustrates in *Safari Dreams*, remain paramount: use enough gun; know your gun; and choose the correct bullet. Lastly, but most importantly, do not take a compromising shot that could lead to non-fatal wounding, unnecessary suffering, and the wasting of an animal. (Know the shot placement for your quarry at hand!) You owe it to the animal to be a marksman and to carry out the task with as much precision and accuracy as possible. It is not to be taken light-heartedly. While human mistakes are often made, it's the *careless* mistakes that need to be avoided.

Having hunted with Royce in the field and after sitting with him for many an evening's campfire under the African sky, I know that he has tackled this book with a passion, not forsaking differing opinions nor shying away from controversial themes. Combining all this with up-to-date hard information, Royce has forged *Safari Dreams* into a "must read" for all those who wish to be well-informed, successful African hunters.

Safari Dreams covers many topics, not one of which in the big scheme of things is more important than the other. Someone once said, *"The whole is more important than the sum of its parts!"* This is very true when it comes to planning and executing a hunt. Royce clearly illustrates that it is pointless to get lost in the small details during your safari, such as a delay at the airport, a bumpy ride, etc. These minor details, if focused on, can make for a negative overall safari experience.

Safari Dreams highlights the fact that there is never a perfect hunting area, PH, tracker, gun, bullet, animal, 4x4, etc. (Although numerous things are not going to be like home, surprisingly, many will be.) Make the most of every situation, as you have travelled half the globe to come to Africa for this challenging, once-in-a-lifetime hunting experience!

As a professional hunter — and, before that, having had a lifelong passion for hunting — I have to say that Royce clearly defines my three most important aspects of hunting: **conservation, ethics, and safety.** *I.e.*, harvest animals only where there are more than enough present to sustain a thriving herd, do so in a sporting, ethical fashion, and hunt in a responsible manner that does not endanger others.

Such will enable future generations to share in this privilege for years to come, a point Royce brings home in a very unique and effective manner with his fairly controversial approach. You will get a healthy push into thinking on a different plane. *Safari Dreams* is a most useful planning and preparation guide, and is guaranteed to whet your appetite for at last making your African hunting safari happen.

Enjoy your read, and I hope to see you in Africa!

Mark Ivy
Professional Hunter and family man
IVY SAFARIS (www.ivysafaris.com)

INTRODUCTION

Breathes there a man with a soul so dead that he never to himself hath said, ". . . someday, somehow, I am going to make that Africa hunt."

— author unknown

The hunter's horn sounds early for some, I thought, later for others. For some unfortunates, imprisoned by city sidewalks and sentenced to a cement jungle more horrifying than anything to be found in Tanganyika, the horn of the hunter never winds at all. But deep in the guts of most men is buried the involuntary response to the hunter's horn, a prickle of the nape hairs, an acceleration of the pulse, an atavistic memory of his fathers, who killed first with stone, and then with the club, and then with spear, and then with bow, and then with gun, and finally by formulae. How meek the man is no importance; somewhere in the pigeon chest of the clerk is still the vestigial remnant of the hunter's heart; somewhere in his nostrils the half-forgotten smell of blood...

Hunting is simple. Animals are simple. Man himself is simple inside himself....

A man and a gun and a star and a beast are still ponderable in a world of imponderables. The essence of the simple ponderable is man's potential ability to slay a lion. It is an opportunity that comes to a few, but the urge is always present. Never forget that man is not a dehydrated nellie under his silly striped pants. He is a direct descendent of the hairy fellow who tore his meat raw from the pulsing flanks of just-slain beasts...

— Robert C. Ruark, *Horn of the Hunter* (1954), pp. 22-24

Any man worth his weight in gunpowder has dreamt of Africa. Any serious hunter has dreamt quite a lot about it. Hunting is in a man's blood, and to hunt Africa is hunting's highest calling. He cannot help it, nor would he want to.

But you will have to *do* something about it. Dreaming is not enough. Reading books is not enough. Buying a rifle for Africa is not enough. You must first *commit* to your safari, and then you must carve out the *time* for it.

> Today the African hunt is expensive, though not prohibitively so . . . The most prominent single obstacle to the African hunt is the decision to make it. Many enthusiastic hunters have reached the conclusion that the African hunt is only for the very rich, and thus beyond their reach. Actually time is more of an obstacle than expense . . . When one complains that he has not enough time, he is simply stating that he is unwilling to make the time. This is just as well, because without great desire fulfillment is vapid.
> — Jeff Cooper, C Stories (2004), p. 148

Humans have only one thing in common: 24 hours in a day. If I ever meet anybody who has but 20, then I'll believe his "*no time*" excuse. Everyone says to himself "*some day*." Well, "*some day*" is "*no day*." You will just have to commit to doing it, and when you have, things will begin to fall into place. The cosmos are simply waiting for a firm decision. *Your* firm decision. The entire universe is waiting in traffic — waiting for your green light. It will *not* proceed through your red light.

"*Oh, but it's so expensive to take a safari!*"

Not really. "Expensive" is when the experience is not worth the money. A safari is not cheap, but for the richness of experience it's a bargain. Also, if it were easily affordable, every slob hunter you've ever loathed would be going to Africa. So, be thankful that the high cover charge guarantees a (somewhat) better clientele than the average whitetail hunt.

Besides, money is a pygmy's hurdle. Save $300/month for three years, and you can collect a half-dozen South African plains game animals. If your safari dream is not worth $10/day for three-fourths of a presidential term, then it is not yet a big enough dream. There are bus drivers who spend $3000+ each year on season tickets to watch strangers from out-of-town play sports. For any middle-class guy without a gambling habit, money is not the problem.

A lack of *will* is the problem. Conquer that and you'll be amazed at how quickly your savings will accumulate.

All time and costs told, from preparation to execution, my first safari took a month and $18,000 of my life. I had not an abundance of spare time or money, but it was important to me. Anything worthwhile in life must be *fought* for, must be *made* to happen. You have to carve out space in life for what is important to you, otherwise life carves from you.

Like dancing, you can either lead or you can follow. If you're not leading, then you're following. (And there is no spectating, either.) **When you lead, life follows.**

If your first African hunt is important to you, then you must choose to take the lead over your life and do it. I wrote this book to make the whole thing easier for you, to knock you out of your rut, and persuade you that you can *do* this!

Action turns daydreams into memories.

Don't percolate for years about it. None of us is getting younger. The best game are *disappearing*. Prices are rising. You must go *now* to Africa, while you *can*. The VISA card you can pay off later. You must go now, while you're still allowed to take your own rifle across the ocean on a Boeing. This privilege will not likely last into the next generation for the middle class.

> But if honestly attempted, it is still a prime adventure, a staggering experience, and a daily recital of astounding beauty and unimaginable peace, accompanied by moments of almost unbearable excitement and drama.
> — Robert Ruark's *Africa* (1991), p. 39

WHO IS THIS BOOK FOR?

Africa is flesh and blood, and the hunt is ever a love affair.
— Isak Dinessen

First of all, *Safari Dreams* is about *hunting,* not taking a "camera safari" — which is like kissing your sister. While taking pictures is a great supplement to hunting, it is no substitute. A camera has no recoil, no sound, and no risk. It is not hunting, and this is a book about hunting.

I will assume that you have at least a fair amount of hunting experience, but have not necessarily traveled internationally (much less to Africa). I also assume that you are in sufficient physical shape to comfortably walk at least 10 miles per day with your rifle and gear.

If you've never hunted, and/or you are unfit, then you are not ready for Africa! *Get in shape!* Hunt deer and elk for at least two seasons. Only then should you contemplate your first safari. It is an experience you must *earn* vs. merely pay for. Only then have you the right to such an experience.

> [Adventure] *is not for the heat sensitive nor for those with tender feet. But few things of value in this world are available just for the asking. Those who are prepared to face a little heat or cold, a little thirst or weariness, will live a richer life for it.*
> —Jeff Cooper, *Fireworks*, p. 75

While you won't have to read further on calibers, rifles, ammo, what to pack, and how to fly, *Safari Dreams* does not go into exhaustive detail on wildlife anatomy and hunting techniques. There are many other books on those subjects by people far more knowledgeable in their subtleties.

However, my book will help you cross the Ts and dot the Is to evaporate any remaining apprehension you understandably would have about planning the hunt of a lifetime.

The Swahili word *safari* means "*a walking forth.*" Your first step of that walking forth begins in your own mind with a commitment to go. I hope that my book will be that final nudge you need.

Good hunting!

Kenneth W. Royce (aka Boston T. Party)
Winter 2007, Wyoming

> NOTE: Quote protocol is unique. **My added emphasis is in bold.** Original emphasis by the author is underlined.

❖ 1
ETHICS OF HUNTING

THE ANTI-HUNTING ATTITUDE

What is most difficult to explain to a religious nonhunter is that there is no paradox between loving animals and hunting them. In fact, I purport that the spiritually ethical hunter loves Nature the most and understands it the best.

A good friend's wife is a bright Eastern liberal (though living in the West with her husband who now regularly hunts). She believed that hunting was about *domination*, and that there were bloodless alternatives (such as riding horses). This floored me momentarily, as I'd never heard of such a thing, much less felt it. She was also of the opinion that trophy hunters routinely took only the antlers and left the meat to rot on the ground. (Wow. The stamina of that myth is amazing.)

Try to find a recent book on Africa in which "safari" is also taken to include hunting activity. It is nearly impossible. Today, safaris mean bird-watching and wildlife photography. The hunting concept is foreign to the modern eco-moralist, due to intellectual cowardice. Take this passage, for example:

> **No hunting.** Trophy hunting — an upmarket tourist activity in many countries — is so badly regulated and prone to corruption regarding animal quotas that there's no telling the damage you'd be doing to the ecosystem by going hunting. There's also a moral question regarding local populations: the best hunting grounds were formerly village lands, whose inhabitants will likely have been deprived of their traditional hunting areas.
> —Jens Finke, *First Time Africa* (2007), p. 322

This is a breathtakingly underinformed statement by somebody allegedly experienced about Africa. By his "logic" the natives never overhunted before the whites stole the land.

In the tribal trust areas, the land has been completely *denuded* of game. Not even a rabbit survives. Everything has been wiped out: not by white hunters, but by the *natives*. They could restock the game and practice managed conservation for subsistence living, but they don't. They would rather poach on the game ranch across the road, and they'd clean *that* out too if allowed. In Kenya, where hunting was outlawed 30 years ago, the natives are wiping out their local game, and elephant poaching is rampant. The native appetite for meat (*nyama*) is limitless because "tomorrow" is a theoretical concept.

There is only Today.

However, when the private property incentive is allowed for ranch game, there is good management and poaching control. Professional hunters (PHs) and clients want the game to always thrive, and thus have no interest in killing *everything*.

Tomorrow and time horizons are Western concepts, and *only these* can save the renewable resource of wild game. Foreign hunters (who are comparatively wealthy and thus indirectly pay for most conservation costs) are *needed* in Africa. The socialist native bureaucrats and dictators are loathe to admit that because it points to their own stalled development.

> The nation of Kenya, once the crown jewel of African safari destinations, is once again debating repealing its thirty-year-old ban on hunting.
> Tourists who see abundant wildlife in Kenya's national parks rarely hear about the fact that wildlife numbers in Kenya's unprotected areas have fallen by at least two-thirds over the last three decades. **Experts blame heavy poaching by locals for bush meat and destruction of wildlife habitat.**
> . . . little of the money generated by wildlife viewing and photo safaris finds its way into the hands of communities that must coexist with the animals, **compared with the much greater percentage of revenue from hunting that goes to locals.**
> — from the *Financial Times*

Hunting as a form of tourism contributes enormously to the economy of South Africa. Some 70,000 jobs have been created on game farms and directly from professional hunting. In the 2005 hunting

> season, 8,000 clients, inclusive of non-hunters in each hunting group, hunted in South Africa, having a total of 58,341 hunting days. A total of 39,561 animals were hunted. This amounts to a total revenue from daily rates, animals hunted and taxidermy work of US$100 million (R650 million).
> — www.professionalhunters.co.za/index.php?pid=3

> With international assistance, restraint on incursions into wildlife habitats, incentives for landholders, and an effective anti-poaching policy, there is still an opportunity to arrest drastic wildlife declines and preserve Africa's unique heritage.
> — Brian Herne, *White Hunters* (1999), p. 416

What about conservation through nonhunting safaris? While this does help a *small* bit (less than 10%), no sandal-clad photographer from Vermont is going to pay $300-1000 in daily rates as do hunters. He's not going to pay a $200 permit fee for his camera in Tanzania as a hunter does for his rifle. And he certainly is not going to pay trophy fees for each picture.

Finally, the fact that game ranches and public land concessions are hunted regularly by *armed* PH/client teams is what keeps poaching even partially at bay.

All this is instantly provable by the *facts*, if anybody truly cares to understand the vitality of hunting for conservation.

Yes, there *are* ethical black hunters and slob white hunters, but as far as *generalities* go what I tell you is true.

WHY I HUNT, AND MUST

> *No se caza para matar, sino, al revés, se mata para haber cazado.*
> *(One does not hunt in order to kill, rather, one kills in order to have hunted.)*
> -- José Ortega y Gasset, *Meditations on Hunting*

Nursing a beer at one of my regular watering holes in 2005, a couple sat next to me. They pleasantly struck up a conversation. Somehow, my plans for a first African safari were mentioned in the course of things. The wildlife biologist fellow began looking at me with some intensity as his date asked me what I was going to hunt. (This was after I had cleared up the inevitable misnotion that I was going there merely to take pictures of animals, vs. hunt/kill/eat them.) "*Plains game. A Cape buffalo I hope, and possibly even a lion.*"

At the word "lion" the tousled-haired wildlife biologist blanched and almost fell off the barstool. His reaction, impolite (if not impossible) to ignore, compelled me to ask, "*I guess you have a problem with the hunting of lions?*"

"*I'm having a problem with all of this,*" he wearily replied.

Ah, good. Now we could have a very interesting conversation. I ordered another beer. (Conversing, along with dancing, racing, and hunting are the four great categories of felicitous occupation — and here I was conversing about hunting. Dandy.) He continued, "*Anyone can go to Africa and take stacks of pictures of lions from daybreak to sunset, so why would anyone want to kill them?*"

First I quoted Ortega y Gasset, "*One does not hunt in order to kill, rather, one kills in order to have hunted.*" When this obviously sank not in, I explained:

> Whether by creation or by evolution, or even by some combination, I am a predatory omnivorous creature. My flesh-tearing teeth are ample proof of that. I have binocular vision, weapon-making capacity, problem-solving ability, the unique capacity for abstract thought, and stalking skills. As a Homo Sapien, I am at the top of Nature's food chain, and at least occasionally I wish to remind myself of it by hunting, killing, and eating animals which are not. Hunting is, for me, a biological, emotional, and spiritual imperative. I truly do not have a choice in the matter — nor would I ever want one.

After a bit of parrying, they finally countered that they have no philosophical qualm with *well-managed* hunting in general, as long as the hunter has a "reverence" for his animal.

They had a point there. Too many hunters are "slob hunters" who have utterly no respect for where they are or what they are hunting. (If I caught some slob hunter wounding deer at 800yds, I don't know if I could restrain myself.)

Properly, every successful hunt should involve a considerable ration of sadness over the animal's death. I confessed to them that I can get pretty solemn after all my kills, and that hunting is such a profoundly moving experience for me that I don't have to take an animal every year. This made an impression on them, but they persisted in wondering why, if I obviously respected animals, must I *kill* them.

> Look, nothing in Nature — especially in Africa — dies a gentle, painless death. Take the grand old buffalo bull I intend to kill. I will spend days tracking his herd, until I find them. I will carefully select an old bachelor. I will choose him and only him because of his venerable magnificence, a royal status he has earned through years of vigilance, combat, and valor. He has sired all the calves he ever will — he's now too old and cantankerous to mate. He's only waiting for a final worthy adversary.
>
> That he is in my sights is the highest praise I can bestow. I have spent years preparing for *Syncerus caffer*, and for him alone. I have studied his terrain, his anatomy, his temperament. I have spent countless hours choosing the proper rifle most suited for our encounter, and practicing with it on the range until it is an extension of my being — for this is his due. As his predator, I will not demean him on that day by being unprepared, sloppy, irresolute, incompetent, or even lucky. My rifle will function perfectly, my aim will be quick and true, and my bullet immediately effective. As my 2½ tons of .416 caliber energy crash into his noble, fearless heart, I will honor this bull by giving him the quickest and most painless death possible on the African plain. If I perform my task correctly, I will turn him off at once — like a light-switch — where he stands.

My wildlife biologist companion replied, "*That's hardly a fair encounter because you have a rifle. You have a vast advantage!*"

Well, not really. No rifle can guarantee success against the African buffalo. *Syncerus caffer* has his weaponry, and I have mine, however, my rifle cannot ensure victory. I've heard dozens of tales where a buff was hit well and hard with a proper solid-core bullet of sufficient caliber and weight... to little or no visible effect. Many hunters have died from buffs unconvinced that they had been mortally wounded. And nothing in Nature loathes like a mortally wounded *Syncerus caffer*. He will align every molecule of his seething locomotive body in trampling his attacker with those axe-head sharp hooves the size of salad plates. (If allowed to, he will wear the unrecognizably mangled hunter on his massive horns until, after a few days, the Cabela's clad corpse has finally rotted sufficiently to at last fall off.)

Nothing in Africa takes a bullet more personally than *Syncerus caffer*. His last pair of firing neurons will be expended in hate — and he often wins, even against experienced men with very large rifles. A true hunter revels in that rare and perilous encounter. From what I read, one is never more alive than when seconds away from death by a mortally wounded buff.

Ortega y Gasset wrote that man has always hunted because it involves his eager descent into Nature — his voluntary attenuation of his superior status. In his "*vacation from the human condition*" a true hunter returns to his Paleolithic roots and *wants* the animal to have a sporting chance:

> Hunting is what an animal does to take possession, dead or alive, of some other being that belongs to a species basically inferior to its own. Vice versa, if there is to be a hunt, this superiority of the hunter over the prey cannot be absolute.

This notion has been codified as the **Rules of Fair Chase**:

❶ Animals that are hunted for sport must be free-ranging, self-sustaining animals that are in areas large enough for them to be able to escape the hunter.

❷ There must be no shooting from or near any mechanical vehicle—nor should there be any chasing of animals by vehicles.

❸ There will be no use of electronic nightvision equipment.

❹ In the interests of conservation, there should be minimum disturbance of breeding groups, with no shooting of females or immature animals.

❺ Rifles must be of appropriate caliber and bullet to effect one-shot kills.

Without me, however, my animal is destined for a typically African death by a pack of hyenas when he becomes too sick and frail to defend himself. My animal deserves much better than that. He deserves death by proper foe — honorably — and not by a pack of opportunistic, cowardly scavengers.

> The lion hates [the hyena] — because, like the native, the lion knows that the hyena will eventually get him. It is cynically humorous that, one way or another, the king of beasts always finds his tomb inside the knave. It is the crowning indignity to a regal life that the aged and weakened lion is pulled down and consumed, while still alive, by a stinking, snarling, cowardly outcast . . .
> — Robert C. Ruark, *Horn of the Hunter*, p. 118

The wildfire biologist shook his head in polite disgust and exclaimed, "*Yeah, but that's Nature!*"

I replied, "*Yes, and . . . I . . . am . . . part . . . of Nature, too!*"

This dedicated disciple of Darwinism could not absorb it. He would prefer his beloved African lion torn asunder by a pack of hyenas rather than cleanly dispatched by a human hunter. I cannot comprehend a view so perverse, that we descended from the African savanna yet somehow are not entitled to return there as hunters. In summary, I scored quite a few points, but never actually changed his mind.

What a happy thing, however, that I didn't convert him into a hunter. It is already expensive and crowded enough as it is. Hunting is the 21st century's best kept secret for a Man, while it lasts. That we are still able to hunt in Africa is one of the very few compensations to Life in the Common Age. And responsible, managed hunting is what keeps many African nations and their people afloat.

By the way, this encounter had a happy prequel. One of my local readers, who is now a very good friend, is a gun student of mine. Politically, he could fairly be described as a Left-libertarian. Before knowing me, he had never owned a gun, much less hunted. In 2003 he took his first animal, a buck mule deer. The next year he packed around his own Winchester Model 70 .308. He didn't get his deer, but he was *hunting*. He now *understands*. After tramping around in the woods with 8lbs of steel and wood in his numbed hands, all senses keen, his excitement incendiary — he understands.

"Hunting changed my life!" he exclaimed.

Yep, it tends to do that. The *"barefoot boy with cheek of tan"* and his .22 out hunting squirrels understands more about animals and himself than that wildlife biologist ever will.

Why does man hunt? As y Gasset so beautifully explained:

> ... *hunting is a relationship that certain animals impose on man, to the point where not trying to hunt them demands the intervention of our deliberate will. The graphic symbol for the hunting relationship would have to be ... the arrow ... drawn emerging from the animal.* [Hunters see animals] *as what they really are — creatures gifted with marvelous powers of evasion, to the point where they are, essentially, 'that which escapes,' the unsubmissive, the surly, the fugitive, which is generally hidden, absent, unobtainable, wrapped in solitude. ... Thus they automatically convert any normal man who comes upon them into a hunter. The only adequate response to a being that lives obsessed with avoiding capture is to try to catch it.*

You doubt the truth of this? Try this, then. Find a street cop, act startled to see him, and take off running. He *will* chase after you. "*The only adequate response to a being that lives obsessed with avoiding capture is to try to catch it.*" He can't help it, for you have imposed the same relationship on him.

That's one part of the answer to why man hunts. The other is this. As the renowned PH Harry Selby once said, "*You are not shooting to kill. You are shooting to make immortal the thing you shoot. To kill just anything is a sin. To kill something that will be dead soon, but is so fine as to give you pleasure for years, is wonderful.*"

I go to Africa to make some worthy animals immortal. Their beautiful horns will live decades longer in my mind and on my wall than they would have trampled into dust on the Kalahari plain. It is a Win-Win situation. My animals get a clean and respectful death followed by immortality.

"*One does not hunt in order to kill, rather, one kills in order to have hunted.*" That is the deal, and it has been the deal for all time.

Hunting is, for me, a biological, emotional, and spiritual imperative. I truly do not have a choice in the matter — nor would I ever want one.

> [A] fascinating mystery of Nature is manifested in the universal fact of hunting: the inexorable hierarchy among living beings. Every animal is in a relationship of superiority or inferiority with regard to every other. Strict equality is exceedingly improbable and anomalous. Life is a terrible conflict, a grandiose and atrocious confluence. Hunting submerges man deliberately in that formidable mystery and therefore contains something of religious rite and emotion in which homage is paid to what is divine, transcendent, in the laws of Nature.

I guess they don't teach y Gasset in wildlife classes these days.

Hunting saves game and changes lives. As Frank Miniter of *The Politically Incorrect Guide to Hunting* wrote, it builds character, inculcates values, and develops virtues in respect to the natural world that no other sport can. Hunting camps bring generations of families together every fall.

Perhaps most usefully, it is impossible to be a hunter and still remain a eco-moralist liberal!

❖ 2

THE GOLDEN AGE

The generation to which I belong has seen Africa yield up her secrets. I have loved the chase not only for its own sake, but even more for where it has taken me. I possess memories I would not exchange for all the wealth and distinction the world can give. I love these years in Africa as I do the shade of palms and the sound of waters after the dust and toil of a desert march. You go out to Africa to see savages, and you find them only on your return.
— Sir Alfred Pease, *The Book of the Lion* (1915)

Just to illustrate some of what we've lost in Africa, and why you should prioritize your first safari, here is how it was done about a century ago. Fifty years from now your 14 days in Namibia may seem nearly as extravagant and fantastic.

LORD RANDOLPH CHURCHILL, 1892

Winston Churchill's father embarked on the first of the lavish celebrity safaris. Dying of syphilis, his marriage and political career over, Lord Randolph sought recovery in Africa during six months in the bush. He would cover 2,500 miles.

In what would become not uncommon procedure, part of his trip was underwritten by stories sold to the press. His fee of £100/article was the highest then paid to an English journalist.

Seven wagons and a cart groaned under the 20 tons of freight, including 24 long guns and a *piano*. (Mid-through, he condescended to lighten his load with a four-day auction.)

Although "*characteristically difficult and disgruntled for much of the time*," Lord Randolph was a keen critic of the Boers' harsh treatment of Africans as less than human. (In Pretoria, the Afrikaners burned Churchill's effigy.)

THEODORE ROOSEVELT, 1909

In hunting, the finding and killing of the game is after all but a part of the whole. The free, self-reliant, adventurous life, with its rugged and stalwart democracy; the wild surrounding, the grand beauty of the scenery, the chance to study the ways and habits of the woodland creatures — all these unite to give to the career of the wilderness hunter its peculiar charm. The chase is among the best of all national pastimes; it cultivates that vigorous manliness for the lack of which in a nation, as in an individual, the possession of no other qualities can possibly atone.

— Theodore Roosevelt

Rather than seek an unprecedented third presidential term (which he clearly would have won), TR chose instead to enjoy his first African safari with son Kermit. Just 19 days after departing the White House, Roosevelt embarked in grand style from New York harbor on the steamship *Hamburg* for Naples, arriving on 5 April 1909. There, F.C. Selous met him and they boarded the *Admiral* for Mombosa, Kenya, arriving 21 April.

Ten months later, they left for home from Khartoum.

Andrew Carnegie bankrolled the $75,000 ($1.5m in 2007 currency) nine-month safari in anticipation of TR's writing success. *African Game Trails* was indeed that, with an advance of $50,000 ($1,000,000 today!) and a 20% royalty. It won the 1910 "Book of the Year" by the *Herald Tribune*.

While TR was not a *bon vivant* of the likes of Lord Randolph, his safari was lavish in the sheer number of trophies to be collected for the Smithsonian Institution in Washington, D.C. and the American Museum of Natural History in New York. Accompanying this veritable scientific mission were three professional field naturalists, two of them taxidermists. (They would be kept quite busy with thousands of skins and heads.) Outfitted by Newland & Tarlton, the hunt began with 265 porters, and later grew to 500.

TR's three rifles are well-known in safari lore: a Springfield M1903 in .30-06, a Winchester 1895 in .405, and a lovely Holland & Holland .500/.450. All three rifles still exist today — and are rightfully now in museums.

Under Kenya's game licensing system, each elephant cost $85 ($1700 today) and each rhino or hippo $15 ($300). Lion and leopard, considered pests at the time, needed no license.

It is with lament that I report that Roosevelt was a rather poor shot. Much of that was due to a blind left eye from a boxing match in 1905 with one of his aides, Captain Dan Tyler Moore. The officer only learned in *1917* of the injury he caused back when he commanded the 310th Field Artillery at Camp Meade:

> But could you ask for any better proof of the man's sportsmanship than the fact that he never told me what I had done to him, never told anybody else that I know of — at least, it never got around to me till I saw in the papers the other day that he had said that he lost the sight of his eye while boxing with a captain of artillery who was his aide. He didn't name anybody then, but I knew that he must have meant me, for I happen to have been the only boxing aide he had who was in the artillery.

Poor eyesight notwithstanding, TR did tend to let the lead fly at excessive distances (past 300yds, including missing a lion at over 600yds). He wounded many animals with *"ranging fire"*. His bag of nine white rhino was considered overly much, even then. Stalking was not his style: *"Colonel Roosevelt's bulk and conversational powers somewhat preclude him from tracking"* as Lord Cranworth sweetly put it. (The natives dubbed him *Bwana Tumbo*. Sir Stomach, an honorific.)

After only five weeks on safari, Roosevelt plied another $30,000 ($600,000!) out of Carnegie. (It's good to have a benefactor.) The Roosevelts hunted with the finest shots of the day, such as Cuninghame, Delamere, Quentin Grogan, Cole, and Percival. Hunting through four countries, the expedition was a grand success even for 1910, and would be impossible to repeat today.

> During the safari the President and Kermit bagged 512 animals of over eighty species, including 17 lion, 11 elephant, 20 rhinoceros and 10 buffalo. Altogether the expedition collected and shipped home to the Smithsonian 4,900 mammals, 4,000 birds, 500 fish and 2,000 reptiles. Some of Roosevelt's specimens are still on display, and not all the original packing cases have yet been opened.
> — Bartle Bull, *Safari: A Chronicle of Adventure* (1988), p. 173

> *One reason that he appeared to be the living embodiment of human enthusiasm is that he became what he loved — the hunt, the land, the country, his kids.*
> — Roger Rosenblatt

Theodore Roosevelt was America's most famous boy, and none have ever hunted Africa with such relish:

> *...the red sunset paled to amber and opal and all the vast, mysterious African landscape grew to wonderful beauty in the dying twilight.*
> — *African Game Trails*

The Roosevelt legacy lives on in Africa, as grandson Kermit took his son in the 1960s, and as TR-4 took TR-5 in 1986 (nicely seen in the film *In The Blood*). Neither safari could match that of *Bwana Tumbo*, a grand relic of a passing age.

> *Such experiences as are related here are largely unrepeatable in today's Africa — and certainly not for the same cost. Alas, the environment has changed radically, and little can now be done to bring it back. Enormous increases in human populations have denuded the land of its assets — its forests and its water resources and, above all, its valuable wildlife. Subsistence economies have seen to that. To be fair, there was little or no alternative. Few, if any, of the African countries granted independence from colonial powers were prepared for the responsibility of government in such a short time, and they were without the infrastructure to plan for the future.*
> — John Kingsley-Heath, *Hunting The Dangerous Game of Africa*, p. 2

A 28-day TR-style hunt in Tanzania with 70 porters and no motor vehicles is being offered these days by Ballatine & Smalling Safari, Ltd. at 425-888-4872 or jayballant@aol.com. Be sure to wear that huge TR pith helmet.

❖ 3
PLANNING & PRICING

Booking a safari isn't all that unlike contracting for a wedding. You supply the money and the main participants and somebody else will be delighted to do the most work of putting the whole show together.
— Peter Capstick, *Safari* (1984), p. 32

Don't go to Africa unless you understand that once is not enough.
— anybody who has already been there

Safari companies vary in price and service, and government fees vary per country. My experience so far is three safaris: a 7-day 2x1 Selous buffalo hunt in Tanzania, and two plains game ranch hunts in South Africa (totaling 40 days). Twenty-four animals total. Having done the two most common safaris and countries, I can help make *your* first time the best it can be, especially since I was recently in your shoes. Your concerns, issues, and questions were mine until just a few years ago. The veteran safari hunter, however, has long since forgotten them.

In retrospect, I should have gone plains game hunting first, and saved Selous buffalo for the next time. South Africa is a better way to dip your toe in, and much less expensive.

a few terms to know
safari outfitter
They hire (or are) the PH, own or lease the hunting area, provide vehicles, trackers, skinners, etc. Generally, you get what you pay for. Extremely low daily rates should be looked at with some skepticism. (Are they using poor concessions with sparse game, and then passing the "savings" on to you? How is the food? Are they serving franks and beans to cut costs?)

Always remember that they are a "one-trick pony" with nothing to sell but their own hunts. Until you have personal experience with an outfitter worthy of returning to, you're likely better off going through a booking agent.

References are paramount! Contact clients directly and ask what they did *not* like. Would they book their hunt again? Good outfitters enjoy a 50+% repeat factor.

Get in writing *whom* your PH will be. Very important!

booking agent

They cost you nothing extra, and are paid a commission directly by the outfitter. (A similar service and arrangement to a travel agent.) Booking agents should represent several different outfitters (vs. only one), which will provide you a better selection. You will not have much (or any) leverage to haggle on price, as the outfitter must charge full fare to pay for the agent's commission. A good option for first-timers.

However, if you've already heard great things about a particular outfitter and have decided to go with them (do check client and guild references first!), then you don't *need* an agent. In fact, you will be able to directly negotiate on price, and you *should*. (A 10-20% discount may be yours for the asking.) Websites and email have made possible for outfitters to more easily handle bookings themselves.

PH (professional hunter)

WANTED: Young, active man interested in low and infrequent pay to play bwana in remote bushveld. Must be proven raconteur and socialite without liver trouble, expert card player, bartender, caterer, barbecuer, philosopher, African historian.

Experience in sanitary engineering, local architecture, labor relations, navigation, medicine and pharmacology, botany, zoology ichthyology, mineralogy, entomology, butchery, taxidermy, dietetics, optics, photography and radio operation essential. Applicant should speak at least two black African languages fluently as well as English and one other modern European tongue. A solid knowledge of mechanics, driving, gunsmithing, toxicology, ballistics, tracking, marksmanship, handloading and experience as a professional bodyguard are required.

Benefits are twenty-four-hour day, unlimited fresh air, including rain, sun and dust; no medical, dental or life insurance and no retirement benefits. Applicant should supply his own rifles. Vehicles on a per diem basis.

— Peter Capstick, *Safari* (1984)

He is the most important personality of your safari. A good PH can make a good hunt from a slim area. A bad one can ruin what would have been an idyllic time. Creating a situation where the client can shoot well is his primary task. Most countries require a rigorous course and certification, but this will not guarantee the position's vital flexibility and affability.

Working PHs are generally very capable people. They are hardy and courageous (3 in 4 get hurt or killed during their career). Their range of skills and knowledge is astounding, and especially includes diplomacy (with hunters and local officials). Your PH must be a *"businessman, leader, psychologist, linguist, hero, and a nice fellow, all rolled into one."* If friction develops between hunters, he must somehow hold the group together.

His knowledge of trophy animals must be *keen,* as this is not something you will be able to do for yourself at first (if ever). Book only with a PH who hunts his areas continuously. Nothing beats local intel and experience. (Many Tanzanian hunts are guided by South African PHs who merely fly in every year. Find a good East African PH who speaks Swahili.)

If you can, meet your PH in person beforehand (*e.g.*, at SCI). Also, be sure to check with PHASA, APHA, or other guild for his membership in good standing.

Important question for your prospective PH: *What is your opinion on shooting from the vehicle?* Trust me on this, you want a PH who will *not* allow it. "Diesel stalking" is not hunting, and anybody who permits it cheats their clients.

plains game

This has come to mean everything that is *not* dangerous game (DG: elephant, buffalo, rhino, leopard, and lion). It includes zebra, wildebeest, the antelopes, warthog, etc. Even though bushbuck and waterbuck are not technically "plains" game, they are still lumped together in that category.

1x1 hunt

One hunter and one PH.

2x1 hunt

Two hunters sharing a PH. There are even 2x2s and 3x2s.

daily rate

This will comprise the bulk of your fixed cost. It includes camp lodging, meals, drinks (and perhaps alcohol in moderation), laundry, PH, driving, camp and vehicle staff. You will pay this regardless of what animals you take (or not).

This will be multiplied by the number of days the government has decreed for the species you are hunting. Some countries allow fairly short hunt lengths (buffalo: Zimbabwe 5 days, with 7 days in South Africa, Tanzania, and Zambia). Other countries require longer hunts (10 days in Botswana).

Game ranches generally don't have a set minimum, though their outfitters won't likely let you swoop in for just two days for a Rowland Ward kudu. Such trophies they reserve for clients who stay more than a week.

The daily rate is just the "cover charge" to hunt.

trophy fee

This is cost per animal (which ranges from $50 to many thousands). Trophy fees vary tremendously by country. Low trophy fees are usually offset by the requirement of longer hunts, and vice versa. South Africa has very reasonable daily rates but *very* high trophy fees ($10,000+ for buff).

It is paid only if your bullet strikes an animal. If any blood is found, it's *yours* — that's the deal. One *drop,* and you pay. In *general* it's the fairest way. An animal that has run off after being hit, after leaving even a little blood, is either grazed or mortally wounded. If it's never found, how could anyone tell if it survived or died? **Blood = money.** Know this now and don't whine about it later, claiming that your merely grazed animal ran off for an inevitable and quick recovery.

My Limpopo Province PH Mark Ivy charges 10% of trophy fee for any *missed* shot, learning from experience that 1 in 10 will wound (though without sound or blood spoor, seemingly a clear miss). This seems a very logical policy, though I imagine it rankles some clients.

Tanzania has much higher daily rates (often double that of the RSA), but their buffalo is only $1100 (which tempts the hunter to try for *two* on a 10-day hunt).

In short, to decide which country is the best choice, you must add up *all* the costs. Don't be lured solely by a low daily rate, or repelled by an high trophy fee.

dipping/crating/packing fee

This is the trophy prep/preservation for your taxidermist. (The lasting quality of your mounts depends on this being done right.) It *excludes* air freight, customs fees, closing costs, etc.

choosing your game and hunting area
the game
Stick with plains game for your first safari: the various antelope, warthog, and zebra. They offer plenty of variety as far as different stalks, shot distances, and overall experiences. Yes, buffalo hunting is very exciting, but it's better to "earn" your way up to that with impala, wildebeest, and then kudu.

various countries and their hunting areas
One could hunt in *many* different terrains, but for your first time I highly recommend the northern Limpopo Province bushveld and its 50-200yd animals. Your trusty .308 or .30-06 is all you need, vs. a .338 Win Mag for 300yd Kalahari gemsbok. Basically, we're talking South Africa's provinces near the Kruger National Park (KNP). There are many outfitters there, most of them with private game ranches.

Save the Namibian desert and its 300yd shots for your second safari, hunting gemsbok in their natural terrain.

Zimbabwe still has very good hunting with quality PHs, but you'll pay more for travel and daily rates, and the country is tottering on disaster from a quarter century of Communist rule by dictator Mugabe. The infrastructure (roads, especially) has been largely consumed. All your supplies must be trucked in, as there is little internally. Petrol, parts, etc. are scarce. As of late 2007, the country is approaching starvation. For your third or fourth safari, Zim could be a good choice. Time will tell.

Jagplase private game ranches (4,000+ acre)
Two-thirds of all game in South Africa is privately owned behind 8' electrified fences. Since legislation in the 1970s allowed this, cattle ranchers have switched to game, which "*pays its own way, eats nearly anything, is more resistant to disease and predators, and generally produces a higher and better use of the land*" (Capstick). Game is purchased as needed at auctions (very interesting to attend!), and trucked in.

There you will have an easier hunt (twice I got an animal just minutes after my breakfast) and good accommodations. Assurance is high on what kind of game is present, and the average time required to hunt them.

But with smaller areas and fences, are game ranches selling "canned" hunts? Generally, *no*. As long as the animals do not have an engineered or enforced encounter, and enjoy sufficient room (it varies per species) to escape, it *is* fair chase hunting. (I once visited a 1000-acre game ranch with tower blinds, and the disgraceful situation was *far* from fair chase. It is something to see *once* in order to sear your memory. If your ranch doesn't provide fair chase conditions, you'll know it.)

You will be nearby a province capital for supplies, banking, air travel, or medical care. The ranch I hunted on was 8000 acres (12½ miles^2, or about 3½ miles per side) and provided true fair chase conditions. Only twice (in 20 animals) did I ever have to hunt within 100yds of any boundary (which was of no issue with that animal).

Connecting flights are 40 minutes from Johannesburg. It all makes for a convenient, yet exciting, first safari. The hunting is sufficiently challenging, but not grueling. A 10-14 day 1x1 hunt will provide you with many nice animals.

public land concession

> . . . . *given a choice I lean towards the traditional safari in remote areas, especially for a first safari. The old Africa is going quickly, and while I think the ranch hunting is often excellent, it will be available for a long time to come. I like to see a hunter go for the traditional African hunt — or as close an approximation as possible — the first time around.* (at 265)
> — Craig Boddington, *From Mount Kenya to the Cape* (1987)

He makes a good point. It is more difficult to find quality outfitters and PHs for such hunts, but if you do, the experience cannot be matched.

For my first safari, I hunted in the largest game reserve in the world, Tanzania's Selous. The cost is nearly *double,* the hunting is *much* harder, and the animals are much more spread out, but it's a *marvelous* experience. From the tented camps it *feels* like the true safari it is! You'll see elephant nearly every day, as wild and free as elephants are on the planet today. The demented giggle of the spotted hyena you'll be imitating long after you've flown home. Your third hunt should be for buffalo in the Selous or the Masailand.

I would *strongly* recommend against hunting in a new concession. The roads haven't been cleared, the camp is being sorted out, and the PH is still learning where the game are. Wait until their third season.

SOUTH AFRICA or TANZANIA?

There are many good hunting countries in Africa, but the first timer should probably focus on one of these two for their convenience and relative political stability. (Namibia and Botswana are also satisfactory, but beware Zimbabwe.)

South Africa

South Africa is a better choice for more plentiful (and cheaper) plains game (*i.e.*, varieties of antelope). While it has very good buffalo, they charge $10,000+ for it (vs. $1100 in Tanzania). So, if you aren't quite ready for buffalo (you'll need a .416 or .458 heavy rifle), a South African hunt is a good way to "dip your toe." They have some 6,000 game ranches!

South Africa is a huge country (471,446 miles^2), and larger than Arizona, California, Oregon, and Washington combined. Hunting terrain is quite varied, from desert to forest to savanna. While not the best choice for Big Five, it's tops for plains game. (30% of the land is devoted to game.) Infrastructure is the best in Africa, which eases your first safari.

brief history of South Africa

The first inhabitants of Africa's southern tip were the San (Bushmen, or KhoiKhoi) hunter-gatherers, concentrating in the Western and Northern Cape. These were displaced by migrating black tribes from the north which envied all that underutilized grazing land for their cattle.

In the 1600s hardy Dutch farmers (the Boers) began settling the Cape coast. By the 1770s their eastern expansion had them running into and fighting the Xhosa at the Fish River.

Once the English turned their colonial eye toward South Africa in the early 1800s, many Boers relocated eastward to the interior (the Great Trek of 1836-1854) in what is now KZN. The Boers then established their republics of the Transvaal and Orange Free State after the British annexed the Natal. The years 1838-1854 saw conflict between Brits, Boers, and Zulus. The first Anglo-Boer war of 1880-1881 left intact the independence of the Transvaal Republic.

When gold was discovered in the Transvaal in 1886, the British decided to grab that area as well, kicking off the second Anglo-Boer War (1899-1902). This was a hard-fought guerrilla campaign tying down hundreds of thousands of British troops. Lord Kitchener resorted to a scorched-earth policy and concentration camps for the Boer women and children (where many thousands died). The Boer leaders had no choice but to capitulate. The South African Union of two former republics and two former colonies was proclaimed by the British in 1910.

When WWI broke out, Afrikaners formed the National Party (NP) in protest of South Africa fighting for England. Racial laws were increasingly passed limiting the rights of blacks and Indians. In 1948, the NP won the general election and the era of *apartheid* began.

In 1961 South Africa left the commonwealth and became a republic. The white government increasingly tightened restrictions on blacks, finally sparking the Soweto riot of 1976 in which 600 were killed. Government repression increased, and a state of emergency was declared in 1986. The situation was tumultuous through 1990, until President F.W. de Klerk released Nelson Mandela after 27 years in prison (after which the newly unbanned ANC suspended its armed struggle). International sanctions were lifted.

Apartheid legislation was repealed in stages, and a White referendum allowed de Klerk to negotiate for a new South Africa. There was tremendous tension in 1993, as the country was poised for violence from *some* camp: the right-wing AWB, the Zulu *Inkatha*, or the Communists. In 1994, the first nonracial, multiparty general election was held, Mandela winning 62%. A new constitution was ratified in 1997, the ANC won a 70% majority in the re-election of 1999, at which point Mandela retired (succeeded by his deputy Thabo Mbeki).

By some miracle, South Africa has escaped civil war since 1990, and the country is now breathing relief that the hardest stage has passed (and all without international tribunals or peacekeeping forces). The future remains troubled on many fronts, but the country is trying to increasingly unite her varied peoples and continue the current strong economic growth.

The black government is getting pretty silly about renaming everything to erase evidence of 342 years of white rule. Pietersberg is now Polokwane, Pretoria is now Tshwane, etc. (Transitional maps are sagging with parenthetical asides.) If you speak to a black, say Polokwane/Pietersberg. If you speak to an Afrikaner, say Pietersberg/Polokwane. Get it?

South Africa was chosen for soccer's 2010 World Cup,

which currently has the entire nation atitter. (I would try to hunt *before* then!)

when to hunt South Africa (seasons are opposite ours)

July is overall the best month, though up to mid-September isn't bad. (For a grand time, hunt S.A. in July, Botswana in August, and Tanzania in September.)

where to hunt in South Africa

First-timers should concentrate in the Limpopo and Mpumalanga provinces. Natal is nice, too. Leave the more challenging Cape for future hunts.

Tanzania

Tanzania is on the east coast, just under the equator below Kenya (which prohibited hunting in 1977). It's quite large — twice the size of California. While its Selous buffalo aren't typically 45", there are plenty of very nice 38-40" bulls to be had. And the $1100 trophy fee is a *great* deal. Zebra, hartebeest, and wildebeest abound. For me, the classic tented camp of East Africa symbolizes a true safari, and these camps are extremely well-staffed as a matter of long tradition. I *highly* recommend Tanzania to first timers for buffalo.

English is widely spoken, the people are very friendly and cheerful, the land fascinating, and the prices very affordable. I had absolutely no trouble getting my rifle in or out.

brief history of Tanzania

Until Germany lost its colonies after WWI, it was known as German East Africa. It saw lots of fighting from forces of British East Africa (now Kenya), with a brilliant delaying action spanning two years by General Paul von Lettow-Vorbeck and his outnumbered, outgunned German troops and native *askaris*. His guerrilla campaign ended with only himself, 30 officers, 125 white troops, and 1,165 fiercely loyal *askaris*. As a measure of respect, he and his officers were allowed to retain their weapons — an act of chivalry rarely repeated since.

The great African hunter and explorer Frederick Courteney Selous (lead scout for Cecil Rhodes) was felled at age 65 by a bullet in 1917 from a German *askari*. His grave may still be visited today in the Selous Game Reserve.

If you've time to see a bit of Tanzania, try to visit the rusting hulk of the cruiser *Königsberg* in the Rufiji delta. Its 10 guns were stripped by Lettow-Vorbeck's men, requiring 400 porters. (Novelist Wilbur Smith's *Shout At The Devil* was based on the story of the cruiser's sinking in 1915.)

Lettow-Vorbeck was the only general accorded a hero's welcome at war's end in Berlin. He scorned the Nazis, and barely survived through WWII but through food parcels sent by his old adversaries in Africa. Things rebounded for him after the war, and he visited Tanganyika in 1953 and met up with some of his old *Schutztruppe*. He died in 1964, at age 94. That same year the *Bundestag* finally paid his surviving *askaris* their back pay for the past 50 years. These vets were identified as being able to perform the German drill-at-arms flawlessly. Not a single aged claimant failed.

After WWI, Kenya's growing safari industry began to stretch southward into Tanganyika. Hemingway's first safari was led by Theodore Roosevelt's PH, Philip Percival (who mentored PH Harry Selby who guided Robert Ruark in his first safari of 1951).

Without notice, Tanganyika — now Tanzania — closed hunting in 1973 but fortunately reopened in 1981. Hunting is pretty well managed now, and those caught clearly poaching are executed on the spot (quite the deterrent).

By the 1970s neighboring Kenya had badly mismanaged its game and PH certification, and international pressure from the bunny-huggers forced Kenya to close hunting in 1977. Recently, however, there is serious talk of ending the ban. Properly managed, game hunting *works*.

Tanzania hunts

The licensing system allows a 7-day (one area, one buffalo, plus several plains game), 10-day (as 7-day, but with a second buffalo), 16-day (as 10-day, but with one cat), and 21- or 28-day hunt with full bag and multiple areas.

Most hunting areas require a bush charter plane, which adds considerably to the cost. (In South Africa, one simply flies to Polokwane or Nelspruit, and the PH picks you up.)

Selous Game Reserve

This is where I hunted. There are 47 concessions in this 20,000 mile^2 reserve, the largest one in the world. It is literally the size of Switzerland. In no other place is game so wild and free. To hunt there in the 21st century is an utter privilege.

A protected game reserve since 1905 (when Tanzania was German East Africa), the Selous was named by the British in 1922 in honor of hunter/explorer F.C. Selous. Game warden C.J.P. Ionides is to be credited for the creation of this self-sustaining hunting reserve where safari clients can hunt virgin country offering truly wild game in fair chase conditions. What made the game so plentiful was a half-century moratorium on human habitation and hunting in the 1800s because of rampant sleeping sickness (*encephalitis*, born by the tsetse fly). By 1905 the game was thriving, and the Germans declared it a reserve.

We had a 3,500 mile^2 block two-thirds the size of Connecticut all to ourselves, with a dozen staff people working just for us! It took nearly a month back home for it to dawn on me how special the experience truly was.

Masailand

Up northeast in the highlands, with perfect weather and few mosquitos, this is a better area for larger buffalo with thicker bosses. I'd like to hunt this next for the variety.

Visually, the area screams *Africa!* with its upside down acacia tortilla trees, open savanna, and Mt. Kilimanjaro. Since we cannot yet hunt in Kenya, the Masailand and Serengeti Desert is the next closest thing.

Rungwa Game Reserve

A lower and hotter region than the Selous, but with very good roan and sable. Good, though scarce, kudu and eland.

when to hunt Tanzania

You don't want to go too early (because of the tall grass and abundant water) or too late (because the game have become wary of hunters) in the season (which runs July-December).

For a Selous buffalo hunt anything prior to September can be too early (especially if they have late rains, which you won't know about when you book your flight and hunt months in advance), and anything past November is too late.

Forget **July**, as you'll be blazing new roads and trails, and burning grass. Later hunters will benefit, but not you.

Late **August** is the earliest you should contemplate.

September is a nice month, especially the second half.

My PH highly recommended **October and November**, as the lesser watering holes have by then dried up and the smaller herds combine into large ones in search of water. It will be quite a bit hotter then, but there's no free lunch in life.

You should of course query your outfitter, but remember that they are trying to fill their season. Don't be lured by a July or early August discount. You are there to *hunt*, not wade through grass 8' high.

go to a hunters' convention
Safari Club International

If you go to SCI (www.safariclub.org) in Reno (January) there will be *hundreds* of outfitters vying for your hunting business. There, you can personally meet dozens of PHs and outfitters. It is, for the most part, a buyer's market. You'll have many choices, but expect some *Sign now!* sales pressure. (That *is* why they've come all the way from Africa.)

I highly recommend attending an SCI convention before you book your first safari. (You must be a member to attend, but can join at the door. Then, your 4-day pass will cost $325.) You'll learn things you never knew to ask about. Do not, however, book there unless if you've previously done some homework. (Write up a questionnaire before you go, otherwise you'll get lost in the hugeness of it all!) Flight costs rise significantly just after SCI, so book ASAP.

I went in 2007, got to visit with both my previous outfitters, met many guys such as Craig Boddington, Peter Flack, Terry Wieland, Robin Hurt, Kevin Robertson, etc. (Take their books with you for them to sign.) It was a great time, even if I didn't need to go for research!

Dallas Safari Club
A smaller and lower-pressure event, held just before or after SCI (so that African PHs can attend both).

Jagd und Hund in Dortmund
The largest venue in Europe. I expect it is a highly formalized event, given the training and polish required of German hunters.

IMPORTANT QUESTIONS TO ASK

Know before you go! It is your first hunt in Africa, so don't be shy about asking dozens of questions. This is easily accomplished through email (vs. writing letters just 10 years ago, the exchanges requiring weeks). Some very good questions were gleaned from Richard Conrad's *Safari Guide*:

questions for the agent

1) How long have you been booking hunts in Africa?

2) Have you hunted with these outfitters? Seen their facilities?

3) What airlines do you book with? How do they treat hunters and guns? Do they allow stopovers en route (*i.e.,* will they store your guns)?

4) Do you have a detailed brochure explaining all costs? Can I speak with the PH I'll be hunting with before the safari?

5) Do the daily rates and trophy fees include all costs associated with the hunt, such as special licenses, taxes and fees? If not, can you supply me with an itemized list of these additional charges?

6) Are transfers to the camp included, or is this extra? What options are available (land, scheduled air, charted air), and what do they cost?

7) What is the rate for 2x1 hunts?

8) What is the charge for nonhunting observers?

9) Can I take my wife and children? What are the safety issues?

10) How long in advance must I book my hunt?

11) How much of a deposit is required to book my hunt? (50% is max.)

12) What is your policy on refunds if I have to cancel? What if the safari company cancels? Can I rebook with my deposit for next season?

13) Can you book a hotel room (for at least the day) for me to recover from the long flight?

14) Do you handle all travel arrangements to the country where I'll be hunting, including air travel?

15) Are there game preserves or other tourist attractions to consider? Do you handle such arrangements?

16) Can you provide names of people you have booked hunts for as references?

17) Do you book the kind of hunt I'm interested in?

18) What are the accommodations like in your hunting camp(s)?

19) About how many hunters have you sent to Africa? How many to the outfitter you are recommending for my hunt?

20) Can you recommend an insurance provider for my guns, health, and trip cancellation?

21) Will someone meet me at my arrival point to help me clear customs and get the necessary permits?

22) Do I need a visa? How do I get it?

23) Does the hunt start the day I arrive? When does it end?

questions for the outfitter

1) Are all of your PHs licensed for the game I want to hunt?

2) How much experience does my PH have? What is his background, and what is he like personally?

3) What calibers do you recommend? What are typical distances?

4) What kind of hunting vehicles do you use?

5) Is bird hunting or fishing included in your safaris, and at what cost?

6) Can I rent firearms (shotgun, buffalo rifle), or must I bring my own?

7) What camp staff will be available on my hunt?

8) What level of physical effort is required on this hunt? How much walking and climbing, and in what temperatures?

9) What are your success rates for the animals I'll be hunting? What trophy quality can I expect?

10) Are alcoholic beverages included in the daily rate?

11) Will I have to travel between hunting camps to get all the game I want? How much are these transfers? What are the alternatives?

12) How and when do I pay for the deposit and balance of the safari? What currency and means do you accept?

13) Can you provide any references of satisfied clients?

14) How many hunters will be using the same camp while I'm there?

15) What hunting methods do your PHs use to hunt my preferred game?

16) Will you be in the USA in the near future so that I can meet with you?

17) What do you charge for field prep of trophies for shipment home?

18) How many actual days of hunting will I get on my safari?
19) What are some suggestions for gratuities for my PH and staff?
20) Is there anything I can bring you from home? Flashlight bulbs, etc.?
21) How is the cuisine? Will my game be prepared for our dinners?
22) What is distance/conditions of shots? What caliber/bullet weight?
23) What brand of travelers check should I buy at home? (Important!)

VARIOUS TIPS

Call previous clients! *"Would you book that hunt again?"*
Understand your hunting area, and contract for *that*.
Meet your PH first, and contract for *him*.
Get the cancellation/refund/credit policy in writing in advance.
Go during the best or second best month.
Get into your best possible physical condition.
Save up extra cash for extra animals.
≥ .30, heaviest/2nd heaviest *quality* bullets at 2400-2700fps MV
Book a 10-14 — not just 7 — day hunt. (You can afford it, and should!)
Enjoy a week of non-hunt time in Africa (4 days before/3 days after).

PRICE NEGOTIATIONS

Nearly everything in this world is negotiable, especially in Africa. (Except for all *government* fees, such as trophy fees, firearm license, hunting license, daily concession fee, and conservation fee.) Firm negotiations are the easiest way to "make" money. Remember, however, to remain polite. Avoid any acrimony. They must make a fair profit; you must reach a fair deal. As long as you don't take things too seriously and too far, you'll be respected for your business acumen.

daily rate

Depending on how busy they are, you may be able to grind them in advance for a 10-25% discount, especially if you are a returning client who was pleasant, honest, and fair.

If your hunt was somehow *significantly* marred by an act of the company, then you have some real leverage for negotiation when settling up. (General whining about a lack of game, however, does not qualify.) PHASA can help if needed.

In Tanzania, for example, the government sends official hunters out to harvest meat for the villagers. As long as they do so *after* the commercial hunting season is over in December, fine. (Or, if they do so during the season but only on those travel days where commercial hunters are not in the field, that *may* be tolerable, but only just.) However, they should *not* be in the field when you are. This happened to us one afternoon, and they scared off a pair of hartebeest we were glassing. On-the-spot negotiations with the official got him to cease hunting while *we* were there, but I doubt we solved the matter for *future* hunters that season.

While not enough to ruin the trip (although that afternoon was a wash), if you are hunting in Tanzania, *get written assurance in advance* that this will *not* happen to you in your hunting block, and what the adjustment will be if it does. You did not fly all the way to Africa to compete with government poachers within your own hunting block! I mention this matter here as it was the only issue which our company had (or *should* have had) control over that negatively affected our hunt.

dipping/crating/packing fee

Our Tanzanian firm charged $1000/person in our 2x1 hunt, but not $2000 for a 1x1 hunt. Since we took a total of only 4 animals (easily within the reach of a 1x1 hunt), we politely argued that collecting the full $2000 was unreasonable. The manager explained that $200 of that $1000 was a government fee charged per hunter, but did wipe off the remaining $800. Thus, we paid $600 each and were assured that all four animals would be flown to America in just one crate, thus saving us additional funds. A fair resolution.

You may want to negotiate in advance a per/animal fee for this (on top of the $200 government bite, of course). Some game is less expensive to process than others.

charter flight fee

Selous camps in Tanzania will require a charter into the bush. There is *great* variance here in what different companies charge. Usually it is $2000-3000 per flight (80 minutes, 218nm in my case), the expense divided between the hunters. Assuming full flights (*i.e.*, four hunters each), the outfitter charging $3000 per hunt will make about a tidy profit over his charter costs. You should let them have this if they gave you a break on the daily rate and packing fee.

what is *not* included:

Expenses before/after your hunt, such as hotels and transportation beyond local airport pickup. Taxidermy.

THE SAFARI CONTRACT

Your outfitter's website or brochure is *not* a contract. You will need to negotiate and agree on all terms and prices, and sign a written contract. From the www.accuratereloading.com forum, Terry Carr posted a good overview:

> Before paying a deposit, you should have a detailed written contract with the outfitter. The contract should, at a minimum, include the following:
>
> 1. The specific dates of the safari.
> 2. Are arrival and departure days counted as hunting days?
> 3. The number of hunters and PHs (1x1, 2x1, etc).
> 4. The name of the PH.
> 5. The area(s) to be hunted.
> 6. The daily rate.
> 7. The observer rate.
> 8. All applicable taxes.
> 9. Any licensing, permit or other fees or costs.
> 10. The animals to be hunted.
> 11. The applicable trophy fees.
> 12. The cancellation and return of deposit policies.
> 13. The services to be provided by the outfitter. Airport pick up and return. Field preparation of trophies and delivery to a taxidermist/shipping agent. Services of a fully licensed PH. Hunting vehicle. Tracker, skinner and camp staff. Meals, alcoholic beverages, lodging and laundry service.
>
> Just because it is in the brochure is not good enough; it must be in the written contract. If the brochure says that you will be "the only hunting party in camp and on the hunting concession," then put that in the contract. If the accommodations are described as having "en suite bathrooms with hot and cold shower and flush toilet," put that in the contract.
>
> It may be wise to add a provision that the there will be no change in the PH or the concession without your prior written consent.
>
> Duplicate originals of the contract should be executed. Keep one original contract, and the other original contract goes to the outfitter.

GET INTO *SHAPE!*

Poor hunter fitness is the #1 gripe of PHs, and rightfully so. (#2 is poor choice of calibers, usually throwing too light bullets too fast.) Many Americans who go to Africa cannot walk several miles each day, and thus lose out on 80% of the game (which does not hang around the roads waiting for a bullet).

I heard a story about one 400lb behemoth who couldn't walk more than 25yds from the truck to dart his rhino, so he chartered a *helicopter* to haul His Lardness into the air to make the shot! (The wealth:obesity correlation astonishes me.)

Start hiking *months in advance* back home with rifle and gear until you are as fit as a mountain goat. *Then,* your PH can guide you to all the choice game spots.

typical American hunter shortcomings

From Jeff Cooper's *Gargantuan Gunsite Gossip 2* is a list (pp. 466-7) from a PH symposium compiled by Layne Simpson:

1. Bringing more gun than one can shoot accurately.
2. Poor physical condition.
3. Inability to spot game in heavy brush.
4. Inability to shoot accurately from the offhand position.
5. Shooting offhand when a natural rest is available.
6. Inability to shoot quickly.
7. Choosing a bullet that goes to pieces without penetrating.
8. Unsafe gunhandling.
9. Unfamiliarity with animal anatomy.
10. Admiring the first shot instead of shooting until the animal is down.

Four of 10 are related to shooting and gun handling! My South African PH has no problem with ❷ since he does not accept out-of-shape clients who plead for "diesel stalking" (hunting from the Land Rover), but he *did* mention ❻, ❼, and ❾. (His website stresses slow/heavy bullets vs. 150gr at 3000+fps.) I was initially mediocre on animal anatomy, but got better quickly. By the end of my second hunt there, I was surgical in my bullet placement with one-shot kills.

DOCUMENTS

passport

A hundred years ago passports were quite uncommon and rarely required. Today, they are required nearly everywhere. (Since 2007, Americans must produce their passport returning from Canada, Mexico, and the Bahamas.)

Only 1 in 6 Americans has a passport. Even if you've never travelled and Africa is still years away, get your passport now! Certainly apply for it *the moment* you decide on a hunt. You never know when you may want to leave the country, and a passport is your freedom to do just that.

At no extra cost you can order a 48-page passport (24 is standard). Some countries really fill up the pages with their silly stamps and import/export documentation. (It's been my experience that the more insecure the country, the larger their visa stamps and/or the stronger their ink. The rightfully defunct East Germany was by far the worst strong-ink offender, with visas bleeding through the page.) Since passports are valid for 10 years, a puny 24-pager can get filled up before then.

Your passport must have two clean facing pages and be valid for at *least* 30 days after your South African departure, and the boarding agent *will* check. (To be totally on the safe side, 6 months is preferred. Renew before you go if necessary.)

international driver's license

Your local AAA can issue one for $20. Even if you don't plan to drive in Africa, some occasion may arise where you must, and this inexpensive translation of your American DL could prove invaluable. Who knows, you may be taken with the idea of renting a moped on Zanzibar, or renting a car in Joburg instead of booking a connecting flight?

South African Police gun permit

This is mandatory, but free. While it can be done at Joburg airport when you arrive, processing can take *hours* if they are busy and you could miss your connecting flight.

Get it done *for* you 30+ days in advance through PHASA or www.riflepermits.com. The $90-110 is well worth it. You're in and out of the airport police office within 10 minutes while other hunters have only just begun to fill out their forms (which they should have done in advance).

If staying overnight in Joburg before flying to your hunting camp, then you'll have time to DIY at the airport, saving the $110 and DHL courier fee, which will pay for your hotel room. Your choice.

The SAPS 520 Form is online. It's formatted in A4 size paper (which is longer than our 8½"x11"), so print it out on legal and trim to length. You *must* supply a copy of the below 4457. Print out *two* copies, fill them out in black ink, sign one and send it. (Take the unsigned one with you just in case your permit somehow was not received or processed.)

If having the application processed in advance for you, you can save on the $100 DHL cost by sending it for $7 by U.S. Global Airmail. Even though service is a claimed 5-7 days, allow for 6 weeks, and give yourself a 45-day window to DHL a replacement form if necessary.

U.S. Customs Form 4457

The purpose of this form is to have evidence that you are not importing your rifle back home and that you actually left with it on your trip. It's a simple form, with no fee, and no record is kept by U.S. Customs. **Do *not* wait to accomplish this a few hours before you board your outbound flight!** Though it's only a 10-minute procedure, get it done *months* prior (because most foreign gun permits will require a copy). Any airport with a "Customs and Border Protection" office (or whatever they're calling it these days) can handle it. Once you have your form, laminate it (no expiration date) and you can use it whenever you go back and forth to Africa with your rifle.

Log in your American-purchased valuables (guns, scope, camera, laptop, radio, rangefinder, binos, etc.) as proof that you did not buy them overseas. It will save you possible duty and hassle upon returning home.

A notarized list will likely accomplish the same thing if the feds haven't an office near you, but check with your permit liaison company first.

A final tip for hunting buddies is for *one* of you to handle the 4457s, as if he owned *both* rifles. This makes good sense for insurance purposes, and for also dealing singularly with the Dutch in getting transit permission.

BUFFALO HUNT COST OVERVIEW

This is a completely no-frills accounting, assuming no side trip to Zanzibar, no shopping, and no extra days in Tanzania. (Realistically, you should plan at least $1,000 extra for such and make your trip special.) It also assumes that you don't have to buy much gear for your trip.

Finally, it assumes that you pay full retail prices and do not negotiate on a few things able to be discounted (which I'll discuss in detail shortly).

Here is generally what I paid in 2005 for a 7-day buffalo hunt in Tanzania, sharing your PH on a 2x1. Trophy fees since then have risen about 20%, so check before you commit.

fixed costs (*i.e.*, not including any game taken)

rifle w/1-4x scope	$1,500 (this is about minimum)
ammo (up to 50rds)	$ 200
insurance	$ 500 (incl. trip cancellation)
vaccinations/meds	$ 500 (for the full spread)
daily rate (7x$600)	$4,200 (likely negotiable)
USA—>Dar—>USA airfare	$2,500 (economy class KLM)
Dar—>Selous—>Dar charter	$1,500 (half of $3,000)
hunting permit	$ 450
concession fee (7x$100)	$ 700
gun permit	$ 200
hunt gratuities	$ 500 (each hunter)
buffalo trophy fee	$ 900
15% anti-poaching fee	$ 135
zebra trophy fee	$ 888
15% anti-poaching fee	$ 133
Dar hotel/misc.	$ 100
clothes/gear/misc.	$ 200 (depends on you)
fixed cost total	**$15,106**

variable trophy costs (*e.g.*, buffalo and zebra)

dipping/packing/crating fee	$1,000 (max; haggle on this)
trophies Dar—>USA taxidermist	$1,600 (each hunter)
taxidermy	$1,000 (minimum)
variable cost total	**$3,600**
total hunt (buffalo and zebra)	**$18,706**

A 7-day buffalo hunt would be difficult for under $19,000, and I can't see where I could have saved any real money in 2005. And, I still had many things to do, *quickly*:

> acquire a heavy-caliber, dangerous-game (DG) rifle, and add optics
> handload the ammo; acquire bits of gear
> book an affordable flight
> get vaccinations
> research and buy insurance
> study up on Tanzania to plan pre/post-hunt excursions
> get personal and business affairs in order (*e.g.*, update my will)

PLAINS GAME HUNT COST

Here is generally what you'd expect to pay (minimum) for a 10-day plains game 1x1 hunt (8 animals) in South Africa:

fixed costs (*i.e.*, not including taxidermy)

.308/.30-06 rifle with scope	$ 600	(this is about minimum)
ammo (up to 50rds)	$ 100	(using premium bullets)
insurance	$ 500	(incl. trip cancellation)
vaccinations/meds	$ 500	(for the full spread)
daily rate (10x$400)	$4,000	(estimated, can vary)
USA—>RSA—>USA airfare	$2,300	(economy class)
RSA connecting flight	$ 300	(less if booked simult.)
hunt gratuities	$ 400	(10% of daily rate)
trophy fees	$3,000	(estimated)
clothes/gear/misc.	$ 200	(depends on you)

fixed cost total   **$11,900**

variable trophy costs (*e.g.*, 8 various animals)

taxidermy	$2,500	(estimated)
trophies RSA—>USA	$1,000	(estimated)
US Customs duties, etc.	$ 300	(estimated)

variable cost total   **$3,800**

total hunt   **$15,700**

A 7-day hunt with a less expensive outfitter, and forsaking all trophies would cut costs by several thousand dollars. This may be necessary for those on an extremely tight budget.

❖ 4
INSURANCE & HEALTH

Insurance is for pessimists.
   — Karen Blixen, *Out of Africa* (after she lost her farm to fire)

You will be traveling around the world to a very poor country. I strongly advise you to purchase insurance. There are basically three areas to cover: trip cancellation, baggage loss, and health. The first two are often covered under a common policy. Health insurance (including a bit of life insurance) will usually be a separate policy.

In short, you want a no-B.S. policy from a large, reputable company which is familiar with safari hunters' needs. I bought very good total coverage for just $200.

trip/baggage insurance
trip cancellation insurance

You'll have paid at least a 50% safari deposit, as well as your full airfare in advance, and these costs are usually nonrefundable. Add to this your $500 of vaccinations, your specialized rifle, etc. and you could be easily dangling for $10,000+ in otherwise nonrecoverable expenses if you, for some reason, can't make your trip. You should contemplate trip cancellation and interruption insurance. Get quotes from:

Sportsman's Travel Protection Plan	www.travelguard.com
Insure My Trip	www.insuremytrip.com
Total Travel Insurance	www.totaltravelinsurance.com
AAA's plan	www.accessamerica.com
Magellan's	www.magellans.com

How much coverage you purchase is up to you. For the minimum $38 plan, $500 of coverage is included. $10,000 of coverage would have cost $408, which I thought excessive, so I settled on a quasi self-insured deal: I bought $4000 of coverage for $167. (The rates really take off from $5000 on.) Besides, I purchased the policy the week of my flight, so by that time I was sure I'd make my trip. The $4000 of coverage was the minimum catastrophic coverage needed, just in case.

It's preferable, however, not to procrastinate, as you'll get other benefits if you sign up within 15 days of hunt deposit.

baggage loss insurance

The above policy covered $2500 of lost/damaged/stolen luggage, $200 of baggage delay (you may want more, in case your rifles are delayed), and $1000 travel delay. You can print baggage tags online with your policy number and name.

Retriever Luggage Tags from www.magellans.com may assist in the recovery of your lost luggage.

travel assistance

The Sportsman Travel Protection plan also includes pre-trip advisories, rebooking, BagTrak, emergency message relay, and emergency cash transfers.

health insurance

The above plan allowed for $25,000 in medical expenses, but I wanted more coverage. A mere $25,000 would be quickly exhausted after a real mauling or bad GSW (gunshot wound). Be *extravagant* here (you just may need it). Buy an extra policy for comprehensive medical coverage. (What does your current domestic policy cover?)

emergency evacuation to nearest primary care hospital

Some safari companies include in their fees an emergency flight to Joburg, Dar, or Nairobi. If not, then you'll need to buy this coverage independently. The above Plan covers $300,000 of emergency medical transportation (that would pay for a 24k gold-plated helicopter to haul me out of the bush to catch my own chartered Gulfstream V).

Medjet Assistance   www.medjetassistance.com
MARS (Medical Air Rescue Services)   www.mars.co.zw

medical bills (www.worldtrips.com)

I bought $1,000,000 worth of 16-day medical coverage with a $2500 deductible (which would be taken care of by that $25,000 coverage in my other policy) for just $30.

pre-notification requirements

This company (and others) requires a phone call from you or your doctor before evacuation, hospitalization, etc. If you don't pre-notify, medical expenses will be reduced by 50% and all other coverage will be forfeited.

You or your buddy will likely forget to do this during an emergency. **So, give all your insurance info to the safari outfitter with strict instructions to pre-notify.** If something happens, your PH will sat phone to someone at his office, who will arrange all matters of insurance and medevac.

direct vs. indirect disbursement

This is a vital consideration. Does the insurance company directly pay the hospital, or merely reimburse you *after* you've already paid? Find out *exactly* how this works before you go.

HEALTH

What can a sick man say but that he is sick?
—Samuel Johnson

All told, I spent about $500 in preventative measures each trip. What a bargain... Good information sources:

> www.thehuntdoctors.com
> www.mdtravelhealth.com
> www.cdc.gov

get a dental checkup before you go!

Dental work is not pleasant even at its best back home, so imagine your discomfort in Africa. Get it done before safari.

vaccinations

Although only yellow fever is required for Tanzania, it is commonly advised to get "jabs" for hepatitis A & B, IPV, typhoid, and tetanus.

One warning about vaccinations in general. Beware and avoid *any* shot containing something called "squalene" (an oil-based adjuvant which triggers the immune system into a quicker and more vigorous response). Squalene has been shown to induce autoimmune diseases such as lupus, MS, and rheumatoid arthritis. **It is *highly* suspected as the cause of Gulf War Syndrome.** I would demand written assurance that any vaccination you are about get contains absolutely *no* squalene. An excellent book on the matter is *Vaccine-A: The Covert Government Experiment that's Killing Our Soldiers* (ISBN 0-645-04400-X) www.Vaccine-A.com

malaria

Malaria is endemic to tropical Africa and kills a million every year, but fewer than 1:100 infected actually die from it. Largely preventable and treatable (when caught early), it is a blood-borne *Plasmodium* parasite (there are four varieties, but 95% in Africa is *P. falciparum*). It is transmitted by the night biting female *Anopheles* mosquito (also carrier of dengue, yellow fever, and lymphatic filariasis).

When an infected mosquito bites, malarial parasites are injected in the bloodstream and carried to the liver, where they multiply. One to three weeks later (but sometimes up to a *year*), these parasites leave the liver for individual red blood cells, destroying them. This is when malaria becomes symptomatic with the typical fever, aches, chills, and shakes. (These will be much reduced if you've been taking malaria-prevention pills, so don't pass them off as merely a cold or the flu.)

Since malaria takes at least a week to re-enter the bloodstream from the liver, any symptoms within that time are not malarial. But thereafter, if you ever become the *slightest* bit unwell during your safari, tell the PH immediately! A malarial blood test can be done nearly anywhere in Africa from a simple finger prick, and early treatment is very effective.

While all of Tanzania sees malaria, only northeast South Africa and northern Namibia do. Even there, the risk of malaria above 4600' (1400m) is very slight, and above 5900-6560' (1800-2000m) nonexistent. Also, since you'll likely be hunting during the African winter months (June-August), the *mozzies* are very much reduced then. Ask your outfitter the elevation of his camp, and if he recommends taking malarial prophylactics. (While he's no doctor, he does *live* there.) South Africa's Limpopo Province is not at high risk for malaria, especially just outside of Pietersberg/Polokwane. My PH has spent his entire life there without contracting it. Nonetheless, I took Malarone for my first hunt. The following year I was there even earlier in their winter, and thus skipped Malarone entirely. I didn't have a single mosquito bite.

Malarone (a combination of Atovaquone and Proguanil)

This drug has the fewest side effects and is effective against multidrug resistant strains. These $5 daily tablets will begin 2 days before you land in Africa (showing any early reaction to the drug) and continue after you leave for 7 more days. Do not miss a single day taking them, else you'll risk contracting malaria.

Larium (Mefloquine)

Cheaper than Malarone for longer trips, but it does have more side effects and has generated considerable controversy. Research this drug at www.suggskelly.com/larium and test your reaction before leaving home.

avoiding mosquito bites

Your malarial prevention plan doesn't stop just with Malarone. You must treat your clothes with Permethrin (an insect neurotoxin lasting through two detergent washings, but store clothes in a black trash bag as much as possible since UV breaks down Permethrin). Wear long sleeve shirt and pants.

Treat yourself with 20-30% DEET (effectiveness maxes out at 35%). Cream base is best (avoid aerosols which evaporate), concentrating on hands, wrists, face, neck, and ears. (DEET doesn't work on clothing.) Reapply every four hours, and after your evening shower. Store in ZipLoc bags as DEET can chemically dissolve many common materials (such as camera lens housings and Swiss Army knife handles).

Wear pants and long-sleeve shirts as much as possible. Sleep under mosquito netting if necessary (it was on Zanzibar). In the Selous I had nearly no mosquito bites, and did not come down with malaria. (Tse-tse flies are not malaria carriers, and they are hardly repelled by DEET.)

trypanosomiasis (sleeping sickness, *tyrps*)

Here's where the tsetse fly can be dangerous, especially if you get swarm bitten. (Don't wear blue or dark colors, as tsetse flies mistake such for their favorite wildebeest.) There is no vaccine. If a bite area swells, becomes inflamed or forms a chancre, or your neck lymph nodes swell up, or if you develop headache or an irregular fever, speak up immediately! Early treatment can get you back hunting in a week. **Don't *ever* be stoic about not feeling well!**

yellow fever

Not present south of Tanzania and central Africa, but it's good to get inoculated in case an infected person from elsewhere is bitten by your local mosquito.

schistosomiasis (bilharzia, schisto)

This parasitic disease is caused by a tiny worm from freshwater snails. After several *months* you will suffer abdominal pain or blood in your urine and feces. A single dose of praziquantel is required.

Stay *out* of ponds, lakes, rivers, and streams. If you do get wet, vigorously dry off immediately (the worm takes 10 minutes to bore through your skin).

diarrhea

I pack Immodium (or generic) liquid. In three trips to Africa and ten weeks there I've never had even a twinge of stomach upset or queasiness. Washing your hands with an antibacterial soap every chance you get is the key. Your hunting camp food will most likely be quite safe, but beware street vendor salads and vegetables.

If you get the runs, you must replace lost fluids. A teaspoon of salt with eight teaspoons of sugar per liter of water. (Two glasses after each episode is what you'll need to "keep up." Dark urine indicates dehydration.) Get lots of rest. Eat bread, rice, boiled potatoes, and bananas (while avoiding dairy products, fruits and veggies). A single 500mg of Cipro with some Immodium will often give immediate relief. However, if you suffer from fever, vomiting, or diarrhea lasting longer than a week, see a doctor.

dysentery (diarrhea with blood/mucus in it)
Ciprofloxacin
$10 bought me 18 Cipro 500mg tablets, which I happily never had to use.

get this $6 book!
Healthy Travel — Africa from www.lonelyplanet.com. Its small 3"x4½" pocket size will fit in your cargo pocket or ruck.

final comments on prescription drugs
Always keep them in the *original* packaging and within their expiration date, and never take excessive quantities else you could be accused of smuggling.

prescription eyeglasses/contacts
Have a few extra pairs with you, especially if you'll be in a hunting camp far away from a city.

GSW blood clot powder (www.quikclot.com)
If somebody in your party suffers a gunshot wound, this amazing product is a lifesaver. It reportedly burns like hell, but you won't leak out. Well tested in Iraq. Only $15 per serving.

DISCLAIMER
I am not a doctor dispensing medical advice. While every effort was made to ensure the accuracy of this chapter's information at time of press, recommendations and drugs do change so please see a qualified travel doctor before your trip.

Neither the author nor the publisher accept responsibility for any loss, injury, or illness resulting from use of information in this chapter.

❖ 5

TRANSPORTATION

I've been overseas dozens of times, and to Africa thrice, so I've some experience at this. While an excellent travel agent is important, you have to become almost your own travel agent in order to ask the right questions and discern the best flights.

As expensive as airfare seems these days, it's actually cheaper (in 2007 dollars) than some 50 years ago (not to mention the improved service):

	Economy	1st Class
1956	$8,350	$12,027
2007	$2,300	$ 9,500

BOOKING YOUR FLIGHT

To "book" a flight is to pay for a flight that you reserved. *I.e.*, it's not yours until you *book* it. A reservation is not a property right, but a booked ticket *is*.

Economy, Business, or First Class?

During peak season (May-Sept., for most safaris), Economy Class will run about $2300 (in 2007). Business Class is $6600 (although Air Namibia is only $4300), and First Class $9500+. While most readers will probably fly Economy (also called "Coach"), I'll mention the more luxurious options.

First Class vs. Business Class

I've flown First Class to Europe and India, and while the comfort was top-notch I felt almost inconvenienced by the flood of amenities and service. For me, it was really *too* much. I believe Business Class is the better balance of value vs. comfort.

Business vs. Economy Class

You'll pay at least $4000 extra for 40-50 hours of wider seats (which recline almost flat for easy sleeping), and 5-18 hours of Business Class lounge use (which will spoil you!). The food is better, and the drinks are free. It's worth splurging on at least once in your life, and perhaps for your first hunt. I enjoyed Lufthansa's service recently, and being able to shower, shave, and change clothes in Frankfurt during the 9-hour layover was quite the treat.

don't rely on your airline miles for Africa!

Yes, they *will* honor them, but you *won't* get a smooth USA-Europe-Johannesburg ticket. Oh, *no*. You'll get the worst flights on the worst airlines with the longest layovers. One friend missed out on safari because his airline bumped him to an alternate itinerary so horrendous that I thought he was kidding me. We're talking *several days* of travel each way, and through Egypt, Cameroon, and Malawi. No more sadistic arrangement was possible.

Internet vs. a travel agent
do *not* book your safari flight on the Internet

While you can certainly discover some good bargains on the Net, the reservation and booking process are combined. You'll have little-to-no customer service, and your odds of being bumped or experiencing snags are higher. Also, you'll rarely be able to pick your own seats, which is vital for optimal comfort.

use a travel agent for Africa!

A travel agent, however, can reserve your first itinerary while you fine-tune things before you actually book the ticket. Also, the agent can arrange for a European vacation layover or other things requiring more flexibility than an Internet ticket. He will also know of a dozen tips and advisories that you'd never have been aware of otherwise. Finally, booking your ticket through a travel agency really isn't much more expensive than the Internet. The extra $100 is well worth the personalized service and experience, especially if you've an problem later on.

www.gracytravel.com specializes in safaris, and each ticket comes with a very thorough info packet on your African country. They gave me excellent service. I can't envision any compelling reason *not* to use Gracy Travel.

have a *sharp* travel agent who *listens*

One indy I worked with screwed up things so badly that I wouldn't buy a bus pass from her now. I did *all* of the ground work and told her to book a *very* particular itinerary. For one of the legs she booked a *different* flight, getting me in camp too late to hunt that day. Then, she cobbed up the replacement, *twice*, while insisting on flying me through the *Orient* for a better price (never comprehending that I wouldn't be able to travel with my *rifle* through there). I could have done better myself online.

websites with good airline and seat information

SkyTrax   www.airlinequality.com/index.htm
SeatGuru   www.seatguru.com
Airliners.net   www.airliners.net

Book as *early* as possible!

Avoid flying on these South African holidays:
27 April   1 May   16 June   9 August   24 September

FLYING TO SOUTH AFRICA

Unless otherwise stated, quoted times assume Denver. Domestic/foreign airline partners are United/Lufthansa/SAA, American/British Airways, Northwest/KLM, and Delta/Air France. The two best ways to go are either Johannesburg direct from the USA (SAA), or connecting through Frankfurt (SAA, Lufthansa). Others have figured this out, and these popular flights sell out within 2-3 months of departure, so book early!

Other countries/airports/airlines involve increased hassle or cost. Keep your booking simple, with as few flights as possible (reducing risk of bag delay/loss). That Internet "bargain" using six flights and four airlines is Snag City.

If you return through Europe, ask your travel agent if you can place your gun case (with *all* gun-related items) in customs bond and spend some time in Europe for a vacation.

United/South Africa Airways   (Airbus 319, 346)
     NYC, DC, Chicago —> Joburg   (domestic + 15:15/18:05)

These are nonstop flights which get you to RSA the next afternoon (vs. early morning 2 days later). After a short layover in Dulles (*ugh!*), a 15:15 flight. (From Denver figure only 20:10 Very quick!) The Joburg/Dulles return is *18* hours because of a Dakar refueling stop and slower flying into headwinds, totaling 25:29. 15-18 hours in the air nonstop is a *grind* (especially with an uncomfortable seat or poor seatmate) and may require more recuperation time than it saves in Euro layovers.

So, consider returning through Europe if you can layover shorter than 5 hours (such as Lufthansa from Joburg to Munich to Denver, with a mere 2-hour layover, totaling just 23:30). You can even get a ticket with a nonstop flight out, but return on Lufthansa connecting through Europe (thus making a separate vacation if you place your rifles in customs bond meanwhile).

I flew their Airbus 346 from Frankfurt and enjoyed it very much. What a lovely airplane! Each seat has its own video screen (one channel features a real-time camera in the vertical stabilizer, so you can watch your plane on final approach and landing), and the aircraft exudes quality. Excellent service, too.

Prices are $300 higher than other airlines, but SAA does not levy an excess baggage fee on rifle cases, as does KLM and Lufthansa, saving you $250.

While SAA offers good service to/from Joburg, the **domestic connections at Tambo are a *mess*.** Wait right by your gate and *do not rely on* the departure screen. (My 2007 domestic flight was not even listed until after it had nearly departed with 20% of its passengers not yet onboard!)

For your return connection to Joburg, I would allow enough time to rent a car and *drive* to Tambo if necessary. (You may consider staying in Joburg the night before. Afton House is a fine B&B catering to hunters.) My flight was merged into a later one, giving me only 45 minutes to complete the transfer and international check-in. (With assistance of airport staff, I did make it, though barely. If stressful for this very seasoned traveler, the experience would have done-in a newbie.)

In summary, SAA's quality is slipping noticeably. While it remains a top choice, this may not be forever.

United/Lufthansa (Boeing 747-400)
　　USA —> Frankfurt —> Johannesburg　　　(30:00/28:25)
　　　　　　　　　　　　　　9:35 + 9:45 layover + 10:40
　　　　　　　　　　　　　　10:45 + 7:15 layover + 10:25

This is the best European connection (often in conjunction with SAA). Usually only two flights (vs. three or even *four*), a great airline, and no gun permit needed through Frankfurt (though you'll pay $127 each way for the rifle case). Lufthansa is very familiar with service to Africa, and it's my second choice (even with the long layovers). You may be able to fly through Munich.

　　For this author writing about safari travel, the boarding gate staff at Denver very kindly upgraded me to Business Class. The flight was nearly twice as comfortable, and the 9-hour European layovers in a Business Class lounge are a true joy. There, one can enjoy a hot shower and fresh change of clothes, Internet, newspapers, and complimentary beer, wine, fruits, and snacks. (The First Class lounges must be even nicer, but I cannot quite envision *how*. Perhaps a personal masseur?) If you want to splurge on yourself, this is a fine way to arrive in a capital frame of mind!

　　Service in Economy class, however, is a little brusque:

"Beef or chicken?"
　"Do you have—?"
"Beef...or...chicken?!
　"Well, then...beef."
"Vee are out of beef!"
　"OK...chicken."
"Gut choice!"

Northwest/KLM
　　Minneapolis —> Amsterdam —> Joburg　　　(25:45/28:40)

Very nice service, with short 1:10-4:00 layovers in Amsterdam. (Your domestic layovers will likely be longer.) You'll pay a $150 gun case surcharge, and have to get gun transit permission from Dutch Customs in advance (described later herein).

Virgin Atlantic (Airbus 346)
　　Boston, DC, JFK, Miami, LAX, Vegas —> London —> Joburg

Fairly new service and bargain fares. The London connection doesn't work for *me,* but Your Mileage May Vary.

Delta/Air France**Boeing 767, 777, Airbus 332)**
Detroit —> Paris —> Johannesburg(23:30/23:08)
8:45 + 3:55 layover + 10:35
18:20 + 1:45 layover + 2:03

You'll outbound on AF through Paris (with a tight 1:25-3:55 connection), and return to Atlanta with a plane change from Joburg at Dakar (1:15 delay) for a 23:08 total time.

Previously not a top choice, Air France is improving.

American/British Airways**(Boeing 777, 747-400)**
USA —> London —> Johannesburg(26:35/29:10)

Requires a 7-9 hour layover at Heathrow. BA is overly fussy about guns, and the UK is a security hassle (although I'd heard at SCI 2007 that conditions are improving). BA is *very* fussy about excess baggage, down to even 0.1kg. (That's 4 ounces!) Until further notice, I'd pass on both BA (regardless of connection) and flying through London (regardless of airline).

Air Emirates

My UK friends enjoy their Joburg service from London, so you may want to give them a try.

Air Iberia**(Airbus 319, 346)**
Chicago —> Madrid —> Johannesburg(39:15/28:25)

Madrid layover is a ridiculous 16:50, then departing for Joburg at 12:35AM. (One hunter vehemently panned Air Iberia, saying that even —*grimace* — British Airways was better.)

European layover in comfort

Many airline lounges are available by yearly pass, even for economy class travelers. (Tip: A WiFi signal is often accessible outside their walls.) Also, most airport hotels offer a reasonable day rate, giving you a chance to shower, nap, and change clothes. Spend your layover in some comfort.

Joburg (Tambo) International layover

The Premier Club lounge (R140/$20) has free sandwiches, drinks, and nice seating. After passport control, turn right, go to near end of terminal, take escalator on right, left upstairs.

FLYING TO TANZANIA

Unless you are hunting up north in the Masailand (thus landing at Arusha), your destination is the capital of Tanzania, Dar-es-Salaam. From Dar's Old Terminal (*i.e.*, not the new one) you will catch your charter flight into the bush.

Northwest/KLM, via Amsterdam

I had good flights with them. They were on-time (though packed full), and no bags were lost or delayed.

On the way to Dar you will land in Arusha for a 30-minute stop. (On the way back to Amsterdam, it is nonstop.) Very good service, a pleasant airport, and no firearms hassles. (The Dutch customs *do* require transit permission, as soon explained.) There is a $127 excess baggage fee (each way) for rifle cases.

This is my first choice, because others require a stop-through Nairobi, Kenya, increasing risk of luggage delay/loss.

SwissAir via Zurich and Nairobi

A very fine airline, to be sure, but about 30% more expensive than the KLM flight and a Kenyan stop-through is required. The Swiss should be accommodating about rifles.

United/Lufthansa/SAA via Frankfurt and Nairobi

About the same cost and quality as SwissAir. You should have no firearm hassles going through Frankfurt. You'll pay a $127 surcharge each way for your rifle case.

American/British Airways via London and Nairobi

Although the UK isn't (yet) overly finicky about your rifles, the very fussy British Airways has a few forms you'll need to fill out.

Ethiopian Air   (Boeing 767)
D.C. Dulles to Dar 4x/week

Gracy Travel reports that EA *"have advised they will ensure passengers traveling with sporting weapons will get the attention and service they require."* If you're on an extreme budget and don't mind a possible "adventure," then this may be for you. I'm not recommending this flight by any means, but mention it nonetheless out of thoroughness. If you fly EA, please email me about your experience. (A hunter at SCI raved about his $1000 First Class flight from Frankfurt to Nairobi back in 2005, with three days at the Addis Ababa Hilton.)

PREFLIGHT GOVT. PAPERWORK

the US Customs 4457 gun form

As described in the Planning chapter, you should have one for all possible safari guns. Cameras, laptops, etc. should also be 4457ed to avoid any Customs hassles back home.

Dutch transit license for your rifles

Since summer 2005 the Dutch have required *advance* permission to fly through Holland with firearms — even if only passing through. I heard about this just 3 weeks before my flight, and 3 weeks was reported to be the average processing time. Hence, I was thrown into a bit of a panic. (My safari outfitters had loaner rifles available in Africa, but my dream was to hunt with my *own* rifle.)

The Dutch form is available on several websites, such as:

www.gracytravel.com/dutchconsent.htm

and requires a *stamped* accompanying U.S. Customs 4457 (or a letter from your police chief or sheriff attesting that the rifles are yours). Fax in both forms, and be prepared to intersperse your nervous wait with a bit of regular phone calling to the Dutch Customs office in Groningen:

011-31-50-523-2183 fax
011-31-50-523-2600 phone

They were all very polite and helpful, although locating an English-speaking colleague was often difficult.

Once at Amsterdam's Schiphol, I thought it wise to be proactive on the gun transit issue, so I sought out officialdom. Immigration knew nothing of it, and sent me to the airport police. They'd never heard of this new form, but were very helpful in sorting matters out by summoning Customs for me. Two very polite fellows showed up, and they *had* heard of the new transit form. Phone calls and faxes were made, my rifle was released to KLM, and I went off to find some overpriced airport beer in celebration.

The transit permission is now valid also for your return flight home, but *do* be proactive and seek out a Customs office when passing through Amsterdam, making *sure* that your rifles are cleared. Do *not* assume that since you got them to Africa via Holland that the Dutch will automatically let them pass through back home. (By the time you read this and actually make your own KLM flight, matters will likely be fairly routine. I was a pioneer on this, as the law was only months old then.)

At Schiphol airport, the nearest Customs office for me was near the entrance to the F gates, just behind the flowershop (look for the VAT sign). Be sure the fellow actually calls KLM, vs. merely stamping an already stamped form (because he thought that's all you wanted).

One final bit of info on all this is that the Dutch apparently process the forms based on who needs them most urgently. So, just because you faxed yours months in advance is no guarantee that you'll get them back long before your flight. Feel free to phone them in moderation, *and be polite.* For government people, they're really not bad folks, and put our federalies to shame. Learn a couple of Dutch phrases:

Hello, do you speak English?	*Hallo, sprect oo engels?*
Please	*Alst oo bleeft*
Yes/No	*Ya/Nay*
Thank you very much.	*Dank oo vel.*

I sent the Dutch official a postcard in thanks. Nobody does this, and it will smoothen things for the rest of you. If your experience with them was good, send a postcard from Africa.

Tanzanian visa

This is easily obtained at Dar airport by filling out a short form and coughing up a $50 bill. (Do *not* get your visa stateside by sending off your passport! An unnecessary risk and wait.) The Tanzanian gun permit is handled on the spot at the airport; no advance application is necessary (though this may change).

visas for other African countries

Not required for South Africa. Other countries, check in advance. Requirements are often fluid. Your travel agent (especially Gracy) will know.

TRAVEL DOCUMENT FOLDER

This is something vital to create in advance, and having all your safari paperwork under one roof might save your bacon. I've always done this, and so has accuratereloading forummeister Terry Carr (whose tips I combine with my own).

calendar
airline itinerary
aircraft seating chart (with copy for travel mate)
airlines' and TSA *Traveling with Firearms* (extra copy for ticket agent)
hotel and rental car reservation confirmation
1-page itinerary with flight schedules, travel agent/hotel/safari contacts
    (give copy to relatives, and put a copy in each piece of luggage)
printed emails to/from outfitter, PH, travel agent, etc.
safari contract
insurance policies (travel, medical, evac)
trophy fees schedule
trophy shipping instructions
small map of your hunting country
10 passport size photos (for visas, or in case passport is lost or stolen)
some envelopes receipts, boarding passes, received business cards

Copies of:
drivers license (USA and International from AAA)
Form 4457
passport (I prefer notarized)
airline tickets
credit cards
travelers' checks
Medjet Card
insurance card (with African contact phone #, not just the USA 800 #)
supplemental insurance policy (with African phone #, not just USA 800 #)
hunting invitation letter from PH (required in RSA)
blank and filled-out (black ink, though unsigned) copies of your firearms
    permit application (just in case)
printed description/color picture of luggage (and CD with such .jpg files)

All of these documents I also backup on a USB drive and CD. This may seem anal-retentive, but sloppiness is usually paid for in a trip like this. Give Murphy no obvious inroads to goof up your safari.

AT THE AIRPORT

confirm your flight and reservation within 48-72 hours!
Some airlines require this. Your travel agent will advise. Do not skip this vital step, as your flight could have been cancelled or merged into another, or your reservation lost.

at the airport, *verify* boarding/departure times
My Dulles-Joburg flight left 20 minutes earlier than ticketed, and I barely noticed it in time. (*That* was exciting.)

board *early*
The masses arrive late and wait. Breeze through earlier. This also gives you plenty of time to unravel any snags.

beware excess baggage weight fees!
You're allowed two checked bags, weight 50lbs each. Between 50-70lbs they will charge you $50, but over 70lbs is a whopping $540. Weigh your bags *before* you leave home, and allow extra space in your carry-on in case you need it.

A tip on foiling the excess baggage fee: Leave extra space in your rifle case. If your other checked bag is overweight, remove some books, ammo boxes, etc. Put them (for now) in your carry-on. You will then receive baggage tags for both checked pieces. The rifle case won't go on the conveyor belt with the other bag, because TSA must first seal it. A porter will accompany you to the TSA office, *and on the way there* is when you transfer those excess items from your carry-on to the rifle case. The porter won't care (especially if you tip him), TSA won't care, and the airline won't know because they previously weighed it and already affixed a baggage tag. Cute, huh?

Most hunters won't need to pack so much for a mere 7-14 day safari (unless you're taking over some liquor or extra ammo to leave with your PH), but my last trip to Africa lasted six weeks, and even 70lbs/bag wasn't sufficient.

When the airlines become logical about the weight issue and thus begin to charge excess for obese *passengers*, then I'll shut up. Everyone should step on a scale with their bags and be given the first 400lbs free. Charge $1/lb after that. Simple.

remove your baggage claim stubs from ticket jacket
Place these *immediately* in your neck pouch. Do not step away from the ticket counter until you've done this!

detach your return ticket and place in neck pouch
If you don't, it can easily become separated and lost.

do not walk about with your passport or ticket in hand
Keep these secured until you must provide them.

security tips

Modern airport security installs a steel door on a grass hut, since the airport workers go through far less screening. Also, the *shoes-off, no-shampoo* drill is no doubt calculated to dehumanize and condition passengers. (What indignity will people *not* put up with these days?) While you can't avoid the process, reduce its unpleasantness by packing in this fashion:

front pants pocket
Outbound ticket and ID only. Remove all metallic items.

neck pouch inside the shirt
This contains all vital paperwork: passport, baggage claim checks, return ticket, cash, travelers' checks, and a spare credit card. Have nothing metallic inside so you can wear it through the detector.

belt pack
All pocket metallic items go in here: coins, watch, keys, cell, etc. Your goal is to pass the detector without beeping.

going through the metal detector
I place my things in trays in this order: shoes, belt, belt pack, vest/jacket, laptop, rucksack. Thus, I am dressing on the other side while they are screening my rucksack (which has the most items and takes the longest to clear). The reverse order begs for trouble, and it's embarrassing to have to wait for your belt, etc. while the TSA agent is opening up your carry-on bag.

tips for comfort in Economy Class

While you may not be wealthy, you can at least be clever. This will greatly increase your comfort and convenience.

know your airplane!
Seating configurations vary widely by aircraft, and even airlines using the same equipment. Some passengers prefer to be near the lavatories, while other do not. Most airline websites

have seating diagrams. Print them out while making flight/seat reservations.

ask at the ticket and/or boarding gate for Business Class

The best way to improve Economy Class comfort is to get bumped up to Business. Though the airlines are getting increasingly chintzy, free upgrades do still occur. An author, journalist, or other airline-advantageous person has a bit of leverage for this. Also, anybody celebrating their birthday or anniversary has a decent chance.

Dressing nicely will go a *long* way in making this happen. (Another reason for not wearing yard clothes on international flights.) *I.e.*, dress and act like you *belong* in Business Class, vs. some rube who will likely embarrass himself (and others) there.

You'll have to wait until about the last minute, as the airline naturally prefers to *sell* the upgrade, or at least use a passenger's frequent flyer miles, rather than giving it away. My Lufthansa upgrade (travel book author *and* birthday boy!) was made in the final minutes, and I was the last person to board. Though a bit dicey timing, it certainly added to the savoriness.

Once given a Business Class boarding pass by the agent, the aircrew won't be able to discern your free upgrade, so don't be shy (but try not to gloat). Enjoy the novelty of pre/during-takeoff drinks, something never allowed the *hoi polloi*.

Keep your boarding pass stub, as it will allow you into the Business Class lounge during your layover.

get exit row seats

These will have quite a bit more legroom, almost as much as business class (but with skinny seats). If you cannot reserve such when you book your flight, then ask the ticket (or boarding gate) agent to reseat you. The earlier you check in, the better the odds. On full flights, exit rows were reserved long ago.

if no exit row, then an empty center row

On those rare flights less than 70% full, this may be possible. Stretching out across four or five empty center row seats is as comfortable as Business Class. Be prepared to defend "your" row against others keen on sharing. Stretch out as soon as you can and claim that row. When you leave for the lavatory, place items in all "your" seats.

choose the most forward row
This decreases your boarding and deboarding time.

rows to avoid: in front of exit rows and bulkheads
These seats do not recline. While not an issue on a 2-hour domestic flight, such is devastating after 7-15 hours.

get window seats
You'll have the bulkhead to nap against, and avoid seatmates skittering past you to the lavatory. With an inflatable pillow and something to prop your feet on, this makes for a most tolerable flight (especially in an exit row).

seats to avoid: aisle and center
Aisle seats get constantly bumped by aisle traffic, and should be avoided unless you've a bladder control issue.

Center seats are just awful on long flights.

if you get stuck with a truly lousy seat
Such as a nonreclining center seat by the rear lavatory with a flatulent fat man in aisle and a mom with screaming baby in window, ask the flight attendant to move you ASAP. Very few flights are 100% full, so empty seats do remain.

If your situation is egregious *and* the airline's fault, then ask for a Business upgrade. Make your problem *their* problem.

use the overhead bin across the aisle, not above you
Then you can keep an eye on your bag from your seat.

sleep as much as possible!
The time passes far more quickly, and you'll suffer less dyschronia (jet lag) upon arrival. (During your first day in Africa, stay awake until bedtime.)

use the lavatory on the off cycle
Such as *before* meals are served, vs. just afterwards.

are your checked bags *onboard*?
Upon arriving at your domestic connection (DC, NYC, Chicago, Atlanta, etc.), ask the boarding agent of your overseas flight if your checked bags are in their custody. (With computers, this can be verified nearly instantly.) Find out *before* you board, and you may be able to resolve any snags while your plane is still on the ground. Do the same for any European connection.

MY AFRICAN TRAVEL EXPERIENCES
Tanzania
KLM flight USA—>Amsterdam
The rifle check-in wasn't terribly painful. An airline rep escorted me over to a special room of "Homeland Security" where my rifle case was X-rayed. When I asked why, the answer was *"To check for any weapons."* Uh, OK... This feat accomplished, the case was sealed with TSA decals, and I was escorted back to the ticket gate to give the case to the airline.

KLM flight Amsterdam—>Dar-es-Salaam
Having confirmed that my bags had made it across the Atlantic, and that my rifle had been released from Dutch customs to KLM, I was feeling very relaxed about the trip.

KLM planes have monitors which update (in Dutch and English) the passengers on location, speed (*snelheid*), altitude (*hoogte*), and ETA. Well, these two words for some odd reason seemed funny. As we began to taxi, my seatmate said with perfect deadpan visage, "We are gaining *snelheid*." I replied, "Yes, but I'd like to see some more *hoogte*." During the 9-hour flight we traded many such wisecracks. During our descent I mock panicked, "We're losing *hoogte*, we're losing *hoogte!*"

The plane's monitors also have a map with your flight's location, updated every few minutes. Since I'd never before crossed the equator, I snapped a nice photo just when I had reached the southern hemisphere.

Happily, the flight was only half full, and just after takeoff I grabbed my own empty 4-seat row. Pull back the armrests and you've got a makeshift little bed. I got 5 hours of good sleep. Only when we began to lose *hoogte* did I wake up.

Dar to Zanzibar and back
Coastal Aviation in Dar's *old* terminal (not the new one handling international flights) is the sort of Southwest Airlines of Tanzania. They link the capital to the islands (Zanzibar, Pemba, and Mafia), Arusha, and the Selous.

A round-trip to Zanzibar is $110. It is a 12-minute hop, the shortest commercial flight I'd ever made. Outbound was a lovely Pilatus PC12 turboprop. Beautiful ship, but with a very surly pilot. My seatmate was a black man from the RSA, some sort of mid-level government functionary. His oily disdain for me was not, however, mid-level. Every ill and ache of Africa, including the decades of slaughter in Rwanda, he attributed at least indirectly to white colonists. (He conveniently omitted that tribal warfare was in full swing long before white explorers, much less colonists, ever arrived.) Good thing it was a 12 minute flight. Had it been 13, I'd have opened the exit door in midflight. (Not for me—for *him*.) This was the only racially charged conversation I had on my trip. Not surprisingly, it came from a *bureaucrat*. Black people who *work* for a living were universally friendly to me in Tanzania.

The return flight to Dar was with a better pilot and passengers, though not in that Pilatus PC12. Our "copilot" was a 6-year-old Belgian girl who was allowed to actually take control of the yoke over the ocean. Although the pilot had to rudder for her since she couldn't reach the pedals, she otherwise flew the plane. (Try *that* in America!) She was even allowed to help taxi, and wheeled us into a perfect wingtip-to-wingtip position. A very impressive little girl. She was calm and asked detailed questions before did anything, wanting to confirm exactly what was expected of her. She wants to be a pilot when she grows up, and I've no doubt that she will!

charter flights in/out of the Selous Game Reserve

I was really looking forward to this. My very own twin for the 218 nautical mile flight. I had returned to Dar from Zanzibar with a planned one-hour layover at the Old Terminal before our flight. Perfect.

***Soft* bags only!** These are small Pipers and Cessnas, and hard bags are too unwieldy. (My safari outfitter kept my hard rifle case for me at their Dar office.) Lots of camp supplies also onboard: eggs, beer, water, etc. Nothing but what is flown or trucked in exists at camp.

If the pilot had a larynx, I wouldn't have known it. A surly little Parisian, Remy stuck in his iPod earphones after takeoff and trimming, and his passengers ceased to exist. He said not a word during the entire 80-minute flight in his ratty Piper Aztec. (I later heard that such experience was typical.)

None of this, however, sullied the joy at actually arriving in the bush. The grass airstrip at Mbuga was a thrill to land on, and part of it was still on fire from the last reburning. All the village children are aviation fans who visit every flight and swarm the grass hut "terminal" to gape at the newest *bwanas*.

The four departing hunters (a family of ungrateful, drunken sods with dot-com money) were there to enjoy Remy's cheer back to Dar. I asked one of them, an 18 y/o kid, how his hunt was. *"Uh, OK."* This punk got a *21-day* hunt for his worthless birthday, shot everything from buffalo to leopard, and *that's* his reaction. (When I turned 18, I'd have been delighted just to go deer hunting.) The others whined that the camp wasn't all that great, that their PHs didn't find them enough easy animals, etc. You get the idea. I had been in the Rover for just minutes and the two PHs began to cheer over the exodus of that group. (When I explained that I was thrilled just to *be* in Africa, game notwithstanding, my PH was very pleased.) Too many American hunters are fat, lazy, wealthy, and completely inappreciative of being able to safari. (If you are of this ilk, please do not mention my book!)

The return flight featured a newer ship and a nicer pilot. He cheerfully explained things below I'd missed coming in, such as hippos floating in the Rufiji river from a mile up.

South Africa

One main advantage to hunting in the RSA over Tanzania is that you avoid expensive charter flights into the bush. From Joburg you will have to connect with a domestic turboprop to a provincial capital nearest your outfitter (who will pick you up at the airport), but these flights are under an hour. (Another reason to book with a safari-experienced travel agent, is that these domestic add-ons are $200 cheaper than booking separately from an Internet ticket.)

I sampled both Lufthansa and SAA, and recommend them (though Frankfurt layovers are 8-10 hours). All were on time, and no bags were delayed or lost.

The next year, out of experiential thoroughness, I booked a Joburg nonstop on SAA from Dulles. It was 15 hours in the air, and *felt* like it. After my 18-hour return I laid over few days in order to teach a shooting class in Virginia, see friends, and tour D.C. Would I book those direct flights again? Not likely. I loathe the jumbled, humid mess of Dulles, and those long flights are very hard on travelers (unless you fly Business or First). If you can spend the extra outbound day of travel required to connect through Europe, I urge you to do so.

GROUND TRANSPORTATION

My first South Africa hunt saw no off-campus travel around the country except for a day hunt in the mountains. The next year, after a month hunting, I rented a car for two weeks and 2100 miles. In Tanzania I had several car trips within Dar.

South Africa

The RSA is a large country, being twice the area of California. In my two weeks I toured the provinces of Limpopo, Mpumalanga, KwaZuluNatal, and Gauteng. (Hadn't enough time to see Cape Town, alas.)

renting a car and driving about

This is not as dicey as it seems. South Africa has an excellent roadnet, clear signage, and ubiquitous fuel stations (all of which are full-serve). Go for it! It's a great way to see the country, and your travels will be remarked on by the locals. If you've an auto GPS, take it with you and download local maps.

My Nissan Tiida (unknown here) was a compact 4-door, but it had great pep and a nice stereo. I drove it hard and fast (80mph) and it got over 30mpg (nearly the same economy as a subcompact, but with much more power). Cost for two weeks (including excess mileage premium) was $500. There is a mandatory insurance policy ($100) with R3000 ($429) deductible, but you can (and should) pay for the full coverage.

If there is a chance that you will tour a foreign country (*i.e.*, Mozambique, Zimbabwe, Botswana, Swaziland, Lesotho, or Namibia) you must first get the rental agency's permission form at the desk. While a mere formality, you'll certainly need it in case of accident or theft outside South Africa.

The rental car agent was pretty new, but most professional. I could not, however, resist a last minute joke as he showed me my car. Pointing to the 5-speed stick, I deadpanned, "*Do you have an automatic? I cannot drive a manual.*" Consternation flooded his face until I grinned widely and shook my head that I was kidding. He laughed heartily (and with great relief). Africans have a great sense of humor, so don't forget to clown around occasionally.

Driving on the left side of the road (which derives from the Roman practice of keeping the righthand sword arm close to your foe) takes a bit of practice. Constantly tell yourself the mantra of a well-dressed Socialist: *Keep left —look right!* After a few days (if you survive), it'll start to feel quite natural.

Traffic enforcement policy for speeding allows 10% over. The excellent highways have a 120km/h limit, so that means you're likely safe from the flashing lights up to 132. Photo radar is used, and your ticket will likely end up at your rental car office (which will ding your credit card for the fine per the small print on your contract).

Carjacking is common in South Africa, though a compact rental car won't likely attract attention. Carjackers there are a very serious lot. Typically, four guys with AK47s will pile out. That is a tough problem to solve, even with alertness and a .45.

Final caveat: don't drive at night if you can avoid it. Things get weird and risky. An hour past sunset I nearly plowed into some cattle crossing the road. If you must drive at night, tell your friends between A and B, and have some assistance in between lined up. And have a prepaid cell phone!

Tanzania
from airport to hotel

Most safari packages include "meet and greet" to assist your entry into the country and process your gun permits. Such folks will have their own car for you. Be sure to tip the driver, as well as the man who got you through Customs.

getting around Dar

Your safari company will likely have a car and driver for you to use (if no charge, tip your driver handsomely). Our driver, Urussa, wheeled us around for an afternoon, helping us to shop for local goods. After asking the safari manager's advice, we tipped Urussa $30, and he seemed very grateful. (Moral: Take *care* of people who take care of *you*. You'll never miss an extra $1 or $10 here and there, but in a country where a middle class wage is $10/day, you're helping entire families.)

taxis

Some specific routes are set price by the government (your safari company can inform you), while others are subject to negotiation. Always settle on the price *before* you get in!

And haggle at least a little bit. If the driver says Tsh6,000 ($6), offer 4,000 and you'll arrive at 5,000. You won't get as good a deal to/from the nicer hotels (because your fellow Western guests usually pay full fare, or more, thus ruining it for you).

Taxis are all privately owned, and there is quite a variety in age and cleanliness. Never agree on a driver until you've seen his *car*, and you might as well choose the newest one around. I learned this through experience after a few ratty rides. (My nicest taxi was in Zanzibar, a Toyota Camry.)

avoid the *dalla-dallas* minibuses

While a cheap way to get around, sometimes too cheap becomes expensive. They're very crowded, and petty thefts and assaults are quite common. Take a taxi for $3-7 per trip.

GOING HOME

> There was a part of me, of us, back there on a hill in Tanganyika, in a swamp in Tanganyika, in a tent and on a river and by a mountain in Tanganyika. There was a part of me out there that would stay out there until I came back to ransom that part of me. It would never live in a city again, that part of me, nor be content, the other part, to be in a city. There are no tiny gleaming campfires in a city.
>
> We got on the plane one day and pointed back to Paris and New York and work and cocktail parties and penthouse and expensive, fashionable saloons. Our first stop was in Addis Ababa. The natives were just as ugly, and there were even more flies than I remembered. I was sure New York would be worse.
>
> — Robert C. Ruark, *Horn of the Hunter* (1954), pp. 315

packing for the airport

pack your rifle hard case with as much as possible

In mine went my three knives, binos, and plenty of shopping goodies I'd acquired. It would barely close, and that was the point. Tufpaks hold more than Pelicans, but are not as convenient to remove your rifles during customs checks.

Have no ammo on your person or in carry-on luggage!

I knew this very well, but was careless packing up in Dar. I left the two bullets and spent cases from my hartebeest in my fanny pack, and forgot about them entirely until we went through security in Amsterdam for the USA flight. The Dutch people were *eventually* reasonable about it, though not before a few dicey minutes passed as they considered confiscation.

Although I was prepared to raise a righteous stink about the matter (*i.e.,* demanding to mail them home, etc.), it was preferable that I had simply packed them appropriately in the first place. I don't make many mistakes during travel (having been to three dozen countries), but if I can, so can you. Be careful and thorough in your packing.

get a VAT refund at Joburg airport
If your purchased goods (not dinners or rental car) totaled at least R250, and you can show them (and their receipts) to the tax clerk, you will get the VAT (*i.e.*, sales tax) refunded.

There is a big snag to this, however. You must have the goods with you in your *carry-on* bag, as this office is inside the security zone. Pack accordingly if you've a big VAT refund due.

dealing with officials
Never be pushy or impatient, as they have much more power and time than you do (and they know it). Politeness and empathy (*"Busy day?"*) will usually speed you along. A cigarette, candy, biltong, or soft drink can go a long way in greasing the bureaucratic wheels. Relax and smile often.

back in the USA
the US Customs declaration form
Returning Americans are allowed $800 of duty-free articles. Most of you won't likely exceed that. On your flight to the USA you will be provided a U.S. Customs declaration form. Itemize every last trinket, and you'll have little problem.

You will be asked if you are importing any elephant products, including elephant hair bracelets. Know before you go! (Lion and leopard products must be accompanied by a CITES permit.) Simian products (*e.g.,* baboon) require paperwork from the CDC and are a *huge* hassle.

You will not be allowed to bring back *any* of your game meat, and they will specifically ask if you have any biltong (as if they throw away what they confiscate).

As a hunter, I was treated quite respectfully, even by U.S. personnel. African safari hunting is still echoic of a wealthy man's game, and I was never hassled.

the US Customs 4457 gun form
I was asked only coming back from South Africa, and my rifle's serial number was compared to the form's. The year

before, from Tanzania, I was not asked for the form but my rifle was inspected for unloaded status.

Department of Fish & Game

Since the threat of rinderpest here is a severe one (which would wipe out 90% of cattle infected), your shoes will be sprayed upon return. This is a Good Thing, and one of the few I can attribute to government operations at airports.

❖ 6

2x1 HUNTS

> *Things are very simple in the African veld. You is or you ain't. You are a courageous man or you are a coward, and it takes a very short time to decide, and for everyone you know to detect it. You can learn more about people in three days on safari than you might run down in a lifetime of polite association under "civilized" circumstances. That is why few foreign visitors are speaking to each other when they finish a long trip into the bush.*
> — Robert Ruark's *Africa* (1991), p. 71

A 1x1 hunt means that the hunter has a PH all to himself. 2x1 hunters must share the PH, and the game. While a *bit* cheaper than two hunters enjoying their own 1x1 hunts, it's not by much. For example, a typical 7-day Tanzania buffalo hunt would be $850/day for 1x1 and $600/day for 2x1. So, sharing a PH will save each hunter $250/day.

If game is plentiful, *and* you're both not expecting 3-5 animals each within 7 days, then a 2x1 hunt can work. However, if the game is thin and/or your expectations high, you'll each wish you'd had your own PH.

Depending on how busy your safari company is, it may not even have an extra PH for two simultaneous 1x1 hunts, and you'll be forced to go 2x1 (as I was). Nonetheless, our block within the Selous was 3,500 miles^2, or 42% larger than Delaware and Rhode Island combined; it was an area nearly half the size of New Jersey. And we had it *all* to ourselves.

HUNT ALONE OR WITH OTHERS?

going alone in a 1x1 hunt
The only advantage I can see to this is that you will have all the game to yourself. But *if* there is enough game for *two* during the time allotted, then a 1x1 hunt has no real advantage.

Its main disadvantage is experiential loneliness. You will have no friend with you to share the safari. (And for this, you must add $150+ to the daily rate.)

Most 1x1 hunters probably can't find a buddy with the time and money to go along.

choosing a 2x1 hunting partner
He must be fit: hardy, easygoing, helpful, sociable, experienced in hunting, a good shot, well-traveled, funny, and flush with enough cash to comfortably afford the trip.

He must *not* be: a whiner, out of shape, cantankerous, overtly insecure, a poor shot, afraid to try new things, greedy for attention, a liar, a braggart, lazy, a tightwad ... or a *thief.*

And just *where* do you find such a person? I never did, though I *thought* I had. Months afterwards, my hunting partner was discovered to be a pathological liar with two convictions for theft out of five arrests (and locally suspected of many other thefts). Back home he falsely boasted far and wide of shooting a charging elephant (which our PH had shot *the day before* we even arrived in camp; see the color photo). Also later proven wholly untrue were his alleged combat fighter pilot victories in F-5Es during the Iran/Iraq war.

In short, I'd unknowingly hunted with a *sociopath*.

This was somebody I'd known for three years, and who had up until that time hoodwinked most other friends, too. What is on a person's inside will come out eventually, though it was several months too late for me. Be absolutely sure of your hunting partner's *character*. Had I done a simple criminal/civil background check at the local courthouse, I'd have learned that my "friend" was a serial thief and con artist.

what about taking along your lady?
Regarding a Tanzania hunt, not many women would enjoy days of bouncing around in a Land Rover and 10 mile hikes as an observer. And, there's little to do if they stayed in camp the whole time. Either way, it is expensive at $300/day

($250 daily rate, plus $50 government fee for observers), and you'll be dead-tired every night after hunting, anyway. One option is to leave the ladies in Dar or Zanzibar or Arusha while you hunt. This would save the $300/day fee, and they wouldn't be bored. Your call, obviously, but even 7 days in Zanzibar is stretching things. Unless she also hunts, my advice is to make this guys-only, *or* have her fly over to meet you afterward. This would make for two separate experiences for you, and spending time with your lady following the hunt may just be the way to unwind.

Regarding a South African hunt, she could easily enjoy some time on the coast while you're in the field.

traveling together

From America it is at least two 10-hour flights to Africa, or 15 hours direct to Joburg. With a domestic connecting flight, figure on 25-30 hours. If you and your hunting partner have not traveled extensively on your own, tempers are bound to flare between novices unless great pains are taken to keep things calm, organized, and fun. It's preferable that at least one of you has considerable international travel experience.

spending money together

Much of what you do will be in common, such as taxis, tipping, meals, events, etc. Hence, establish a common fund into which you both pool identical sums, and designate one person to be the "banker." This smoothens matters considerably, and avoids both of you having to dig into your wallets for a common purchase, or trying to keep track of who paid for the last taxi.

hunting together

This will work only if you've already got a very solid working friendship which has been previously tried and tested.

If one of you has already been to Africa, the newbie should be offered the first shot on any animals on both your lists. If you're both newbies, then either flip a coin or agree beforehand who gets first shot at what (thus allowing the game to "decide").

Whichever/whatever, figure this out on your flight over, and not in the field just before a final stalk. If partners alternate between animals, each will end up with about the same number of trophies — assuming no misses.

Misses, however, can pose a problem. If a hunter misses does he "lose his turn" or should he be allowed a second try at the next animal? Discuss this before the hunt, exploring any "what if" scenarios to avoid hard feelings in the bush.

consider a longer hunt

If your hunting concession is, for whatever reason, a bit short on game, then a 7-day hunt may be too short for two hunters' success. Tanzania offers a 10-day hunt (same game as the 7-day hunt, but with a second buffalo), and in retrospect I wish I'd done that. That's 43% more hunting for just $2400. (The daily rate would then go up to $700.) All of your other costs are identical to a 7-day hunt.

take a digital camera for *each* hunter

One camera is not enough, as the photographer will miss out on many random shots of himself. When each hunter has a camera, then both hunters can be equally represented in the photographic perspective.

Or, take a nonhunting observer who will serve as the safari's photographer.

final thoughts

For your first safari, I would *not* recommend a 2x1 hunt. Certainly, travel with a buddy and enjoy your own 1x1 hunts, but too much can go wrong in a 2x1 to not only sour your safari, but also your friendship. Even one hunter suffering from randomly poor luck when it's his turn to cut sign can be enough to cause hard feelings about the trip.

My advice: Spend a bit extra and have your own PH.

❖ 7

PACKING

My advice on packing may seem overly detailed, but what has twice worked well for me should work well for you. Unless you've a proven system of your own, try mine.

MONEY

Most safari companies will require a 50% deposit of their total daily rate to book your hunt. They will usually have an American bank to receive your check, wire, or local deposit. The balance will be paid in Africa upon arrival, and for that you will need cash or travelers' checks. (No credit cards or personal checks are typically accepted by outfitters.) Taking $10,000 or more in cash or *"bearer instruments"* triggers a Customs form.

A variety of cash and travelers' checks (the brand *does* matter!) will serve you well (with a credit card backup). The old rule of taking *"half the clothes you think you need and twice the cash"* remains sound advice. Regarding our own "Federal Reserve Notes" avoid the old "small-head" bills (especially for Tanzania, where they are *not* accepted). Here's an example:

$100 cash ($50 in $1s, and $50 in $5s)
Small dollar bills are scarce, and you should bring your own as a tip supply. Porters should be paid $1-$2 each. A $5 bill (big-head only) is 10 hours of RSA minimum wage and will smooth over most minor difficulties with most minor functionaries (who have big egos).

$200 cash in $10s
A $10 bill or two will usually take care of the more severe troubles. (Your city guide or driver can advise you on this.)

$2000 cash in $20s and $50s

This will serve as your camp tip fund (figure on $500-$1500, depending on the hunt (1x1 or 2x1) and the quality of service), and for other cash needs. The staff are *not* set up to receive travelers' checks as tips, but your PH might be. Take plenty of cash for these folks!

cash-size envelopes for camp staff tips

This will anonymize the amounts given, and reduce potential friction between staff. Also, a few personal words of thanks written on the envelope with perhaps your business card is a kind gesture.

$5000 (or more) in travelers' checks

This is to pay your safari balance at hunt's end in Africa. Take plenty in case it is raining with game. (I had permission for two Selous buffalo in a 7-day hunt because too few had been previously killed. An extra $1035 would have been needed.)

Ask your PH which brand of checks to bring over! For example, AmEx checks are virtually impossible to tender in Tanzania, yet preferred in South Africa. *Know Before Ye Go.*

Join the AAA and you'll save the 1% travelers' checks fee. Calculate what you will likely owe for the remaining balance, game fees, etc. and buy that amount in $1000 denominations (which saves signature time). You will likely have to order them in advance. Buy the remainder in $100s. AAA sells VISA checks, which were accepted without trouble in the RSA.

You should *always* carry the receipts separately from the checks. I used my ankle wallet for the receipts, copies of my passport, some cash, a spare credit card and drivers license. The checks I kept in my neck wallet.

credit cards

Probably indispensable these days, and much easier than travelers' checks. MasterCard is recognized by the Cirrus ATM network, and this is probably the easiest way to get local cash. You should prenotify your card company that you'll be charging in Africa during specific dates.

PACKING FOR AIR TRAVEL

As I wrote earlier, I'll assume you've little/no travel experience internationally. I've had quite a lot, and can save you the needless hassles.

check-through bags

You'll be allowed only *two,* so you must maximize their utility. Here is what I strongly recommend:

rifle hard case (with guns packed in soft sleeves): Pelican or Storm
large soft bag with wheels/handle (and shoulder straps, if possible)

rifle hard case (with wheels)

Along with your rifle (scope side facing handle) goes all valuable gear, such as your knives, binos, etc. A jacket or shirts can be used to fill up any extra space. Be sure that luggage tags are also on the *inside,* as well as the outside. And *triple*-check your gun's unloaded status before you reach the airport! I put strips of bright 2" yellow vinyl tape on my case, writing my name and flight info. Distinctive and good insurance if your bag tag comes off.

Use heavy combination padlocks commonly coded to your friend's locks. (Keys are easily lost.) Or, you can buy TSA locks (www.travelsentry.org) openable by staff, although there should be no reason to subsequently open your inspected/sealed case. (If the case was *not* personally inspected and sealed, your locks *will* be clipped off. Then, the case will be held back because unlocked gun cases are not allowed in transit. It's happened, so beware. You may want to pack inside a *second* pair of padlocks in ZipLoc bag with a note of instructions/thanks.)

I used a wheeled **Pelican 1750** case, and it's served perfectly (though looking worn after three trips to Africa). My guns are well protected, and the case is easily manageable. Holds two long guns and ammo. $250. www.pelican.com

A similar case to Pelican is the **Hardigg Storm im3300** with wheels and four locking tabs (which need reinforcing). www.stormcases.com or only $180 from CheaperThanDirt.

The **SKB ATA Double Rifle** case is a good choice, though the plastic locks are integral and TSA-openable. Try to find the older model with metal latches. www.skbcases.com

Another way to go is the **Tuffpak** container, which looks like a hexagonal golfbag and thus is less conspicuous than a normal hard gun case. The Tuffpak #1049TSA for $355 holds 3 scoped rifles or 5 shotguns, plus clothing and equipment. www.nalpak.com It is not as conveniently unpacked, however, which matters when declaring your guns at airports.

There are nicely made aluminum cases on the market, but these are heavy (say, *33lbs,* and you've 50-70lbs allowed by the airline) and prone to denting. Not my first choice, but **Cabela's Bulletproof** case is one of the best.

soft gun case

Regardless of which hard case you take, remove a layer of foam and use a soft case (required for charter plane and Land Rover travel) to internally pack your rifle within the hard case. The soft case should have an outside pocket, which you'll find very useful in the vehicle to hold misc. items while on the road. (If hunting with a friend, choose different color soft cases to avoid confusion.)

large soft bag with wheels

It must be *soft* because hard bags aren't generally allowed in the small charter planes. It must have *wheels* because that's the only way you'll be able to manage all your luggage.

Make this a *big* bag, as you will likely be bringing back a few souvenirs. A 7000+in^2 sports bag is a good candidate.

Though permitted by **14 CFR 108.203(g),** some airlines insist that ammo be packed in a bag *separate* from your rifle. You may take up to 11lbs (per person, not per gun), but this is rarely scrutinized. (It's never happened to me.) Some airlines are fussy about requiring factory boxes. Polyethylene MTM Case-Guard boxes are great. Bring as *much* as you can, because there is no such thing as "too much" ammo. A buffalo badly shot the first round may need several more to finish him off. (Your nonhunting partner can also pack 11lbs of extra ammo for you.)

Hunters using different calibers should split it with their buddy, so that both have ammo if one bag is delayed or lost.

Idea: If you plan on returning to Africa with the *same* safari outfitter, ask if you can leave your ammo there. That way you have an emergency supply for next time. Also, a box of *assorted* ammo, such as .375H&H, .416 Rem, .416 Rigby, .458 Win, and .458 Lott would make a super gift to your PH, allowing him to save a hapless hunter's bacon who lost his bag.

carry-on luggage and gear

You want to be able to comfortably survive with what you have *with* you, because checked bags are frequently delayed (though rarely lost permanently).

TSA ("*Take Shampoo Away*") www.tsa.gov
A quick aside about the prohibition of carry-on liquids and gels. It's a *sham*. Ostensibly, the TSA is worried that Liquid A and Gel B can be mixed to form a binary-component explosive. So, what's their brilliant safety plan at the airport? To seize your Liquid A and Gel B and toss them into the *same* trash barrel, along with everybody *else's* — many of them *leaking*. That the American public believes this sham is a disgrace.

The rules have relaxed since 2006, and 3oz clear containers in a 1-quart ZipLoc are permitted in carry-on bags.

medium-sized quality backpack
This will serve as your one carry-on bag, so choose the maximum size allowable in overhead storage bins. This will also serve as your truck day pack, so choose something rugged and waterproof. In an exit row seat, it'll serve as a footstool.

Get a nylon backpack with a volume of 2500-3500in^2. It should have wide and thickly padded straps, at least one outside pocket, and an organized interior. Try it out with at least 30lbs of weight for comfort. If there's some African *coup* while you're in country, you may be on your own for a while, and a good pack (no bright colors) then becomes tactical gear.

REI and other quality outdoors stores will have good choices. I like the **Kelty Redwing 3100**. (Most will be made in Asia, but avoid packs made in Vietnam, a Communist nation. Chinese products may be nearly unavoidable these days, but you've no excuse supporting *Hanoi*.) The Vaude Seattle 65 Travel Pack is versatile choice (www.eigerequipment.com).

If the silly 2006 no-liquid/gel rule is ever canceled by the TSA, carry *lots* of water with you for the flight. In 2005 I took 6.5l (nearly 2 gallons). You should drink copious amounts of water, which will ameliorate symptoms of *dyschronia* (jetlag).

In my day pack went the Camelbak Mule (filled with goodies), spare clothes (in case my checked bag got delayed/lost), hat, lots of AA batteries, and several books.

Tip: leave the pack 20% empty in case your checked bag is overweight and you need to empty it of some things.

belt pack

Used for airline travel, and walking about town. I bought a $10 cheapie for bicyclists which included two 500ml polycarbonate water bottles. It's served perfectly for three trips to hold all those little things used for personal comfort, including (back in 2005) evil liquids and gels:

- toothbrush, small tube of toothpaste
- earplugs in a 35mm film can (flying is ear-damaging noisy)
- inflatable neck pillow
- blindfold (for sleeping on the plane)
- safety razor
- Bandaids
- Ziploc bag of unscented baby wipes
- eyedrops
- coughdrops
- Ziploc bag with latex gloves (AIDS is rampant in Africa)
- small bottle of hand disinfectant
- small clear spray bottle mister (very refreshing on long flights)
- malaria tablets, dysentery pills
- the book *Healthy Travel — Africa* from www.lonelyplanet.com
- energy bars
- paperback novel
- small notepad and pen
- digital camera
- one of your two GMRS radios (your partner has the other)
- copies of misc. paperwork (insurance, passport, etc.)

Yes, you *could* keep these things in your day pack, but accessing it frequently from the overhead bin is a hassle. Also, a worn belt pack is less likely to become lost or stolen. If a belt pack isn't your style, then a good safari vest would do the same job.

neck wallet (an absolute *must*)

Protect your passport, international DL, travelers' checks, backup credit card, and some cash.

ankle wallet

This contains travelers' check receipts (always keep separate from the checks!), a spare credit card and drivers license, some cash, copies of passports (yours and your friend's) and any other vital paperwork. If this seems redundant to your neck wallet, trust me that it is not. Modularity and multiple "baskets" for your "eggs" is what protects you against Murphy.

CLOTHES

Most camps will have daily laundry at no charge, and superbly done. So, don't take more than three changes of field clothes (and two *usually* are sufficient, but ask your PH).

footwear (three pairs are all you need)

airport and travel shoes

Given the shoes-off silliness of airport "security" you will enjoy travelling in easily slipped off footwear, such as Roper walking boots. Such can also serve as your about-town shoes, casual or dress-up. Some quality replacement insoles can really make a comfort difference. Try out the gel-packs.

field boots

They must be of good quality, comfortable, grippy, and *well* broken-in. Ankle-high is preferred. You want a flexible sole and not a heavy clumpy one (which animals can hear). **Do not take a *new* pair of boots to Africa!** Take a pair that are *half* worn out (meaning fully worn *in*). I took my pair of lightweight tactical boots which fit me superbly.

While I wasn't in truly wet country, I did occasionally have to step in some muddy puddles in the Selous, so waterproof boots are clearly in order. If you've the room, take a spare set of boots in case your primary pair loses a heel or sole.

Take a travel size GoldBond Medicated Foot Powder. Treat your feet during lunch, airing out your boots and socks.

camp shoes

After being in your boots all day, they are the last things you'll want to wear after your hot shower around the campfire. A cheap, lightweight pair of sandals are just the ticket. They're also great for the beach. Crocs are only $7 in South Africa.

socks

Bring 4-5 pairs of whatever hiking socks work for you. A hemp-blend is comfortable, and absorbent. Easy to find in "hippy" type stores, or you can order them online from www.organicclothes.com. Heavy wool/rayon socks are also good.

gaitors

A very good idea if you wear shorts.

field clothes

"Bwana" clothing festooned with straps, buckles, extra pockets, epaulettes and so on is semi-useless. Straps catch on brush; synthetic fabrics scrape noisily on thorns and twigs and don't breathe; Velcro and sometimes even zippers are noisy. Stick with the tried-and-true: cotton, leather, buttons and laces.
— www.dakotaarms.com/safaritips/index.htm

Your PH will usually be *very* simply dressed in shorts, gaitors, short-sleeved shirt, and ball cap. A leather belt will hold his ammo pouch and small skinner. You'll probably wear more.

A brief word about colors: *dark earth tones only!* Olive, brown, or green. Avoid bone color, as it borders on white and really stands out in the bush. Even tan or khaki can often be too light in color, and I'd avoid such (at least for shirts).

USMC digital camo BDUs (*i.e.*, MARPAT)

These give better concealment than the US Army digital (which have too much gray) or the old woodland (designed for western Europe). If the bush is still lush after the rains, then go green digital. If you're hunting later in the season (*i.e.*, September to November) or in Namibia, then go desert digital. You can't beat the added concealment, ruggedness, and utility. I'm quite sure that my successful stalking was in great part due to my digital camo. An eland herd just 20yds away stared at me for many minutes without spooking, and I surprised very wary animals (duiker, caracal, ostriches) by getting in *very* close.

Before you go, ask your outfitter if camo is permitted in the country you're hunting in. (OK in Tanzania and RSA.)

Carhartt

Great quality and style, and in the right colors. The double-layered pants are a bit overkill, unless for thorny brush.

Bill's Khaki pants

Utterly faithful to the WWII vintage $8\frac{1}{2}oz/yd^2$ cotton twill, Bill Thomas makes probably the world's best cotton pants. You'll look like Burt Lancaster in *From Here To Eternity*. Thomas is also quite a free-market advocate in the style of Ayn Rand (whom he knew). Not cheap; you'll pay $100 for them from www.herringtoncatalog.com, but top quality and a treat.

in Tanzanian tsetse fly country (no blue jeans!)

Try out the twin-mesh BugTamerPlus clothing.

hat
> Everyone has a vision of the "safari hat," a wide-brimmed, sweat-rimmed floppy affair with, in the case of an old Hollywood hand, vague bloodstains, the odd bullet hole, roosting bats and, of course, the inevitable partially moth-ingested leopard-skin band.
> — Peter Capstick, Safari (1984), p. 83

A crushable wide brim safari hat (which can be buttoned up on the side, Australian-style, for a better cheekweld) is a must. Ball caps will do (your PH will likely wear one), but why not look the great white hunter part? Mesh is nice for the hotter months (September-November). OD, brown, or dark tan only. A chin paracord will be appreciated on those windy Land Rover rides.
 www.herringtoncatalog.com; nice mesh hat in olive or khaki with 3" brim for $40. #LS499. Some other good sources:
  www.filson.com/vihats.htm
  www.noggintops.com
  www.randhats.com
  www.hartfordyork.com

wool watch cap
 Carhartt has nice OD cap which I often used.

head net
 If hunting in a river valley, you'll wish you'd brought one. The mosquitoes are as big as B-29s, and the tsetse flies sting like yellowjackets. There are no-seeums which seek the eyes.

windproof jacket and/or sweater
 Your weather and body type will vary. Ask your PH.

fleece or sweat pants
 Just the thing for lounging around the campfire.

gloves
 I took a pair of fleece gloves with me, but it was warm enough even in the mornings not to need them. Some hunters like to wear a pair of thin deerskins.

town outfit and something for the pool/beach

 You may have an evening or two in the city, so slacks, blazer, nice shirt and shoes are worth packing. Jacket and tie are usually optional, except in some restaurants. (Leave at home your dress watch and jewelry, as street crime is common.)

PACKING FOR THE FIELD

Your needs there are much different from airports and cities and beaches.

planning your gear

I firmly believe in modularity. Clothes pockets, belt gear, Camelbak Mule, day pack (left in truck during your walks), and camp luggage. Everything has its place based on when and how often it will be used.

2x1 hunting gear

Several things you can/should share with your partner, to save weight: rangefinder, GPS, gun cleaning kit, broken shell extractor, digital camera, digital voice recorder, books, signal mirror, sunscreen, 1st aid kit, Katadyn, etc. There's no reason to duplicate this weight, space, and expense.

I highly recommend that your rifles be in a common bore diameter or caliber so you can share a Boresnake and broken case extractor.

misc. stuff to take for the field
small hand-held metal detector (my own idea)

This is to locate bullets in your game, which even the most skilled of camp skinners can sometimes fail to find (such as the 400gr Hornady softpoint from my zebra). Any police or security supply catalog will have some for under $100. I took one over in 2007 and it worked beautifully! (Also makes a nice gift if your PH raves about it.) Finding a 180gr bullet in a kudu stomach was its best feat. The skinners thought it nearly magic.

digital voice recorder

You will never want to forget the *sounds* of Africa! Get one (with USB download capability) for note taking and animal sounds (try to record those amazing xylophone frogs).

Lions roaring, hyenas yipping, buffalo grunting — you'll have some .wav files to burn onto your gift photo CDs.

GPS

My Selous PH had one and used it for all it was worth. It saved us a lot of time, and we were able to easily return to proven game areas. Not absolutely vital that you have your own, but it's probably a good idea (if only as an unused spare).

There are dozens of good GPS units out there, from $100 to $500+. Chat up somebody who uses them a lot. And always carry a map and compass for backup.

radios (preferably with GPS, and using AA batteries)

Keep in touch with your hunting partner, tracker, or driver up to 5 miles away, and with GPS be able to send each other's location. (Leave one powered up with your driver. After a kill, power yours up and he can bring the Land Rover right to you, which saves somebody a hike back to fetch him.)

I used Midland GXT500s, which had the maximum transmitting power of 5 watts (up to 14 miles, optimally). 38 privacy codes per 22 channels. *Many* other features. Uses 4AAs Only $60/pair. Get the mic/headphone set.

Garmin has GPS radios: the Rino 120 for $250.

binoculars

A must, and their quality is probably more important than even your scope since you'll use them so much more often. What you can't spot with your bargain binos you won't be able to shoot with your superb scope. Think about that. High quality binos with superior Schott glass and coatings are *well* worth the money. Leave at home your $89 whatevers. Plan on spending at least $300-1,000. You'll be very glad that you did!

A mid-size 8x42 pair is a very sensible compromise between size and weight. I like objectives larger than 24-30mm (though 50mm is a bit much), and 8x is just right for me. My PH prefers 10x42s in order to better judge trophy quality, but 10x may prove too unsteady for you. Try a pair of Leicas, Swarovskis, or Minox (www.deutscheoptik.com). I prefer roof prism binos with individual eyepiece focusing.

Safari #1: **Tasco 7x50s** (a copy of the Steiner Marines). They joked about the extra weight, which happily was no issue with a comfortable neoprene Kolpin strap. An excellent glass for the money, though larger than necessary.

Safari #2: I took a pair of compact **Fuji 8x24s** and a pair of **1970s Zeiss 8x30s**. I liked them about equally.

Safari #3: I enjoyed a fine pair of **8x42 Shepherds**. From the renowned scope company, their $630 binos easily rival Swarovski and Leica of 2-3x the price. They were a favorite of all who tried them. Resolution is an astounding 4.4 seconds (0.08" — the width of two sheets of paper — at *100yds*). Very bright and clear. Just superb! www.shepherdscopes.com

Leica rangefinder

Most distances are short (or at least *should* be if you can stalk like a true hunter), and rangefinders are unnecessary (except to reverse-distance a shot already taken, the longest of which was 225yds). However, if you're plains game hunting, 250+yds is possible and a rangefinder would be handy.

rangefinder binoculars

Leupold has two models (RXB-IV and RB800C) which combine 8x32mm binos with a 500-800yd deer rangefinder. Waterproof rubber armor. Only fair binos. www.leupold.com

If you've $2000 to spare, then Leica Geovids are quite the treat. The binos don't suffer at all. A really lovely piece of gear!

Katadyn water filter

Your camp will be well stocked with bottled water, but (if you can spare the room and weight) you might feel better with a Katadyn just in case. Get the one with ceramic filter. It's good for at least 5000 gallons. Strains out all the bugs, including *giardia*. You'll be able to drink from a Cameroon sewer. Swiss made, and it is The King.

XF7 gun lube from MD Labs

For lubrication and rust prevention, I rely on a product invented by an old friend: XF7 Weapon Lubricant. It bonds to the metal's substrate, and won't melt or burn off. Tested by many spec ops people in extreme cold and heat, it won't wash off even in saltwater. Excellent for semi-auto weapons, especially those known for fouling (AR15, HK91, etc.). I thoroughly treated my M70 with XF7, and not even the barrel rusted after a week of carrying the rifle over my shoulder. Same with my blued Marlin .45-70. An amazing product and "quantum leap" in technology. It's all the rave with our troops in the know.

Available from www.brownells.com (#100-002-242; $12.89)

stubby driver with hollow handle

Hollow in order to hold bits. Home Depot had just what I needed for only $4. In mine I included 6 bits, everything my rifle/base/rings needed. It fit perfectly within my East German surplus belt pouch. I never had to use it, as none of the Loctited screws came loose, but I was prepared. (One loose screw can easily cause a miss. Murphy is alive and well!)

Brownells has one with 4 bits ($20.36; #080-000-023).

misc. on-person field gear
pockets
Should contain the utter essentials, such as compass, signal whistle (orange plastic, and pealess), energy bars, tablets (malaria, dysentery, headache), and a folding knife.

OD large bandana
A must for absorbing sweat, and for softening the weight of your bino strap. (Take *two*: one for wearing while the other is being washed daily.) I bought a bunch of French army surplus large bandanas for only 99¢ each.

on your belt
The next step up in modularity. You may be without your Camelbak, so what's actually on your person is vital.

ammo pouch
Cabelas sells nice leather 10rd pouches. Should be worn front weak side for easiest access during a DG hunt. Place 6 solids first (*i.e.*, next to your centerline), and then 4 softs. (Softs are used generally only for first shots, and solids for all else, hence you'll likely need more solids than softs.)

belt knife
I am accustomed to my **Mad Dog Arizona Hunter** in a front side slip-sheath. It was unobtrusive in the bush, and it also served in town as my carry weapon. The **Mad Dog ATAK2** is a fantastic general purpose utility knife, and chopped through brush with the aplomb of our tracker's *panga* (machete). It *will* skin, though it's not a true skinning knife.

Cold Steel's Master Hunter is a fine affordable skinner. Its Carbon V is good steel, sharpening well and easily. The Kraton grip does not slip amongst the blood and gore.

I took a nice **CRKT Bridger** skinner with curved blade and Kraton grip. My skinner John liked it *so* much, I had to give it to him (with the promise that he would *never* sharpen it on rocks or concrete).

belt pouch
A small soft pouch (I like the East German grenade pouch for its ruggedness, $2 cost, internal pockets, and lack of noisy Velcro) should contain your myriad of small items for the field:

sunscreen
DEET
chapstick with sunblock
moisturizing cream (don't laugh; even biltong dries in the shade)
toilet paper (those from MREs are perfect)
scentless wet wipes
stubby driver with integral bits for your gun/scope rings
Loctite (blue)
Boresnake in Ziploc bag
tiny bottle of gun lube XF7
latex gloves
lemon and cough drops
tweezer with magnifying glass (Brownells; $3)
digital voice recorder
cigarette lighter
compass
cigar cutter

I wore mine in the field every day, and it was unobtrusive and rugged, even during many belly-crawls.

digital camera

I am *thoroughly* pleased with the Canon Power Shot series. I looked long and hard for a camera with the most/best general features, and am confident that I found it. It uses SD cards, AA batteries (I loathe AAAs), has a large view screen, great controls, a clear menu, and it takes phenomenal photos. (Besides, tennis hottie Maria Sharapova says *"Make every shot, a Power Shot!"* — so there.)

In the Selous I took about 500 photos averaging 1-meg each, which filled up only half of my 1-gig SD memory card. (I went through the camera's pair of AAs nearly every day, and barely had enough even with scrounging from the PH. Take *lots* of batteries!) When I got home I culled out about 10% of the photos and burned the remaining 450 on CDs for family and friends. An accompanying .txt Notepad file served as a thorough index of the photos, allowing the viewer to navigate their way through our two weeks in Africa. Next time, I will have .mpg (video) and .wav (sound) files on the CD to really liven things up.

Most of our camp staff had email (though infrequently checked), so be sure to send them some 100k-size photos (don't send 3-megs of stuff to them; connection times are slow!) of themselves when you get home.

In 2007 I upgraded to an A640 with 10 megapixels and a larger 29.2mm lens. Photo printer, too, and all for under $350. My trusty A520 I have retired after great service during two safaris, and it now lives in my motorcycle tankbag.

You may want a larger-lensed camera with SLR body, such as the Canon S3IS, for greatly improved zoom quality. (There's only so much to expect from a 29.2mm lens, after all.) Though not a compact camera, perhaps your observer can tote it about, leaving you with a small digital.

camera pouch

Buy a good quality pouch with a robust belt loop. REI had a perfect one for my digital camera. The zippered flap was quiet, and its Velcro belt strap made relocation easy.

Camelbak Mule

This is the largest thing you'll wear, and it's great gear. Go Camelbak for its quality and best tasting water bladder.

The Mule has a 100oz bladder and two generous pouches. Cinch up the shoulder straps to wear the Camelbak high (which avoids rubbing on your belt gear), and use the chest strap.

Drink from the truck's water bottles while on the road (never share bottles with *anybody*), and save your Camelbak water for walking. (Snake the drinking tube around to your weak side, so not to interfere with your rifle's stockweld.)

The pouches should contain:

multitool (I prefer the Swiss tool)
SureFire flashlight (preferably a 3-cell model)
signal mirror (I made a protective case from an old mousepad)
orange emergency whistle (without pea)
many energy bars (Cliff Bars my favorite)
10rds extra ammo
Leica rangefinder (even though bushveld shots will be <150yds)
pen, small notepad
antibacterial soap
water purification tablets
mini *Perfect Shot* book
lens pen
takedown cleaning rod
broken case extractor
small roll of electrician's tape for muzzle
matches (in bright color waterproof safe)
cable saw (in a round can from snuff or .177 pellets)

length of braided paracord (for spare shoe laces and misc. use)
zip/cable ties (different lengths, can repair many things)
Goldbond foot powder
AA, AAA, 3V lithium batteries (camera, DVC, tac light)
sunglasses and case
Ace bandage
GMRS radio (leave turned off, but the driver's is left on)
rangefinder
GPS (use the MOB function leaving the vehicle)
latex gloves
sharpening stone or steel
cloth tape measure
black Sharpie pen
waxed dental floss and needle (great button thread)
cigars for trophy smokes, right then and there!
passport and cash, if you're nervous about leaving such in the truck

small Ziploc with:
Immodium
aspirin
Bandaids
Neosporin
antihistamine
cortisone cream (anti-itch)
moleskin
toilet paper
handcleaner
unscented baby wipes
eye drops
GSW bloodclot ($15; www.quikclot.com)
burn gauze (silver impregnated nylon hose; amazing stuff!)

This all sounds like a lot, and it is, but it really *does* fit in a Mule. And it's surprisingly comfortable to wear. Mine never tired me out over the 7-10 miles of daily walking.

Other companies now also offer hydration units, so compare before you buy. I like the Mule, but wish that it also came in USMC green digital pattern.

backpack left in truck

The driver will likely be an honest fellow, so you should feel comfortable leaving this behind during your walks.

Katadyn water filter (outside South Africa)
gloves
stocking cap
fleece jacket
reference books
soft gun case
novel, highlighter
vitamins
Swahili or Afrikaans phrasebook
S/W radio
Polaroid camera

spare:
sunglasses
ammo
Cliff bars and candy
sunscreen
socks
water

"Where do I leave my neck and ankle wallets?"

You've only three choices: back in camp, in the truck, or on your person. (Ask your PH for his advice.) I think the best compromise between security and convenience is in your truck backpack. (Your passport and cash won't be any burden in your Camelbak, if that makes you feel more secure.)

On my South Africa game ranch hunt, I secured all my valuables in the locked Pelican rifle case.

TEST *ALL* GEAR TOGETHER *PRIOR* THE HUNT!

Don all of your intended clothes and gear, strap on your rifle and go for a several mile hike in the woods. This is the only way to discover what clinks, rubs, chafes, and squeaks.

MISC. CAMP STUFF

electricity
Most tent camps have but a small generator (our Honda 8kW did it all), so leave most of your 110AC appliances behind. Yes, if *necessary* they can probably recharge your laptop, but why cheat yourself of a simple time? You won't miss your electric shaver and hair dryer after a few days.
Game ranches are all electrified.
South Africa uses three round pins (plugs commonly available there). Tanzania uses the British three square pins.

sat phone
If you've got one, bring it, especially if things are dicey at home. But if neither, then the PH will likely have one, and will likely offer his if you need it.
If he has no sat phone, the camp *will* have a ham radio able to reach the company's HQ (who then can phone or email on your behalf). On game ranches there is often cell service.

they will have everything else for your comfort
Hot meals, cold drinks, laundry, hot showers, clean tents, comfortable beds (I never slept so well!) — it's all there.

health
A very good idea from *African Hunter II* is to bring your own syringes! #4s and #6s. Cheap and potentially lifesaving since you'll avoid dirty needles. Leave them behind as med kit gifts, thus not importing "drug paraphernalia" into the USA.

gifts
gifts for native children
Take a couple of packs of brightly colored balloons. Lightweight, cheap, and great fun. Blow 'em up and let 'em fly! You'll be a colossal hit!

gifts for camp staff
While cash (not travelers' checks!) is always readily accepted, gifts are most welcome (if you've the room to bring them). Inexpensive multi-tools, binoculars, Caylume lightsticks, ball caps, and watches are assured hits with the local staff. Everyone marveled at my digital camera, and decent 2.0 megapixel models are less than $80 now.

For daily treats and rewards, I found that **lemon drops** were very popular (especially with the head tracker, a man you certainly want to keep on your side). Be sure to leave them the bag at hunt's end as part of your gratuity.

One thing to take and leave for the camp is some **blue ice**, preferably those shaped to go between a 6-pack of drinks. Such are not available in Africa, and you'll appreciate having some truly cold beers in the coolbox waiting for your drive back to camp. (It's called a "coolbox" vs. an "icebox" because ice is too much of a luxury out in the bush.) Since the blue ice is reusable, you'll be a real hero with the camp.

gifts for PH

A .416 or .458 Boresnake is hard to find in Africa, but you can order yours from Brownells. Quality scopes and binos. Cigars. Whiskey. 100% maple syrup. Spare gun and archery parts (ask ahead of time). Reloading components (cases and bullets) are especially expensive in Africa, so query the outfit and see what your PH might need.

GOING HOME

Completely scour your carry bag and belt pack for ammo, spent cases, gun parts, etc. Airport personnel have less and less humor, logic, and cheer. You don't want to get snagged with some harmless momento from your hunt at security.

Verify that your firearms are unloaded, and that live ammo is repacked in their boxes.

Take detailed photos of your packed contents in case of loss or theft, and keep them on your traveling person on a USB drive or CD.

Safari Dreams

Kenneth Royce

❖ 8

PLAINS GAME BULLETS CALIBERS RIFLES

> *It should be recognized that not all safari agendas include members of the Big Five. It they don't, there's absolutely no reason for a rifle of .40 caliber or larger; and if eland is not on the list, there's no real need for [even] a .375.*
> — Craig Boddington, *Safari Rifles* (1990), p. 316

You'll likely be taking only one or two rifles, and not three. Thus, your light rifle must provide wider performance than the classic light rifle in a three-rifle elephant hunt.

Meaning, your light rifle must *reliably* take the larger and tougher plains game, such as zebra, wildebeest, eland, oryx, roan, and sable. Most Americans take rifle calibers *far* too light and fast, which tend to wound such animals. Our game is of higher fat content and lighter bone structure, and while the .270 Weatherby is fine 400yd *pronghorn* caliber, its 3300fps 130gr bullet will blow up on a zebra shoulder. For Africa you need greater weight and sectional density, not velocity.

Your caliber and bullet should be easily capable of breaking a shoulder *and* damaging *both* lungs of any African game you intend to shoot at sporting distances.

A good rule of thumb for energy minimum on medium/heavy plains game is 2000fpe at any intended impact distance. (A fine example is the 180-200gr .308 out to 200yds.) To be fair, this will eliminate all calibers between .243 and .270, because only .284/7mm and up can throw 150+gr bullets, and with a sufficient frontal area. (More on this shortly.) Yes, I also like the .243, .260, and .270, but these are really *deer* calibers.

Unless you are *absolutely* topping out at bushbuck, leave at home all rifles under 7mm.

BULLETS

Far too many American hunters remain overly wrapped up in choice of rifle and caliber at the exclusion of a proper choice of bullet. The bullet is the only physical contact you make with your game animal, and a sorry bullet will negate the best rifle and caliber. It happens many times every safari season and is one of PHs' greatest gripes.

In short, you want a *tough* bullet, not an explosive varmit or deer bullet. This means either a *bonded* core (by soldering the core to the jacket, less lead is lost upon impact and retained weight is higher) with controlled expansion (Swift A-Frame or North Fork), or a monolithic copper (Barnes TSX).

I learned this over my first two safaris. My 400gr .416 Hornady bonded cores were OK, but expanded far too much. My 180gr .308 Sierra Game Kings also killed OK, but usually broke up into many pieces. While no bullet caused me to ever lose an animal, I wished in retrospect that I'd hunted with more robust bullets. African game is just plain *tough*. Our classic deer bullets are simply not up to wildebeest, zebra, and eland.

partition bullets

In the 1940s, John Nosler found out that the .300 H&H would send 180gr bullets fast enough to shatter, so he developed his own improved bullet: one with a wall (as in the RWS H-Mantle) between two lead cores to limit how much the expanding nose would peel back (keeping the rear portion intact, like a solid). The Nosler Partition went commercial in 1948, and is popular (though its lead is far too soft, and magazine bullets can deform under recoil). My South African PH Mark is not keen on Partitions after seeing them poorly kill a wildebeest during a 2007 hunt.

A similar (and tougher) construction is used also in Swift A-Frame, which got its start in the .375-.458 market unserved by Nosler at the time. These are *great* African game bullets.

monometal copper solids (*i.e.*, no lead)

For plains game, the metal is copper. (For DG, bronze.) The quintessential plains game solid was the Barnes X, now replaced by their superior Triple Shock X (TSX) which (because of its grooved shank) does not gall barrels as the X bullet did. TSX bullets form four or six "petals" for good expansion, and retain usually near 100% of their weight while penetrating deeply. The TSX has a great reputation in Africa, and PH Mark Ivy uses nothing but 180gr in his .308. Even if the TSX loses all of its petals, it still retains 85% of its weight. A top choice.

North Fork (a Wyoming company) also makes a very good copper solid shank with lead core tip.

Copper solids are long for their weight, which makes excessive seating depth an issue for compressed magnum calibers such as .416 Rem and .458 Win.

designed impact velocity range

This is extremely important, as velocity affects *every* facet of bullet performance: expansion, wound cavity, penetration, and recovered weight. For example, a bullet must expand at a low enough velocity (*i.e.*, 1500-1800fps) to be shot from smaller capacity cases and/or at longer distances, but it also must not shatter if shot within 50yds (a common problem with magnums). Most Africa-tough bullets expand in the 1600-2600fps range, and such a 1000+fps working range was possible only recently (since the 1970s). Prior that, most hunting bullets fragmented too easily or barely expanded at all.

exit wound, or stopping just short of the far hide?

This constitutes a degree-of-penetration issue, and a debate as old as smokeless powder (when impact velocities became high enough to reliably create exit wounds for the first time). To some, exit wounds demonstrate wasted energy, while others assert the advantage of increased blood loss (and spoor for tracking).

My view is this: if the bullet has nicely expanded and reached the far hide, then all energy available to the vitals *was already expended on them*, so no useful energy is "lost" by also creating an exit wound. (Double my emphasis here for DG!)

The only time to avoid an exit is in a thick herd with risk of wounding a second animal after perforating the first. Ask your PH about the herds in your game area.

Bullet Behavior Classification (BBC)

This is a highly useful value from Richard Mann's excellent book *Rifle Bullets for the Hunter* (www.riflebullets.com). It is calculated by dividing retained weight percentage with the expansion ratio of original diameter. For example, my 400gr Hornady .416 bullet: 82.3%/2.5x = 33 BBC. This is nearly in fragmenting class:

FRAGMENTING	EXPANDING			PENETRATING
0-30	30-70			70-100
	maximum	balanced	minimum	
	30-40	40-60	60-70	

Here are few sample game hunted bullets and their BBCs:

Nosler AccuBond	150gr/.308	75%/1.90x	38 BBC
Barnes MRX	180gr/.308	84%/2.03x	41 BBC
Nosler Partition	160gr/7mm	67%/1.58x	42 BBC
Barnes TSX	270gr/.375	99%/2.37x	42 BBC
North Fork	160gr/7mm	84%/1.97x	43 BBC
Swift A-Frame	400gr/.423	95%/1.96x	49 BBC
Barnes TSX	300gr/.458	100%/2.37x	52 BBC
Swift A-Frame	160gr/7mm	93%/1.91x	55 BBC
Barnes TSX	160gr/7mm	100%/1.80x	56 BBC
any solid bullet		100%/1x	100 BBC

no deer bullets for Africa

Do not go to Africa with even great deer bullets such as the Nosler Ballistic Tip or AccuBond. **400+lb animals such as sable, gemsbok, waterbuck, kudu, wildebeest, zebra, and eland need BBC values of 40-60.**

For our deer and elk I'm a fan of Sierra Game Kings, but Africa requires a *tougher* bullet. Highest retained bullet (180gr/2650fps from a 20" Savage Scout) was 90% at 2x expansion (for a 45 BBC). And that was the *highest* BBC seen; the rest vaporized like 3000fps 150 grainers. While they all killed just fine and I never lost an animal to bullet failure, I wouldn't use them there again for anything larger than impala.

what is the *optimum* expansion ratio?   1.6x

It offers a balanced BBC range of 41 (with 65% retention) to 63 (with 100% retention). This 1.6x ratio allows lots of retention percentage leeway, in case your bullet strikes heavy bone, and thus shears. Also, it's a good choice for varied game, performing well on a wide range from impala to eland. www.a-squarecompany.com designs their Dead Tough bullets for a 1.6x ratio to avoid overexpansion and loss of angular momentum (which can cause erratic wound channels).

are boattail bullets necessary?
No, as their flatter trajectory does not come into play until past 300yds, and flat-base bullets shoot flat enough <300yds.

are polymer tips necessary in a tough plains game bullet?
They have the advantages of protecting the bullet in magazine during recoil, shooting *slightly* flatter, and helping to more quickly initiate expansion.

what is the optimum bullet?
> Mostly I've found if you can shoot reasonably well and use a cartridge vaguely suitable for the purpose, it doesn't matter a hell of a lot which BB ["boutique bullet"] you use. (John Barsness)
> — *Rifle Bullets for the Hunter* (2006), p.140

Within the top class of Swift A-Frame, A-Square Dead Tough, North Fork, and Barnes TSX there is no "best" choice. All offer superb terminal ballistics, with BBCs of 40-60. Consider your game, caliber, likely distance, and thus impact velocity. From there, the answer will be pretty clear. And don't forget to query your PH. He's seen/heard what works well and what doesn't.

ethical consideration: never waste meat unnecessarily
The shoulder/heart blasted with a 150gr soft will certainly kill, but several pounds of meat are ruined. Game meat is a valuable resource, and the true sportsman will send a caliber-heavy Barnes TSX or Swift A-Frame into the lungs or brisket. Maximum efficiency. I shot a kudu cow this way with my Marlin .45-70, spoiling no meat at all.

final thoughts
> When it comes to killing game, a $3000 rifle with a $1000 scope is worth no more than its bullet. If the bullet fails, the rest is for naught. When one gets right down to it, killing power depends on two factors: proper bullet placement (in which the rifle and its sights certainly have their part to play), and the behavior of the bullet after it arrives — its terminal ballistics in other words.
> — Finn Aagaard, *Any Shot You Want* (1996), p. 112

Much of your hunt's success will be decided, in advance, by your choice of bullet. In the field, you can improve the quality of your shooting by getting closer and steadier, or by squeezing better — but you cannot improve the quality of your *bullet* just before you pull the trigger.

> *Every battle is won or lost before it is ever fought.*
> — Sun Tzu

The quality of your bullet is the most crucial part of your equipment. ***Everything* eventually depends on it.** It's the very last thing to skimp on. That $9 box of shells at SprawlMart is a totally false economy if your wildebeest laughs them off. Pay $1 each for a *premium* projectile. It's really not optional. If you don't handload, go to www.superiorammo.com, or find somebody who can build you up a great load for you.

> *Notably, every one of these men* (Jack Carter, Art Alphin, Lee Reed, Geoff McDonald, Bill Steigers, John Nosler, Fred Barnes, and Randy Brooks) *was either working on his own or in a small firm. Most were (and are) serious hunters of dangerous game.* **None worked for the big ammunition companies.**
> — Terry Wieland, *Dangerous Game Rifles* (2006), p. 211

choose *one* bullet weight, even for a varied hunt

> *The hunter must carefully balance impact velocity (range), bullet weight and bullet construction to the intended quarry if he is to accomplish a swift, clean kill.*
> — Edward Matunas, *Lyman's Guide to Big Game Cartridges & Rifles* (1993), p. 19

I would choose a superb all-around bullet suitable for 500-600lb animals, develop a <2MOA load, and rely on that. Meaning, for your .30-06, don't load 150gr for impala and 200gr for wildebeest. Settle on the 200gr, as you won't be happy if you mistakenly shoot your wildebeest with a brittle 150gr (exploding on the shoulder, with no penetration to the boiler room). Your 200gr, however, will nicely dispatch a steenbok.

Also, it's too much of a hassle to rezero between different weights, and animals will rarely exhibit themselves based on which you've got loaded that day. **Use the heaviest/2nd-heaviest bullets.** They provide superior penetration, and usually greater impact energies (especially past 150-200yds).

Keep It Simple! One load — one zero. *And know it well!*

7mm (.284)

The below are fine up to 100yd kudu/waterbuck, but I would avoid for 100+yds, or for gemsbok, zebra, wildebeest, or eland. The extra frontal area and 180-200gr mass of the .30-06 is greatly preferred over any 7mm choice.

7mm bullets
Quality 160-175gr bonded bullets will perform well.

(.0633" cross sectional area)	.283 1:10"	.310 sectional density 1:9½" min. recommended twist
Swift A-Frame	160gr	175gr
Barnes TSX	160gr	175gr
A-Square Dead Tough		175gr
North Fork	160gr	

7-08 and 7x57 Mauser (160gr/2600fps)

While very efficient and accurate rounds, they're limited to 100yd kudu/waterbuck even with the best 175gr bullets.

.280 Rem (160gr/2800fps, 175gr/2650fps)

With 175gr, the minimum caliber for a general plains game rifle marginally sufficient for 100yd wildebeest/zebra (and *barely* eland). Great penetration, but shock power is fair at best. It's *slightly* flatter past 300yds than .30-06, but you shouldn't be shooting that far. If you've a .280 and *really* love it, well, OK, but a 200gr .30-06 is far superior for Africa.

.284 Winchester (160gr/2850fps)

A short-action caliber sometimes found in the Win 88/100 and Savage 99. Good 7mm ballistics, but rebated-rim cases are prone to feeding failures. A nearly extinct caliber, anyway.

7mm Rem Mag (160gr/2950fps)

For open country (short grass plains, desert, etc.), these are good ballistics. You'll lose a round of mag capacity, with more muzzle blast than the .280. (.30-06 is a better choice.)

The 7mm Weatherby, STW, etc. are excessive for the <200yd bushveld. The Transvaal is not pronghorn country! Besides, why bother with only a 175gr, anyway? Go .30-.338.

.30

This is my minimum bullet diameter for *all* plains game. I used a 180gr .308 for ten animals (up to kudu and wildebeest, though not including eland) with very good results, and from Sierra Game Kings (not the toughest of bullets for Africa).

.308 bullets

This caliber has a *huge* selection of fine bullets, though topping out at 200gr for most companies.

(.0745" cross sectional area)	.248 1:12"	.271 1:11"	.301 1:10"	.331 sectional density 1:9" minimum twist
Swift A-Frame	165gr	180gr	200gr	
Barnes TSX	165gr	180gr	200gr	
A-Square Dead Tough		180gr		220gr
North Fork		180gr	200gr	
Hornady InterBond	165gr	180gr		

.308 (200gr/2450fps) or .30-06 (200gr/2600fps)

These have very similar ballistics, with nearly interchangeable usefulness on African plains game.

.308 pros

Shorter and lighter actions. Shorter bolt throw. Efficient.

.308 cons

150fps less velocity than .30-06. Common maximum bullet weight is 180gr, which at 2600fps MV will take all but eland with ease. While a 200gr load is reasonable (if your barrel twist is 1:10"), 220gr is a bit too heavy for this 51mm case.

Before the Iraq war, inexpensive 7.62x51 FMJ was widely available for affordable practice. The days of 15¢/rd are *gone*.

.30-06 pros

An extra 200fpe at most distances, which often gives a decided edge in killing power. Can adequately throw 220gr bullets which are best for eland. Wide ammo availability. (For practice, surplus Lake City, Korean, and Greek FMJ is still a bargain at about 31¢/round.) A *century* of effective hunting of everything from varmits to moose to black bear.

.30-06 cons

Heavier by ½lb than most .308 rifles. Longer bolt throw.

conclusion

If you've only a .308 and you are *very* skilled with it, then use 180gr for everything (unless twist is 1:10", to stabilize a preferred 200gr) and know your bullet drops well. A well-placed, tough 180gr *will* perform fine, but it can become marginal at tough angles on tougher animals. Expect this.

However, if you've also a .30-06, take it instead. You'll never notice the extra ½lb of weight, but that extra case capacity for 200grainers is worth it. And, it's the *quintessential* light rifle for Africa. Roosevelt, Hemingway, and Ruark all carried a .30-06, so you'll be in fine company.

recommended .308/.30-06 bullet weights

For open country on small/mid-size game, go 180gr over 165gr for its superior sectional density and ballistic coefficient.

For close cover and/or bigger game, go 200gr spitzer for better penetration and shock. A good 200gr .30-06 handload: 53.3-54.0gr of IMR-4350 for an accurate 2600-2630fps. R19 is also a good powder.

While the roundnose 220gr is adequately thrown by the .30-06, 1:9" twist barrels are rare. A 1:10" will stabilize the 200gr spitzer, which is probably a better compromise of trajectory vs. penetration. A 200gr A-Frame or TSX will penetrate deeply enough.

.30-06 Ackley Improved (200gr/2700fps)

With decreased case taper and a 40° shoulder, the A.I. rounds are good for +70fps and +5%fpe. Regular .30-06 ammo will load and fireform easily. I wouldn't bother in .30-06, but the .338-06 A.I. is well worth handloading.

.300 WSM and SAUM (200gr/2800fps)

Introduced in 2003, these are short-action cases (2.10" and 2.105") with identical ballistics. (Also sold in .270 and 7mm.) Shorter powder columns are slightly more efficient, but the primary advantage to such cases is the shorter bolt throw and reduced receiver weight. (The tradeoff is chunkier feeding and reduced magazine capacity. TANSTAAFL.) This pair offer (barely) .300 H&H magnum velocities. A better WSM choice seems the .325 WSM with higher velocities and SDs.

.300 H&H Mag (200gr/2850fps)

Introduced in 1925, this is a nearly dead cartridge today with no factory rifles. A belted and tapered case with gentle 8.5° shoulder, it will give 250fps over the .30-06. Ammo is rare, so you'd have to handload. (The .300 Win is a better choice.)

.300 Win Mag (200gr/2925fps, 220/2750)
.308 Norma Mag (200gr/2950fps, 220/2800)

These throw a 220gr like the .30-06 throws a 180gr. If you *really* need the flatness of trajectory, or the higher velocity for 220gr, then consider a .300 mag. Many Americans hunt Africa with it, but many of them shoot it *poorly*. Because of excessive muzzle blast and 165gr wounding of game, it is widely disliked by PHs and even their black trackers (who are not caliber buffs). 200-220gr *only* — no 165/180gr! Twist should be 1:10".

The .308 Norma Mag is a better designed case (20% longer neck), but rifles are rare and you won't find ammo in Africa.

.300 Weatherby Mag (200gr/3100fps, 220/2900)

Add another 100fps to the .300 Win Mag. With this level of weight and muzzle blast, I'd go .338 Win Mag instead. (Notice that I didn't even mention the .30-378 Weatherby?)

thoughts on .300 *über* mags

> The lighter rifle wouldn't have to be a .338, **but for the most versatility and efficiency it should shoot flatter than a .375 and be somewhat more powerful than a .30-06 or 7mm magnum.** ...A .300 magnum would fill the bill, especially with well-constructed, heavy (200-220gr) bullets.
> — Craig Boddington, *Safari Rifles* (1990), p. 356

There is now a dizzying array of .300 mags, such as the RUM, WSM, SAUM, etc. Look, 200gr AccuBonds at 3000+fps is great for 400yd desert antelope, but impractical for <150yd bushveld shots. Keep impact velocities under 2600fps!

If you think you need a .300 mag over a .30-06, then you should instead seriously ponder a .338 mag (which will shoot sufficiently flat, but with much better performance). Personally, I'd hunt with a .338 mag over *any* .300 mag. (*250*gr bullets vs. 200-220gr? *.0897"* vs. .0745" frontal area? What choice is *that?*)

8mm (.323)

> [T]he 8mm/.32 family pretty much duplicates the .30/.303 family in terms of capability and variety. One could substitute the .32-20 for the .30 Carbine, the .32 Special for the .30-30, the 8x57JS for the .308 Winchester, the 8mm-06 for the .30-06, the .325 WSM for the .300 WSM, and the 8x68S for the .300 Winchester Magnum and neither the hunter or the game would be able to tell the difference.
> — http://www.chuckhawks.com/8mm_cartridges.htm

8mm is the .30 of Europe and Africa, but never caught on here.

8mm bullets

Actually, the 220gr spitzer 8mm is a *fine* bullet, with .301SD (vs. .331SD in .30) and a .0819" FA (vs. .0745" FA in .30). Thrown at 2400-2800fps, it's a great killer of any plains game. This caliber really needs a 240/250gr bullet (.329/.342 SDs).

(.0819" cross sectional area)	.246	.274	.301 sectional density
	1:10"	1:10"	1:10" min. rec. twist
Swift A-Frame		200gr	220gr
Barnes TSX	180gr	200gr	
A-Square			220gr Mono & D.T.
Winchester PowerPoint			220gr

8x57S (170/2600fps, 220gr/2300fps)

This German military cartridge is equivalent to a .308. Not a personal favorite of mine as it's the least efficient of the standard-length rounds (you could have a .30-06 or .338-06 in the same action). It's fine for 100yd zebra and 150yd kudu.

An 8-08 with 220gr would make for a good wildcat, with better penetration than the excellent .338 Federal.

8mm-06 (220gr/2500fps)

You may run into a rechambered M98 (originally 8x57S) for a song, and this would make a fine plains game rifle. There's nothing wrong with a ".323-06" if you handload. (For the same hassle, however, I'd prefer the 250gr of .338-06 or .35 Whelen.)

8x68S (220gr/2800fps)

The 8x68S flies like a .300 Win but hits more like a .338. A very modern beltless from 1940 (a virtual ".323 Mag") which is nearly unknown here, but greatly respected in Europe.

Bolt face is .512", case length is 2.657" and OAL is 3.425". At 400yds it retains a foot/ton of energy (2008fpe). Only big magnums have that kind of 400yd power, and few are beltless. The 8x68S has it, but not excessively. (Anybody claiming to need a foot/ton of energy at 500yds should learn to stalk closer.) It's a very well balanced round (as is the similar .325 WSM).

handloading the 8x68S (www.reloadersnest.com)

220gr selection isn't abundant, but A-Square and Swift bullets are superb. Hornady has an SP, and Sierra a SPBT. Horneber brass from Huntington's (maybe). Redding dies.

rifles in 8x68S

None new sold here, but you may see a used:

	barrel	price	condition
CZ ZKK 602	25.2"	$ 575	98%
Mauser Model 66SM Magnum	26"	$1925	98%
Sauer & Sohn Model 202 Supreme Magnum		$ 950	98%
Steyr Mannlicher SBS Magnum European	25.6"	$1900	98%
Steyr Mannlicher Model S	26"	$1400	98%
Voere M2165 Rahn "Safari"			

If you find a bargain, quality 8x68S (*e.g.*, $400 ZKK 602) *and* you handload, *then* it would make a *great* medium rifle. You'd certainly be the only one on your block. (Brass/dies *look* before you rifle *leap*!) Still, the .325 WSM is more sensible:

.325 WSM (180/3050, 200/2950, 220/2800)

An American short-action 8x68 with the same great ballistics. Normally I roll my eyes at most new cartridges, but *this* one has a lot of merit. Such a short-action rifle could be about the ultimate package for 300yd plains game, and it retains a foot/ton of energy even at 400yds. From a 2.10" case!

the .325 WSM case

It is optimized for .270-.310 bullets and though does not work for .338, it does well enough for the .323/8mm. Max bullet weight is 220gr, so the .325 WSM *cannot* 250gr compete with the .338 Win (if that's what you need). Nevertheless, its .301SD is very good, and downrange velocities are quite high. It's the killing equal to the 200gr .300 and .338 Win Mags, but in a 7½lb/24" rifle. 300yd elk (or kudu) and 400yd mountain sheep are no problem. Trajectories of the three factory loads (180, 200, 210) are within .7" out to 400yds.

200gr comparison: .325 WSM to .300 Win

I asked Craig Boddington about the .325 at SCI 2007 and he remarked that it *does* kill a bit better than a .300 of the same weight/velocity. (Frontal area makes a difference.) The .325 throws a 200gr as fast as a .300 Win Mag. Downrange energy and drop are comparable.

.325 WSM downsides

It's a fat .532" case, so magazine capacity is only 3 rounds in most rifles. Its rim is slightly rebated, which theoretically increases risk of feeding problems with bolt-over-base overrides. (No reports of this, however.) The sharp 35° shoulder is not conducive to the most reliable feeding, though nobody has complained in print about it. Finally, there have been some reports that velocities are 50-100fps less than published claims. (Even still, the .325 WSM is plenty fast.)

recommended rifles in .325 WSM (generally 24", 3rd)

I personally do not recommend Kimber (erratic quality) or Ruger (heavier cast receiver). Consider the below:

Winchester Model 70 Ultimate Shadow
H-S Precision 2000SA Pro Hunter Rifle
Nosler Model 48

8mm Rem Mag (220gr/2900fps)

100fps more than 8x68S (but in a needlessly inefficient .375 magnum-length action). The 8x68S was "just right" and the 8mm Rem is "too much." Frankly, with such a long case, I'd prefer some kind of .338 or .35 magnum for the 250-280gr. It's a dying caliber, and rightfully so. It's no mystery why Weatherby *et al* never came out with their own 8mm mag.

.338

This is a *very* highly regarded caliber. Case choices are excellent (based on .308, .30-06, and .300 mags). If a .308-.323 just doesn't have the killing power you want in your light rifle, then a .338 is a fine way to go. BCs for 225gr are .380+ so the .338 is a sufficiently flat-shooting caliber for longer distances.

.338 bullets

A *very* fine selection of 225-250gr is available for the .338, as well as a 275gr A-Frame (*the* bullet for eland!). I consider the 225gr the minimum Africa weight, to enjoy a decent .281SD.

(.0897" cross sectional area)	.281 1:10"	.313 1:10"	.344 1:9" sectional density min. recommended twist
Swift A-Frame	225gr	250gr	275gr
Barnes TSX	225gr	250gr	
A-Square Triad		250gr	
North Fork	225gr	240gr (.300 SD)	
Hornady InterBond	225gr		

.338 Federal (225gr/2450fps)

A necked-up .308, it maximizes 200yd performance from that 51mm long case. It's a superb short-action non-magnum caliber suitable for plains game. If you want a light-weight rifle packing a wallop with tolerable recoil, this is a fine choice. (Its only competitors are 200gr/.308 and 220gr/8-08, both with better penetration.) 225gr is max weight for this cartridge.

recommended rifles in .338 Federal

SAKO 85, T/C ProHunter, and Tikka T3.

.338-06 (225gr/2600fps, 250/2500)

The .30-06 necked up, and it's a *very* efficient caliber. Its 250gr bullet has great SD and BC, and at 2450fps it's sufficiently flat shooting for 300yd game. It's probably about as effective on light/medium game as a .338 Win out to 200yds. If you're going after gemsbok, zebra, etc. within 250yds, and/or in close cover, and don't want the extra weight and muzzle blast of a .338 Win, then the .338-06 is a fine choice, but you won't find ammo in Africa. You risk the headstamp/barrel mismatch hassle at the airport (unless .338-06 A-Square, Weatherby, or .338 Hawk brass). The .338 Scovil is another option.

It shoots much flatter than the .35 Whelen (a 200yd caliber), and with superior terminal performance >100yds. (Anticipate your hunting terrain *before* you can choose.) It shoots about as flat as the .30-06, but hits more like the .338 Win. And it's a handloader's dream with medium/slow powders such as IMR4064, IMR4350, N140, H414, RL-19, and RL-15.

The .338-06 has been improved-wildcatted extensively. The Ackley Improved and Hawk (with headstamped brass) squinch another 100fps from the case (rivaling .338 Win), and this is the way I'd go. It's a *great* 300yd African PG caliber.

.338 Win (225gr/2850fps, 250/2700, 275/2450)

My two PHs remarked very favorably on the .338, and with good reason. Throwing a 250gr at 2700fps, it's an excellent general purpose non-DG cartridge (especially if shots past 200yds are likely on zebra, etc.). Bullet selection is superb, and the round is not unpleasant to shoot. (The .338 Win is often respectfully called "*a lady's .375.*") It has more energy at 200yds than does a .30-06 at the *muzzle*.

Boddington recommends this as one's light rifle in a two-rifle battery, because it can handle *all* plains game at *any* sportsmanlike range (*i.e.*, out to 300yds). Sure, you'd be *way* overgunned for 100yd impala, but if your only chance for a zebra was at 285yds, then you'd be very glad you had a .338 Win over a .30-06 or even .300 mag. The .338 Win is no velocity king, so if polar and grizzly bear were also in your future, then you may want a more powerful .338, or even a larger caliber (*e.g.*, .358 Norma or .375 H&H). But for Africa, it's a dandy.

You can get into a used .338 Win for less than rebarreling your .30-06 to .338-06, and for most .338 caliber fans this is the most sensible route. Load it down to .338-06 velocities if the normal recoil is objectionable. A fine caliber since 1958.

.340 Weatherby (250gr/2850fps)
.330 Dakota (250gr/2900fps)
.338 Lapua (250gr/3150fps)
.338 RUM (250gr/3150fps)
.338 Excalibur (250gr/3200fps)

Add another 150-500fps to the .338 Win, and this is what you've got. (They shoot a 250gr flatter than a 160gr 7mm Rem Mag!) If 400yd Kalahari gemsbok is your hunt, then you'll suffer the vicious muzzle blast and recoil. (A 26-28" barrel is necessary.) Few hunters can handle these, so spend some time behind one before you buy, and be sure that you *need* one.

.358 (9mm)

The 9mm rifle cartridges have long been thought limited to short-range; a viewpoint I consider to be erroneous. The widespread belief that a rifle cartridge is of no use at long distance unless its projectile starts at 3,000 feet or better is simply not corroborated by field experience. In my opinion, Colonel Whelen's dictum that 300 yards was an effective working maximum for sportsmanlike use in the field still holds, despite an enormous amount of trash writing to the contrary. I am not inclined to be falsely modest about my personal experience with field shooting - I have a lot of my own, and I have studied the experience of others at great length and over a long period. **While I am satisfied to extend the practical maximum from 300 yards to 300 meters, I am convinced that shots taken beyond that distance are evidence of bad sportsmanship.** *We need not go into details about animals improperly hit. It is enough to say that anyone who has ever seen a deer wandering in the woods with its lower jaw shot off may be impressed enough to give up the whole idea of big game hunting for the rest of his life.*

So we are talking about hitting well, and that means hitting solidly into the boiler room of the target beast under field conditions, including excitement, hurry, wind, bad light, and unstable shooting positions. **Before you take the shot you should be sure of your ability to hit a dinner plate — every time — under the circumstances applying at the time.** *It takes a very good man — a very unusual marksman — to handle that problem beyond 300 meters, and the better members of the 9mm rifle family may be counted on to do better than the shooter can.*

— Jeff Cooper, www.dvc.org.uk/jeff/jeff4_14.html

But for .358 Win and .35 Whelen, all .358s are belted mags. Premium bullet selection is only decent (but likely still to improve), but not as good as .338 (it's biggest competitor). By all accounts, the .35s kill *very* well and wound very seldom. They are all uncommon cartridges, and undeservedly so.

.358 bullets

My main caveat regards their mediocre SDs. The 250gr is .279 (the minimum SD for heavy plains game, about equal to 180gr/.30) — an average penetrator. The 270gr North Fork, 275gr A-Square, and 280gr Swift A-Frame have .300+SDs, but only the .358 Norma and .358 STA have sufficient case capacity to throw them above the "magic" 2400fps threshold. (The .35 Whelen sends 275gr to 2330fps, which is merely adequate.)

Visit www.35cal.com for great info.

A very nice bonus of the .35s is that you can load 125-158gr .357 handgun bullets for practice or varmit shooting.

(.1007" cross sectional area)	.251 1:12"	.279 1:11"	.312 sectional density 1:10" min. rec. twist
Swift A-Frame	225gr	250gr	280gr
Barnes TSX	225gr		
A-Square Triad			275gr (.307SD)
North Fork	225gr	250gr	270gr (.301SD)
Speer Grand Slam		250gr	

.358 Win (225gr/2500fps, 250gr/2400fps)

A necked up .308, and perhaps overly so as 250gr/2400fps is bordering on the slow side (though generally within 150fps of the .35 Whelen in all bullets). Yes, the 250gr has a maximum point blank range (MPBR) of 227yds but penetration isn't great. Few rifles were ever chambered for it (only the BLR and M77 are now), which is unfair to this underrated cartridge. While I prefer the flatter shooting .338 Federal, the .358 Win isn't a bad pick if you must have a <200yd short-action .358. Go Savage 99.

.35 Whelen (225gr/2610fps, 250gr/2500fps)

Wildcatted in 1922 (when there was little between .30-06 and .416 Rigby) and domesticated by Remington in 1987, the .35 Whelen is a fine 200yd round which <100yds kills slightly better than .338-06. (Boddington believes the .35 Whelen is as 200yds effective as a .338 Win.) Good medicine for all non-DG at reasonable ranges, and it will suffice for unwounded lion. Though a 200yd caliber, a good man *could* stretch out to 250 if he made no habit of it.

If you simply want to rebarrel your .30-06 without any bolt face enlargement (*e.g.*, to the .531" case head .358 Norma), then the .35 Whelen is a great idea. (The Ackley Improved, Scovil, and Hawk versions are worth considering.) Its only near competitor is the .338-06, and few experienced hunters could call *that* one for you (though I've more to say shortly). If you weren't hunting past 200yds, and thus positively did not need the extra 100yd range of the .338-06, then the .35 Whelen is fine. If you need more from a .358, then go to the Norma Mag.

In summary, I like the Whelen a lot, and consider it a good .323-.366 non-magnum caliber choice.

.350 Rem Mag (225gr/2575fps, 250gr/2475fps)

The .350 Rem. Mag. remains the only true medium bore (*i.e.*, .33-.375) short magnum cartridge, and offers a useful 260yd MPBR. With <250gr bullets has maybe 50fps on the .35 Whelen, but its rifles are handier. Case capacity is scant for the 250gr, so don't imagine it some .358 Norma. Instead, consider it a belted short-action .35 Whelen.

The original Rem 600 carbines were barreled far too short at 18" to effectively wring out this dandy round, which probably helped to quench sales. Jeff Cooper enjoyed the .350 Rem Mag for his "Lion Scout" (which I've shot out to 300yds at Raton).

.358 Norma (225gr/3000fps, 275gr/2700fps)

A .30-06 length (similar to 9.3x64) belted case with *great* performance. Without a magnum length action, it hits harder than a .338 but shoots flatter than a .375. If big bear is also on your plate, then you may prefer this to any .338. It does not meet the 9.3mm/.375 legal minimum DG caliber, however.

If, however, you *do* have a .416-.458 and thus don't *want* a .375, then a .358 Norma could well serve as your medium rifle, for the entire .338-.375 mag continuum. (*Nobody* will have ammo for it on either continent, so you'll be on your own.) It loads down nicely to 125-225gr for the smaller critters. (Too bad it's not beltless!) A good friend nearly talked me into it but I don't need such a powerful medium for Alaska when I've already a .416. The .358 Norma just doesn't "fit" anywhere in *my* caliber needs, however much I still like it.

.358 STA (225gr/3100fps, 275gr/2850fps)

It's to the .358 Norma what a .340 Wea is to the .338 Win. *Very* flat shooting, but reaching diminishing marginal returns. If you're going to a magnum-length action then just get a .375 or .416 instead (to legally hunt DG).

my thoughts on .358s in general

Unless you're using a magnum case, the .358 is a 200yd caliber. It has its place in North America for woods hunting, but I prefer a flatter-shooting caliber with higher SDs for Africa. Personally, I like the .338-06 and .338 Win much better.

9.3mm (.366) & BEYOND

The **9.3x62** (beats .35 Whelen) and **9.3x64** (beats .375 H&H, and legal for buff in Zim) are not common here, but very well liked in Africa. Large .1052" frontal area and fine .305 SD means great work on all non-DG, and they're both beltless .30-06 length cases. A great medium rifle for zebra and eland in particular.

9.3mm bullets

(.1052" cross sectional area)	.267 1:12"	.305 1:12"	.320 sectional density 1:11" min. rec. twist
Swift A-Frame	250gr		300gr
Barnes TSX	250gr	286gr	
A-Square Dead Tough		286gr	
North Fork	250gr	286gr	
Woodleigh	250gr	286gr	320gr (.341SD)

9.3x62 (286gr/2400fps from 22", 300/2375)

> There isn't really a great deal to say about it. Everybody found it so generally satisfactory that there wasn't anything to start a discussion.
> — John "Pondoro" Taylor, *African Rifles & Cartridges*

> ...the ideal dangerous game rifle for a citizen hunter is either a .375 H&H or a 9.3 x 62. My personal choice is the 9.3 x 62. The 286 grain Woodleigh solids will exit on a buffalo from any angle including a Free State (Texas) heart shot.... The premium soft points available, particularly some excellent flat-pointed ones produced by Ken Stewart, are more than adequate for lion or an initial shot on buffalo. In short, the 9.3 will cleanly kill any animal, and do so with surprisingly mild recoil in an 8lb rifle.
>
> In comparing the 9.3 to a .375 H&H, I've personally never noticed any difference where good quality solids are used, since bullets from both whistle straight through an elephant or buffalo making approximately the same sized hole.
> — Ganyana, "Stopping Power Revisited"

Introduced by Mauser in 1905, this ".366 Whelen Improved" has had a brilliant history of performance in Africa on all plains game. It's even decent on undisturbed buffalo. And all this from a standard length action! While neither the 8x68S nor the superb 9.3x64 is seen here, that old workhorse 9.3x62 can be found on these shores — and ammo is available in Africa. (How tidy to hunt there with a *local* caliber.)

The 286grainer's .305SD is the equal of a 300gr .375, and with similar BC, though velocity is shy by 150fps (not that any critter would notice). As long as distances are within 200yds, the 9.3x62 is an extremely efficient choice of caliber. If a bargain rifle crosses my path, I may snap it up.

handloading the 9.3x62

It's a 1mm shortened .30-06 case with less taper (.025" vs. .030") and a forward shoulder for increased capacity. .30-06 cases can be fireformed, although 9.3x62 brass is available. 3538fpe from 55.5gr of IMR-3031 and 22" barrel is a *deal!* www.superiorammo.com is a good source for loaded ammo.

The 293gr has been hotloaded to 2430fps for 3843fpe, which is within 500fpe of the .375's 300gr/2550fps. That's a *lot* of energy from an '06 case. When I consider that the 9.3x62 is now over a *century* old, I wonder about our so-called "progress." Why invent the .350 SUAM when we should rediscover the 9.3x62? (I mean, are we truly *that* bored, not to mention out of touch with history?) If you can't do it with a .30-06 or .416 Rigby, then the trouble is *not* with these old cartridges.

rifles in 9.3x62

There's a good chance that you'd find one of the below after a few gun shows of searching. The CZs and BRNOs are bargains, and the 1950s Mausers are lovely.

BRNO 98 Standard	23.6"	$ 395	98%
CZ 550 American Classic	23.6"	$ 395	98%
BRNO ZG-47	23.5"	$ 895	98%
Mannlicher Schoenauer Model 1950	24"	$ 775	98%
Mauser Model 66S Standard	24"	$1275	98%
Mauser Model 66 Carbine	21"	$1325	98%
Steyr Mannlicher SBS European Model	23.6"	$1850	98%

9.3x64 (286/2650fps, 300/2550)

10 more grains than a 9.3x62, and we've the excellent ballistics between .358 Norma and .375 H&H. The case head is .496" but it's standard 2.520" length with OAL of 3.370". Rifles and brass are rare (and in Africa it's been undeservedly eclipsed by the .375 since the Germans lost WW2), so Wilhelm Brenneke's fine round of 1910 makes little sense over a .375.

I suspect a growing interest in the 9.3x64mm. 300gr A-Frame at 2550fps (same as .375 H&H but with a .320 vs. .305SD) from a *beltless* 30-06 length? What's *not* to love? And why somebody hasn't wildcatted this great case to .358 is beyond me. (The .376 Steyr is shortened and necked up 9.3x64.)

rifles in 9.3x64 Brenneke

While there are no <$1000 bargains, the rifles are great:

Steyr Mannlicher Model S/T	26" $1575	98%
Mauser Model 66 Magnum	28" $1325	98%

9.3x66 SAKO (286/2750fps, 300/2650)

Only SAKO makes rifles for this new beltless caliber. 100fps additional velocities over the 9.3x64 (which is uncommon enough!). I don't see SAKO's point here...

.375 H&H (270gr/2700fps, 300gr/2550fps)

A DG caliber which will pinch-hit for plains game out to 300yds. You'd be way overgunned for impala, but it's great for wildebeest, zebra, and eland. Load 300gr solids down to 2400fps for less recoil and better terminal ballistics.

.45-70 Marlin (325gr/2050fps, 350gr/1900fps)

A funky, but possibly alluring choice (I know, because I couldn't help myself in 2007), especially for bushbuck and other close-cover game. Go 300gr TSX or 350gr A-Frame. (400gr won't feed or even singly chamber.) Hornady's 325gr LEVERevolution has been downloaded to a mere 1885fps.

My 17" Marlin sends a 350gr A-Frame at 1800fps, and nicely dispatched a 225yd waterbuck with good penetration.

FINAL THOUGHTS

So, there we have a pretty thorough discussion of most calibers from 7mm/.284 through 9.3mm/.366. Much of what you choose should be based on also how/where you hunt in North America. For example, if longer shots here (*i.e.*, 200+yds) are typical, then you may want to lean toward, for example, a .338-06 or .338 Win vs. a .35 Whelen.

On that note, I would point out that while you can *usually* stalk 50yds closer (or, with ample practice, stretch a 250yd gun to 300yds), you can *never* in the field instantly increase your bullet's frontal area or sectional density. So, in close questions between neighboring calibers I would tend to choose the *larger*, all else (*i.e.*, bullet weight, velocity, SI and SPI) being substantially similar. If things are still too narrow to call, *then* consider ammo availability.

a quick word about bullets and ballistics

> *[V]elocity is a positive factor in killing power primarily because [it] increases energy at bullet impact. Using a heavy bullet for a particular caliber is good because it increases SD and thus penetration. There is a trade off here, as the heavier the bullet in any given caliber, the lower the velocity. Attempts to combine high velocity with heavy bullets almost inevitably results in heavy recoil, which degrades the shooter's ability to achieve accurate bullet placement (the most important factor of all). So a balance must be struck between bullet weight, velocity and, ultimately, recoil.*
> — http://www.chuckhawks.com/rifle_killing_power.htm

Welcome to the world of TANSTAAFL. Everything in ballistics involves a trade off, at least in excessive recoil. The below table outlines ballistic parameters to quickly judge any caliber.

	Fair	Good	Excellent
caliber	.284-.307	.308-.323	.338
SA	.0633-.0744"	.0745-.0819"	.0897"
weight	160-175gr	180-200gr	220+gr
SD	.271-.299	.300-.312	.313+
BC	.248-.278	.279-.351	.352+
target V	2000-2149fps	2150-2299fps	2300-2450fps
target E	2000-2299fpe	2300-2599fpe	2600+fpe

Historically, 3000+fps velocities have rarely been necessary since all the classic performers (whether light, medium, or heavy) have been high (.305+) SD bullets impacting at 2200fps (ample, but with tolerable recoil, *i.e.*, balanced). For example, the 160gr 6.5 Mannlicher, the 220gr .30-06, the 286gr 9.3x62, the 400gr .416 Rigby, and the 465gr .458 Lott. All are medium velocity rounds, but with caliber-heavy/long bullets which penetrate deeply to the vitals (the bullet's primary task).

Game is 70% water, and slower/heavier bullets travel more distance than lighter/faster bullets. (Try it at home.)

While none are 300+yd calibers, you must ask yourself what *business* you have shooting at most game at such distances. **Get within 300yds, or pass up the shot.** This mania for 3000+fps has created two generations of flinchers who more often *wound* game with their Weatherbys than kill cleanly. (And, today, Weatherbys have slid to the *middle* of magnums! Our Viceroys of Velocity are never satisfied.) As a sportsman, you are obligated to an adequate caliber as fully powerful as you can reliably place in field conditions — *but no more powerful than that.* If you can shoot a .30-06 just as cleanly as a 7-08, then you are ethically bound to hunt with the .30-06 because it's a better tool for the quickest kill. Conversely, it would be wrong for a known flincher of .340 to hunt with one. **If you can't *place* your shot, all ballistics become *moot*.**

In the end, what caliber to choose depends on how much *you* can handle. If even a .308 is too much, then you've no business hunting large plains game such as wildebeest. (Same applies to the .375 H&H and buffalo.) As Jeff Cooper often quipped, recoil is 80% *mental*. While a .460 Weatherby will ring anybody's bell, I think that any adult can learn to competently shoot a .30-06 and probably a .338 Win. But you won't know your current limits until you test them.

Finally, as I mentioned on page 5 here, why would you ethically choose a meat-wasting caliber/bullet? Technology has given us the right equipment. Ethics must now catch up.

headstamp

If using a wildcat, beware that *some* countries will confirm that your cases' headstamps match the rifle's caliber. Nonmatching ammo can create an airport hassle, causing you to miss your connection or have your ammo withheld.

BUT HOW TO COMPARE?

There are many ballistic minimums for large plains game: .308 caliber quality bullet (for sufficient wound channel diameter), ME of 2700fpe (bullet weight minimum is embedded here), MV of 2400+fps and a .271SD (for reliable penetration). The 100yd kinetic energy of a 180gr .308 (MV 2600fps) is about 2300fpe. I consider this a *reliable* minimum (in caliber, weight, and KE) for all plains game (barely including eland, *if* slipped behind the shoulder). Most PHs would agree that such game, regardless of the caliber and distance, requires this similar minimum of killing power. (Values *over* this are extra insurance for tougher angles and/or tougher animals.)

But how to compare *dissimilar* calibers, weights, SDs, and kinetic energies? Although no perfect formula can be reached, attempts are helpful (if not taken *too* seriously while remembering that bullet performance remains paramount).

One of better formulas was **Wooters Lethality Index**, which is calculated as **KE x SD x caliber**. In my opinion it over emphasized caliber over SD (since caliber values are greater than SD values)—however, it did enjoy a certain tidyness.

calculating RoyceKoV (plains game) index

Basically, I propose *averaging* the two A-Square formulas of Penetration Index and Shock Power Index, both smoothed out by Royce constants for an x:100 ratio to the .308 180gr/2300fpe @ 100yds minimum. If this Royce Knock-out Value (Plains Game) index for any given combination of caliber, bullet, and retained KE is *below* 100, then it's not even as effective as that 180gr .308 at 100yds, and such a load should not be readily used at that distance. (As far as I can tell, my combined penetration/shock power index with a minimum *downrange* ballistic benchmark is an innovation.)

The Royce **Penetration Index** (PI) is calculated by dividing kinetic energy (KE, downrange) with the cross sectional area (SA), then multiplying its quotient by SD, then dividing with 83.66 (a useful constant, soon shown). This assumes no bullet expansion, deformation, or path variance.

The Royce **Shock Power Index** (SPI) is calculated by multiplying the KE by the SA of the bullet, divided with 1.71.

KE kinetic energy = (V^2/450,240)bullet weight in grains
SD sectional density = (gr/7000)/D^2
SA cross sectional area = πr^2
PI Penetration Index = ((KE/SA)SD)/83.66
SPI Shock Power Index = KE(SA)/1.71

OK, let's calculate PI and SPI for our 180gr .308 at 100yds. Why 100yds? First, because *muzzle* energy is irrelevant as nobody shoots plains game at 0yds. What's relevant is *downrange* KE.

KE = 2300fpe   SA = .0745"   SD = .2710638

Royce PI = ((2300/.0745).2710638)/83.66   = 100
Royce SPI = 2300(.0745)/1.71   = 100

The constants of 83.66 and 1.71 level the PI and SPI to 100 as our benchmark. Obviously, in both indexes, the larger the number, the better. Then we average them to take into account both KE (relative to xSA) *and* penetration:

RoyceKoV(PG) = (PI+SPI)/2

Now, we've a base to compare dissimilar calibers, SDs, energies, etc. Let's compare A-Frame bullets: the 180gr and 200gr .308, 220gr 8mm-08, 225gr .338 Federal, and 250gr .358 Win:

cartridge	gr.	SD	SA	KE(@?yds)	Royce PI	Royce SPI	Plains Game RoyceKoV
.308	180	.271	.0745	2300 (100)	100	100	100
.308	200	.301	.0745	2368 (100)	114	103	109
.358 Win	250	.279	.1007	2374 (100)	79	138	109
8-08	220	.301	.0819	2391 (100)	108	115	111
.338 Fed	225	.281	.0897	2490 (100)	93	131	112
.308	180	.271	.0745	1895 (200)	82	83	83
.358 Win	250	.279	.1007	1901 (200)	63	112	88
.308	200	.301	.0745	2007 (200)	96	88	92
.338 Fed	225	.281	.0897	2054 (200)	77	108	93
8-08	220	.301	.0819	2022 (200)	89	97	93
.308	180	.271	.0745	1580 (300)	68	68	68
.358 Win	250	.279	.1007	1509 (300)	50	89	70
.338 Fed	225	.281	.0897	1683 (300)	63	88	76
8-08	220	.301	.0819	1701 (300)	75	81	78
.308	200	.301	.0745	1692 (300)	81	74	78

The moral? That higher case efficiency derives from *higher* SD bullets. Over the .30/180gr, the 200gr gives +68fpe, +14% PI, and +3% SPI. And all from a mere bullet change.

Going to larger calibers does have its limits. A point of diminishing returns is seen with the .358 before 200yds, and the .338 before 300yds. (This illustrates the vitality of anticipating range.) The 8mm-08 is a very nice wildcat, but not quite worth the trouble over the nearly identical 200gr .308. (These two have reciprocal PI:SPI. Very interesting.)

At *some* point, however, a lower PI will translate into wounding game vs. penetrating to/through the vitals. This will depend on the animal and its target angle. (I'd considered weighting PI:SPI at 4:3, but left things 1:1 simple.)

Shock power must be balanced with penetration. SPI without sufficient penetration will not reach the vitals, and penetration without sufficient SPI will not destroy the vitals. When PIs drop below 75, I'd pass on the shot for such distance. Thus, the 63 PI of .338 Federal is inadequate for 300yd Africa. (Same point regarding the .358 Win's 63PI at 200yds.)

When RoyceKoV drops below 100, PI or SPI (or both) has fallen below 100. While I might consider a <100 RoyceKoV *if* the PI remained near 100 (such as a 200gr .308 and its 96 PI and 88 SPI at 200yds), a low PI takes an unnecessary risk.

the 100-400yd RoyceKoV Plains Game table

I've included for comparison Wooter's Lethality Index (WLI) divided with a constant of 1.92 for a new Royce-WLI.

The 2000fpe rule of thumb for impact KE is given a 15% reserve in the 100yd 180gr .308 with its 2300fpe.

For comparison, I included 7-08 and .280 Rem with 175gr. even though I do not recommend 7mm for Africa.

Your choice of bullet *directly* affects downrange KE and thus RoyceKoV. For example, by 250yds the .308's 200gr TSX catches up with the .30-06's 200gr A-Frame! (Note: Barnes TSX published velocities *may* be due to optimistic BCs.) While A-Frames have lower BCs, their proven killing performance may compensate for the 100-300fpe less downrange KE, so I wouldn't automatically choose a TSX for their RoyceKoVs. (Chrono your loads at different distances.) For uniformity, I calculated with A-Frames (except for the 9.3x62 and .45-70).

Also, your bullet choice directly affects *terminal ballistics*. In short, my RoyceKoV table is not to be taken as Gospel, especially considering the variable killing effectiveness of our modern bullet selection. It is a *guide*. (Your hunting experience may differ, but not likely by much.)

Plains Game Bullets, Calibers, & Rifles

cartridge	bullet gr./type	SD	SA	down-range KE	Royce PI	Royce SPI	Royce WLI	Plains Game RoyceKoV
7-08	175A-Fr	.310	.0633	2052	120	76	94	98
.308	180A-Fr	.271	.0745	2300fpe	**100**	**100**	**100**	**100** 100y
.308	200A-Fr	.301	.0745	2368	114	103	114	109
.358 Win	250A-Fr	.279	.1007	2374	79	138	123	109
.338 Fed	225A-Fr	.281	.0897	2490	93	131	126	112
.45-70	325Horn	.221	.1647	2158	23	208	113	115
.280 Rem	175A-Fr	.310	.0633	2409	141	89	110	115
.30-06	200A-Fr	.301	.0745	2568	124	112	124	118
.35 Whelen	250A-Fr	.279	.1007	2828	94	166	147	130
.338-06	250A-Fr	.313	.0897	2941	123	154	162	139
.300 Win	200A-Fr	.301	.0745	3217	155	140	155	148
.325 WSM	220A-Fr	.301	.0819	3227	142	154	163	148
.338-06 A.I.	250A-Fr	.313	.0897	3190	133	167	176	150
.338 Win	250A-Fr	.313	.0897	3449	143	181	190	162
9.3x62	286RN	.305	.1052	3544	123	218	206	171
.308	180A-Fr	.271	.0745	1895	82	83	82	83 **200y**
.358 Win	250A-Fr	.279	.1007	1901	63	112	99	88
.308	200A-Fr	.301	.0745	2007	96	88	97	92
.338 Fed	225A-Fr	.281	.0897	2054	77	108	106	93
.30-06	200A-Fr	.301	.0745	2184	105	95	105	100
.280 Rem	175A-Fr	.310	.0633	2121	124	79	97	101
.35 Whelen	250A-Fr	.279	.1007	2282	75	135	119	105
9.3x62	286RN	.305	.1052	2370	82	146	138	114
.338-06	250A-Fr	.313	.0897	2476	102	130	136	116
.325 WSM	220A-Fr	.301	.0819	2700	118	129	137	124
.300 Win	200A-Fr	.301	.0745	2757	132	119	132	126
.338-06 A.I.	250A-Fr	.313	.0897	2694	112	141	148	127
.338 Win	250A-Fr	.313	.0897	2922	121	153	161	137
.308	180A-Fr	.271	.0745	1570	68	68	68	68 **300y**
.358 Win	250A-Fr	.279	.1007	1509	50	89	79	70
.338 Fed	225A-Fr	.281	.0897	1683	63	88	88	76
.308	200A-Fr	.301	.0745	1692	81	74	82	78
.30-06	200A-Fr	.301	.0745	1846	89	81	89	85
.35 Whelen	250A-Fr	.279	.1007	1692	61	108	88	85
.338-06	250A-Fr	.313	.0897	2071	86	109	114	98
.325 WSM	220A-Fr	.301	.0819	2243	98	108	114	103
.338-06 A.I.	250A-Fr	.313	.0897	2261	94	119	125	107
.300 Win	200A-Fr	.301	.0745	2351	114	103	114	109
.338 Win	250A-Fr	.313	.0897	2459	102	129	135	116
.308	180A-Fr	.271	.0745	1291	56	56	56	56 **400y**
.30-06	200A-Fr	.301	.0745	1551	75	68	78	72
.338-06	250A-Fr	.313	.0897	1722	71	90	95	81
.325 WSM	220A-Fr	.301	.0819	1849	81	88	94	85
.338-06 A.I.	250A-Fr	.313	.0897	1885	79	99	104	89
.300 Win	200A-Fr	.301	.0745	1993	96	87	96	92
.338 Win	250A-Fr	.313	.0897	2057	86	108	113	97

The importance of *balance* between penetration and shock power is clear. The 180gr .308 is a good example, more favoring PI than SPI (except for 160-175gr/7mm and 200gr/.30).

PI : SPI		
1.58 : 1.00	175gr .284/7mm	hugely favors PI over SPI
1.44 : 1.00	160gr .284/7mm	greatly favors PI over SPI
1.10 : 1.00	200gr .30	slightly favors PI over SPI
1 : 1.00	**180gr .30**	**the RoyceKoV benchmark**
1 : 1.09	220gr .323/8mm	slightly favors SPI over PI
1 : 1.26	250gr .338	significantly favors SPI over PI
1 : 1.40	225gr .338	PI insufficient for 300yds
1 : 1.78	250gr .358	PI insufficient past 200yds
1 : 1.98	225gr .358	PI insufficient past 100yds

some misc. remarks

7mm is just too small for *general* use in Africa.

I thought the **225gr .338 Federal** *might* make 200yds, but not quite with a 93 RoyceKoV. (Its .384 BC is the problem, which lowers velocities, energies, and thus PI.

The **200gr .308** acquitted itself *very* well almost out to 200yds. It scored 9% higher than the 180gr at all ranges, which is an easy bonus for simply moving up 20gr in weight.

200gr .30-06 is a great 250yd pick, stretchable to 300yds. At 200yds it equals the 100yd/180gr .308. A *very* efficient load.

looking at things solely from the SD angle:

caliber	Africa *minimum* SD .271+		Africa *preferred* SD .301+	
.284/7mm	160gr	.283SD	175gr	.310SD
.30	180gr	.271SD	200gr	.301SD
.323/8mm	200gr	.274SD	220gr	.301SD
.338	225gr	.281SD	250gr	.313SD
.358/9mm	250gr	.279SD	270gr	.301SD

If your round sends an above bullet at 2400-2700fps MV, then it will perform well in Africa. (Don't stray from these weights.)

The Winners . . .

.325 WSM (220gr)

This is a very well balanced and capable round out to 325yds. Second only to the 250gr .338 Win and 200gr .300 Win.

.338-06 and .338-06 Ackley Improved (250gr)

The *most* efficient use of the standard .30-06 case. The factory .338-06 is a strong 300yd caliber even with slower A-

Frames. For example, the 200gr .30-06, a fine .301SD caliber, scores a 85 at 300yds, which the .338-06 nearly matches at *400*. The .338-06 is within 11% of the 200gr .300 Win at all ranges.

By these figures, the 250gr .338-06 *clearly* beats out the 250gr .35 Whelen (whose 200yd PI is a marginal 75). Higher BC and SD made the difference for the .338 bullet, as the .30-06 case simply cannot throw a 250gr .358 bullet fast enough. The .338-06 is a much more balanced choice. That debate is *over*.

If you want a *true* 300yd non-magnum caliber, go .338-06 Ackley Improved. It is within 200fpe/8% of the .338 Win. The *ultimate* use of the .30-06 case.

.338 Win Mag (250gr)

A factory caliber king. Even at 400yds its A-Frame scores a 97 RoyceKoV, and without .340 Weatherby recoil.

RELIABLE CALIBER MINIMUMS

...the visiting sportsman wants the best representatives he can find of a given species. His time is not unlimited, and he cannot always pick or predict the shot he gets. **He simply must not be undergunned, which means he will often be a bit overgunned — if he's smart!**

— Craig Boddington, *Safari Rifles* (1990), p.24

After scouring many books and opinions I settled on the below matrix of calibers (using heaviest/2nd-heaviest bullets) which I consider to be *conservative* minimums for the ranges and game indicated. **Yes, you *can* do with less, but such would not be as *reliable*.** You'd have no excess margin of power or bullet mass or frontal area for tough animals, or poor shot angles. In Africa, it's always better to have a bit *more* vs. not quite enough.

My minimum RoyceKoVs are 70 for impala, 85 for kudu, 100 for wildebeest, and 115 for eland.

plains game to:		100yds	200yds	300yds
impala/bushbuck	70	.243	.257	.270
kudu/sable/water	85	7-08 (160gr)	.308 (180gr)	.30-06 (200gr)
wilde/oryx/zebra	100	.308 (180gr)	.30-06 (200gr)	.338Win (250gr)
eland	115	.30-06 (200gr)	.338-06 (250gr)	.338Win (250gr)

A 180-200gr .308 *will* take 100yd quartering-away eland, but it's somewhat *marginal*. You're much better off with a 115+ RoyceKoV caliber (such as 200gr .30-06 or 250gr 338-06).

Most sportsmen will rarely take shots past 200yds, and within that range the 200gr .30-06 can do it all. (The 200gr .308 *almost* will, but not quite.)

> Unless you go for buffalo, there is no need to run out and acquire a new rifle for Africa. Your 30-06 will do just fine, and so will your 308. **The 30-06/220 is about perfect for generalized shooting in the African bush.** On one afternoon's stroll you may want to take an impala at about 120lbs, or an eland at perhaps 1500. The 220-grain bullet will harvest your impala without destroying much meat, and it will also drive clear through the vitals of the eland, if it is your good fortune to run across one.
> — Jeff Cooper, *C Stories* (2004), p. 140

The rare 1:9" twist for a 220gr aside, I tend to agree though I think the 200gr spitzer's higher velocity is worth the 20gr less mass. While a .338 offers a decisive power edge over the .30 calibers, it's not necessary (even for eland, except past 200yds). **The answer is not more *power*, but stalking *closer*.**

200yd and 300yd winners for plains game

Below is my Reliable Minimums table, but with other suitable calibers added. The semi-finalists are in **bold**.

plains game to:	100yds	200yds	300yds
impala/bushbuck	.243	.257 7x57	.270 .280
kudu/sable/waterbuck	7-08 (160gr) 7x57 (160gr)	.308 (180gr) 8x57S (180gr)	.30-06 (200gr) 8-06 (220gr) .338-06 .300 mags
wildebeest/oryx/zebra	.308 (180gr) 8x57S (180gr) .280 (160gr)	**.30-06 (200gr)** .338Fed .308 (200gr) 8-06 (220gr) .35 Whelen 9.3x62	**.338Win (250gr)** 8mmRem **.338-06 (250gr)** **.325 WSM (225gr)** 9.3x64 .300 mags (200gr)
eland	.30-06 (200gr) .280 (175gr)	**.338-06 (250gr)** 9.3x62	**.338Win (250gr)** .338-06 A.I. (250gr)

Out to 200yds (and sometimes 250yds) you've the ubiquitous and proven .30-06, two uncommon factory loads (.338-06, .35 Whelen), and the Euro 9.3x62. **For 90% of plains game ranges the 200gr .30-06 is** *ample*.

what about the 200gr .308 out to 200yds?

Although likely sufficient, it *may* (with 92 RoyceKoV) prove too limiting for a tough wildebeest. You might wish for a .30-06 but if you take the .30-06 you'll *never* pine for a .308. (Your .308 is fine, but if you've also a .30-06 take that instead.)

My .308 Savage Scout did well on a 150yd wildebeest, and my PH *would* have allowed a <100yd eland *if* the perfect quartering-away angle had been available. Never, however, did I fool myself into thinking that I was toting a .30-06.

out to 300yds (only for *experienced* hunters)

In our endless flight from the "boring" .30-06, we now have a dozen .300 mags. Instead of getting into shape for 100yd belly crawls to close within a 200yd zebra, we'd rather send 3000+fps mag bullets from *300+*yds. *Über*magnums are *not necessary* unless average distances are beyond 250yds, and few hunters cleanly kill with one shot at that range. **Besides,** *true* **hunting means stalking** *closer!*

A first-timer in Africa should limit himself to 200yd max, and that means a .308 or .30-06 is all he needs. Once you've hunted the 100-150yd bushveld, *then* you can fairly contemplate Namibia or the 250+yds eastern Cape.

Your PH can advise if you need more than a .30-06, and if you do then don't settle for a .300 mag — go **.338 Win** instead. You're better off with a highly versatile .338 Win than a .300. 225-250gr .338s are superior to 200-220gr .30s.

A **220gr .325 WSM** is a solid 103 RoyceKoV. Fine caliber!

For handloaders, the **250 gr A-Frame .338-06** is a good 98 RoyceKoV choice (The .338-06 Ackley Improved is *107*.)

Regardless of caliber, it is imperative to use the heaviest spitzer (preferably with boat tail). Even the mighty .338 Win can be hamstrung by the wrong bullet (*e.g.*, 200gr). It is not advisable to sacrifice a .300+SD for a lighter bullet's slightly flatter trajectory. Slower and heavier is the secret. You can always hold over slightly to compensate for the extra bit of drop, but you cannot make a <.300SD bullet penetrate as well.

between the .338 Win and the .358 Norma

Both are standard-length cases. The .338 Win Mag has a *great* selection of .313SD 250gr bullets, and is a *commonly* available caliber in factory rifles. (At a 2006 gun show I saw a very nice used push-feed Model 70 for just $550. To rebarrel a rifle in .358 Norma would cost about that.)

The .358 Norma has 12% more frontal area, and can throw 125-158gr handgun bullets, but there are no factory rifles and stores haven't the ammo. Handload only.

Their heaviest A-Frame bullets (275gr/.338 and 280gr/.358) both see 2600fps MVs (cases are nearly the same), but the sleeker .338 retains 100-200fpe more downrange KE. (Comparing the two is like the ".338-06 vs. .35 Whelen" debate.)

The Question: Is the commonality, affordability, and slightly greater KE of the .338 Win worth forsaking 12% more frontal area and handgun bullet practice ammo?

Probably not, unless I were also going to often hunt grizzly bears (and even then I'd just use my .416). For a man without any magnum-action .375+ (or desire for one), the .358 Norma makes sense. But for me, it's too extravagant and begins to overlap into .416 territory.

conclusion

So, in *common* calibers, it really boils down to **.308/.30-06 (out to 175/200yds) or .338 Win Mag (300yds).** (Yes, the .308/.30-06 can often be stretched 50yds more, but ...)

What'll be *my* 300yd rifle? .325 WSM? .338-06? .338 Win?

I have a .416 Rem (and eventually a .470 Mbogo) and don't want a .358-.375, although that's a fine general purpose rifle. So, it's a matter of whether I rebarrel my sporterized M1917 to .338-06, vs. buy a new .325 WSM or .338 Win.

I want a true, no-excuses *300*yd medium rifle, which nixes out the very cool, old 9.3x62 and pleasant .35 Whelen. Also, since I'd like the option of 250gr loads, that cancels out the intriguing .325 WSM. This leaves the .338-06 and .338 Win.

The Question: need I a magnum case over a .30-06 case?

Not necessarily. The 250gr A-Frame .338-06 retains 2071fpe at 300yds for a respectable 98 BPKoV. Is 86 PI and 109 SPI viable on zebra? Sure, it'll do fine, with excellent shot placement at a decent angle on an average animal.

Satisfactory ballistics aside, rebarreling my M1917 to .338-06 is a $450 minimum job, plus the wait. I like the .338 Hawk (a mild .338-06 Ackley Improved), but rebarreling is $550. (Or, I could buy a Savage 110 in .30-06 and install myself a $130 MidwayUSA .338-06 barrel.) Odds of finding a used .338-06 are slim.

Once past the "paralysis of analysis," the *reasonable* choice for *me* is a .338 Win Mag. (While the .325 WSM was tempting, mag capacity is lessened by two rounds, and nobody makes 240gr 8mm bullets. Also, 8mm is not a *true* "medium" caliber. The .338 is.)

I should have bought that Model 70 .338, but I didn't have the time to set it up for my second safari (on which I was taking my perfectly adequate .308 Savage Scout, anyway).

African hunting reflections on the . . .
.30-06: 200gr Barnes TSX and Swift A-Frame

I took to Africa my 2600fps handloads (thanks to these companies for their T&E samples). Both bullets performed perfectly: they were <2MOA accurate, tracked like a laser through the animals, and must have expanded nicely because of the significant tissue damage and exit holes.

I recovered *none* of these bullets, which is my benchmark for optimum terminal ballistics. I *want* exits and their superior blood spoor — I never want to see those bullets again. To me, a *recovered* bullet is evidence of suboptimal performance.

While there's nothing really wrong with a 180gr and/or a .308, the 200gr .30-06 is just *magical*. That extra 20gr of bullet and 5gr of powder does provide more reliable results.

Marlin .45-70: 300gr Barnes TSX and 350gr Swift A-Frame

The only bullet recovered was a 300gr TSX from a 225yd waterbuck's neck (entering in an extreme quartered away paunch). Meaning, even that 1800fps slow bullet with a measly .204 SD almost exited *after near-full body travel 225yds* away.

A frontal spine shot on an impala with the 350gr A-Frame exited through the ham. Another such A-Frame sailed through a 125yd double-lunged kudu.

Barnes TSX, Swift A-Frame: why choose anything else?

The only other bullets I'd trust for African plains game are the Northfork and the A-Square Dead Tough.

Royce wildcats
the ".338 Royce" (8.59x60mm)

What would be dandy is a beltless .338 with case capacity of the .338 Win. It would be fatter than .473" (more powder, wider column) but not a .532" (which reduces magazine capacity). The 9.3x64mm case head of .496" is ideal. Length would be no longer than 63mm — about 60mm.

Eureka! A necked-down .376 Steyr! 250gr at 2800fps and 275gr (.344SD!) at 2675fps. These are +100fps over a .338 Win.

Another way to go would be necking down the .375 Ruger.

the ".360 Cooper" (9x60mm)

This fabulous case also has the potential for a great 9x60 throwing 275gr (.307SD) 2650fps/4289fpe. These are about .358 Norma ballistics (if not more), but from a beltless and shorter case. (The 60mm length make possible these long bullets in a .30-06 mag body.) There's a gaping hole in the beltless .358 continuum, and no ".350 SAUM" will suffice. Also, this cartridge could enjoy 9mm/.38 Special/.357 Magnum chamber inserts for plinking or finishing off game.

The .376 Steyr is the proper case for a new .360 Lion Scout. I wish that Jeff were alive to see it. I think he'd have liked the idea of improving his concept with a better round than the .350 Rem, so I name this idea in his honor. The ".360 Cooper" has a nice ring to it — as if the Lion Scout concept has come "full circle" (360°, get it?) from the Scout rifle concept. Besides, any man who's done *that* much for shooting and hunting *deserves* a new cartridge named for him.

A new ".360 Cooper" Lion Scout needs a quality forged steel receiver Mauser M98 action (without mania for <8lb weight), though in the Steyr stock (which is just brilliant). A Schmidt & Bender Scout scope with illuminated reticular BDC. And *damn* the cost! Let the thing be *perfect,* and folks wouldn't quibble about the price.

Whether in .338 or .358, these wildcats would make for the *ultimate* medium in a standard-action, beltless case with tolerable recoil.

OK, enough about *calibers*, let's finally discuss rifles.

PLAINS GAME RIFLES

> *In no country are better sportsmen to be found than in the United States of America, nor does any country posses keener buyers or better men of business, **yet in no country is so much worthless rubbish of the (mass production) gun-factories offered for sale.** The Boers are a race of sportsmen, but it is of no use to offer them rubbish at any price, and the author can hardly believe that the astute American will sacrifice everything to cheapness.*
> — W.W. Greener, *The Gun and its Development* (1910)

1910! The more things change, the more they remain the *same!*

bolt actions

If you've already a proven .308 or .30-06 bolt gun, then you're set for all plains game within 175-200yds. Cooper was right: You don't need to rush out and buy a new rifle for Africa.

Since this game is not dangerous (although some *can* be if wounded, such as roan, sable, gemsbok, and bushbuck), controlled-feed actions are not vital. Any quality push-feed will do fine (though I don't personally care for the Remington bolt, trigger, and extractor). I like Savages and Winchesters.

While the Ruger M77II has many nice features, they are not *forged* steel receivers. Since investment cast receivers have no aligned grain structure or randomly disbursed carbides, they are weaker (pound for pound) than forged steel receivers. Also, these guns feel "dead" in my hands, and have no soul. (For soul, try a pre-64 Winchester Model 70.)

lever actions

While they offer nothing over bolt-actions, if you're a lefty, or simply in love with lever guns, such can serve satisfactorily for plains game however non-African the weapon. (My PH had seen only two in the field: a .308 BLR and a .444 Marlin.)

.30-30

A Winchester 94 or Marlin in .30-30 would normally be a *very* poor choice (anemic caliber and slow roundnose bullets), but the 160gr/2400fps Hornady LEVERevolution "Elastomer Flex Tip" bullet is ballistically superior to flat/round nose and also safe in tubular magazines. Thus, you'd have a 200yd .30-30 for light (but not medium) plains game. www.hornady.com

.308

The Savage 99 and Browning BLR are good. The Winchester 88 is a very strong action, but with a poor trigger. All three guns can use spitzers.

.405 Winchester Model 1895 (400gr/2200fps for 3918fpe)

It's to the .416 Rigby what the .45-70 is to the .458 Lott. If kept within 100yds, this venerable cartridge will suffice. While I wouldn't recommend it for the newbie, for those wanting a taste of Theodore Roosevelt's 1909 safari (now approximated by the outfitter Ballantine, with 80 porters), try a Winchester Model 1895 (once again manufactured) with irons. Due to stock design, even in .30-06, these are *hard* kicking rifles.

.45-70

In .45-70, the Marlin 1895 would be great for close cover hunting (*especially* with XS Sights, or a 2½x Scout scope). Hornady's LEVERevolution load throws a 325gr spitzer at 2050 for 3032fpe. This transforms the .45-70 into a viable African plains game cartridge at moderate distances: 100yds (+3.0" for 1729fps/2158fpe) and 200yds (-4.1" for 1450fps/1516fpe). PIs are abysmal, so target angle and shot placement are critical.

www.grizzlycartridges.com makes a *very* hot load: 460gr/1800fps for 3310fpe. The bullet is a lead flat nose with a huge metplat. (This is like a 400fps downloaded .458 Win.)

Third safari: my handy 17" Marlin got waterbuck, impala, bushpig, and kudu. (I couldn't let my .30-06 M70 have all the fun!) 350gr A-Frame at 1800fps/2519fpe.

pumps

I'm no fan of them, which you already know if you've read my *Boston's Gun Bible*. With their fussy feeding and weak primary extraction, they just don't resonate with me. If you like them and shoot them well in the field, then go for it. (No autoloaders such as BAR allowed in the RSA.)

scopes

While not absolutely necessary for the competent iron-sight man who stalks within 200yds, most hunters should top their rifles with optics. Those hunting the smaller antelope at great distances *certainly* should. If anything, optics can help you more precisely thread your shot through brush.

quality

First, choose at least upper-medium quality such as Burris or Leupold. (*I.e.*, I would *not* go to Africa with a Tasco, Simmons, Bushnell, etc.) IOR makes fine scopes, and their USA customer service has apparently improved since 2004.

If you can afford a Schmidt & Bender or Swarovski, enjoy!

reticle

Both Burris and Leupold offer ranging holdover reticle scopes. If shots past maximum point blank range (MPBR) are likely (this means about 225yds for .308 and 250yds for .30-06), then reticular holdovers are vital.

I have several of the **Burris Ballistic Plex**, and highly recommend them. The 3-12x handgun scope on my .308 Savage Scout worked great in Africa. (www.burrisoptics.com)

Nikon has a new 500yd BDC reticle scope that's worth a look. Their circles subtend to a useful 2MOA.

$600 for a **Shepherd** (www.shepherdscopes.com) will buy you the most useful optic yet designed. How about a one-shot zero? Only with a Shepherd. Then, the reticle will allow you to first *range* your prey, as well as holdover. Also, its patented Dual Reticle System tells you at a glance if the scope has lost its zero from damage. The optics quality is superb, and they hold up in the field. Such a scope is essential on any hunting rifle for 200+yds. I hunted with a Shepherd on my .30-06 Win 70, and loved it. (My PH now wants a 310-P2, as well as a pair of their very fine 10x42mm binos.)

take a spare scope in rings

This is really important if you're hunting with only one rifle. Guns don't break all that often, but optics do. Having a back-up (already zeroed) is very wise insurance. If you can't afford a second scope, then at least have back-up iron sights.

rings

Quick-detach (QD) rings are a must, as you may need to remove your scope in mere seconds (vs. having to dig around for a screwdriver). Do not skimp here! No $10 aluminum Tascos! Buy only quality steel rings, such as Talley or Leupold (QRW or Quick-Release System).

I don't care for see-through mounts because the optic is set too high, requiring a jawweld vs. a proper cheekweld.

www.libertyoptics.com
   Scott Barrish has a great family-owned business carrying many quality brands. His prices are very good, and he shines at no-B.S. customer service. Tell him I sent you!

rifle misc.
trigger
   Your rifle simply *must* have a crisp 2½-4lb trigger. There are trigger adjustments (or drop-in parts) for every bolt-action. Scour the catalog from www.brownells.com.
   Savage's new AccuTrigger is worth buying a new rifle for. (Get a .30-06, to easily rebarrel in .338-06 or .35 Whelen.)

sling
   Learn to sling carry your rifle African style (muzzle down, weak side), and pick a strap most conducive to that.
   Galco's Orion Hunting Sling ($25) is worth considering.
   Also, the Ching Sling found on Steyr Scouts is a *very* nice system, and really braces your shots. (I fashioned my own out of 1¼" nylon strap and Quake swivels for my Savage Scout. Blue LocTite the swivel screws! I didn't, and one of mine backed out.)

spare parts
   Take an extra firing pin/spring and extractor. A broken shell extractor could also save your hunt. I should have had an extra sling swivel (or at least its screw, which I had to replace with heavy wire). I had a second bolt headspaced at the factory for my .308 Savage Scout, and carried it in the field as a spare.

CeraKote (www.RhysPrecisionGunworks.com)
   A baked-on ceramic from the automotive world that held up extremely well on my Win 70 over several weeks in the bush. Just the coating for stainless steel, and no more galling! There are some 31 colors for any taste or need. I chose a fairly light OD which blended in nicely, and many people remarked on how distinctive my rifle looked. I'll have other rifles CeraKoted, especially some older Savages (which rust at a harsh word).
   $200. 4-6 week service from nice folks. Tell 'em I sent you!

SAFARI CLUB INTERNATIONAL

At **Safari Club International** in Reno (every January) you'll meet many famous authors and hunters. Renowned Tanzanian **PH Robin Hurt** helped "set the hook" years ago for Africa with his key part in the 1986 film *In The Blood*.

At SCI 2007 **Craig Boddington** and I chatted about the .325 WSM. Such fellows are accessible and friendly, and keen to answer your questions. Be sure to bring with you any of their books for signing.

Two checked bags (50lbs each without overweight fee, or 70lbs for an extra $50 per bag), and **one carry-on** is all you may take no matter how long your hunt. (Note yellow tape on rifle case, with name/flights penned by Sharpie as backup ID to the tag.) If the checked bags are wheeled, then you can manage all luggage by yourself. (Wearing travel shoes, try out your three bags with a walk around the block. You'll find out then if you've packed too much.)

Your carry-on *must* have shoulder straps, as your hands will be full during travel. The roomy **Kelty 3100 backpack** nicely fits in the overhead bin. Be sure in advance that your carry-on *does* fit, else it will get shunted to the baggage compartment and you'll be deprived of your in-flight comforts.

I prefer the **Airbus 346** over the Boeing 747-400. South African Airways' D.C.—Johannesburg is nonstop; about the world's longest commercial flight. Though the Airbus is quiet and comfortable, it's a memorable relief to deplane after 15 hours, 15 minutes. (Those last 15 minutes are the killer.)

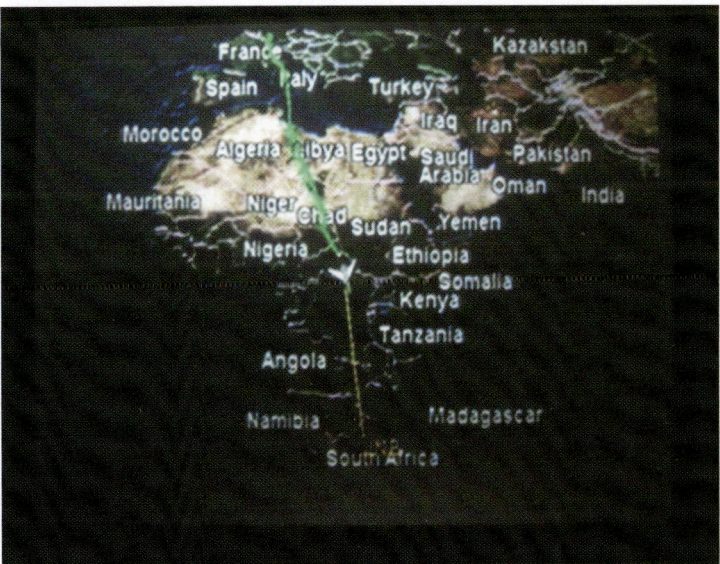

This was during an SAA Frankfurt—Johannesburg flight. Most airliners have a location screen, so you can take a photo of your first **equator crossing**.

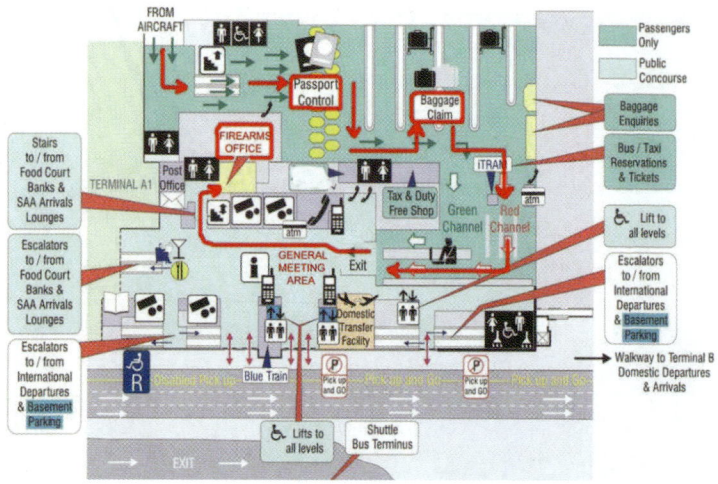

Johannesburg (Tambo) International Airport. After you sign for your rifle case at the kiosk near baggage conveyor #1, it will be taken to the Firearms Office where your gun permit SAPS 520 is tendered. Then, you must hoof it outside 250yds to domestic Terminal B to check in for your connecting flight.

The prop commuter flight is about 45 minutes. Your PH will typically pick you up at his local airport. (If your bags are delayed or lost, he has the experience to sort it out.) After a good night's sleep you'll be hunting the next morning. It will be difficult to believe that you're actually there!

This is a **South African game ranch lodge** in the Limpopo Province. The terrain looks like Arizona. Yes, the thatched roofs are "real" roofs. My quarters were in the *rondavel* on right. Photo taken from a large granite *kopje*.

There are 14 **giraffe** on this game ranch, rarely hunted. Giraffe are usually very docile, and will allow you to walk up to within 50yds of them. It's hardly sporting to shoot one—I could never do it.

Kudu cannot read, so the crossing signs must be pictorial.

A new hunter is typically begun with an **impala**, to gauge the quality of his stalking and shooting, and to help him over any natural case of nerves. This ram would fairly be called "*representative of the species*" (*i.e.,* not a bad trophy, but not a great one either—yet deserving of congratulations).

An inexperienced European hunter shot through this opening, not seeing the branch which deflected his 180gr .30-06. **Be conscientious about brush**, and look *very* carefully for obstructions. High quality optics are a must!

African game is denser, and our fine deer bullets are often not up to the job. In 2006 I used Sierra Game Kings (180gr/2600fps) in my Savage Scout .308. All broke up badly, and only these three bullets were recovered. The next year, I .30-06 hunted only with **200gr/2600fps Barnes TSX and Swift A-Frame**.

You've *no* excuse shooting such poor bullets as these (which often wound because they shed too much mass, going off track to miss the vitals). Instead, **use heavy-for-caliber Barnes, Swift, Northfork, or A-Square**.

Everything about your hunt depends on the bullet, which is more important than rifle or caliber. **Pay the $1/bullet for quality projectiles.** It's the easiest way to increase your chance of success, and you owe it to the game.

Keeping the wind in your face, move stealthily from tree shadow to tree shadow, pausing for at least 30 seconds each time to survey your new vantage point. Bino frequently and you'll have a good chance to see them before they see you.

From 120yds away well concealed in the bush, the blesbok herd could not easily see me. I waited until a ewe was clear, and then carefully threaded a **.30-06 200gr Barnes TSX** to the lungs.

Lung shots are not instant killers, but deadly, and little meat is wasted. This **blesbok ewe** was hit solidly, running only 20yds. Use a heavy-for-caliber, well-constructed bullet to assure an exit wound which will increase blood loss/spoor.

The **Shepherd 8x42 binos** are superb, and everyone praised their clarity. (The best optics deal for $600, in my opinion.) Spend a *painful* amount of money on quality binos, which will make all the difference in spotting and judging game. I'd rather have $1000 binos and a $300 scope than the reverse.

A few excellent .30 bullets
(from left to right)

180gr Swift A-Frame
180gr Barnes TSX
180gr Swift Scirocco II
.30-06 Swift Scirocco II
200gr Swift A-Frame

Fired bullet is a Barnes TSX, with typical 99% weight retention. Swift A-Frame is similarly tough at 95-99%. **Both are my favorites for African plains game.**

While 180gr is OK, 200gr is *noticeably* more effective, especially on larger animals.

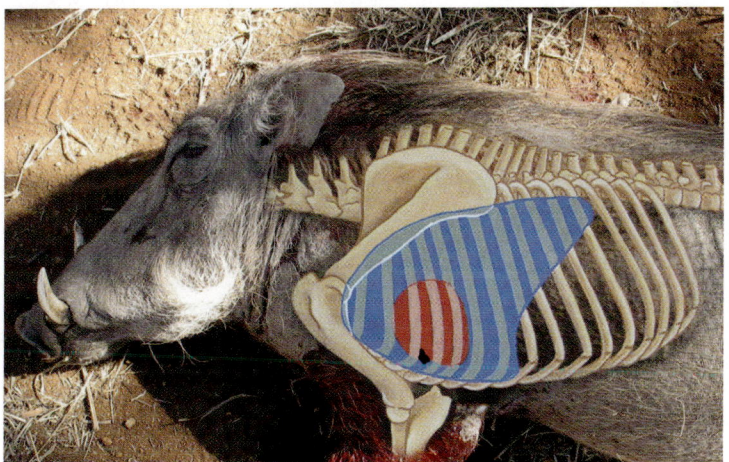

Study your own copy of Dr. Kevin Robertson's fantastic book ***The Perfect Shot*** for accurate game anatomy. This is a **warthog sow** which I shot for the camp. Sows have smaller tusks than boars, but not the second/lower pair of warts. Warthogs are *great* eating. They are often poached, because it's so easy to smoke them out of their burrows.

A **200gr Swift A-Frame .30-06** at 90yds got the lungs and heart, with a large exit wound. She dropped where she stood. 200gr is *the* bullet weight for .308/.30-06. Its .301SD really punches through, but is still plenty flat enough out to 300yds. I wouldn't .30 caliber hunt in Africa with anything lighter.

.308 • .30-06 • .300 H&H Mag • .300 Win Mag • .30-378 Weatherby
.30-06 is all you need (200gr/2600fps) or stalk 50yds closer with a 200gr .308. The H&H and Win mags are not wholly unreasonable, but show up in Africa with an absurd .30-378 Weatherby (220gr/3500fps!) and your PH will have an *immediate* lack of confidence in your caliber judgment and shooting ability.

My favorite plains game caliber family — the **.338**
.338 Federal • .338-06 • .338 Win Mag • .338 Rem Ultra Mag
The highly efficient **.338-06** (250gr/2500fps) is supremely versatile.

Waterbuck was not on my list (much less a cow), but this one had escaped the ranch and had to be put down. Never intending to hunt that **17" barrel .45-70** past 125yds, I overestimated drop at 200+yds and sent many shots too high. I finally ranged her properly and held lower for a one-hit kill. Target angle was very poor at 215°, but the **300gr Barnes TSX** went from paunch to neck (nearly exiting). Astonishing penetration at 225yds from mere 1800fps MV. (This was my only recovered bullet from 2007. Everything else exited.)

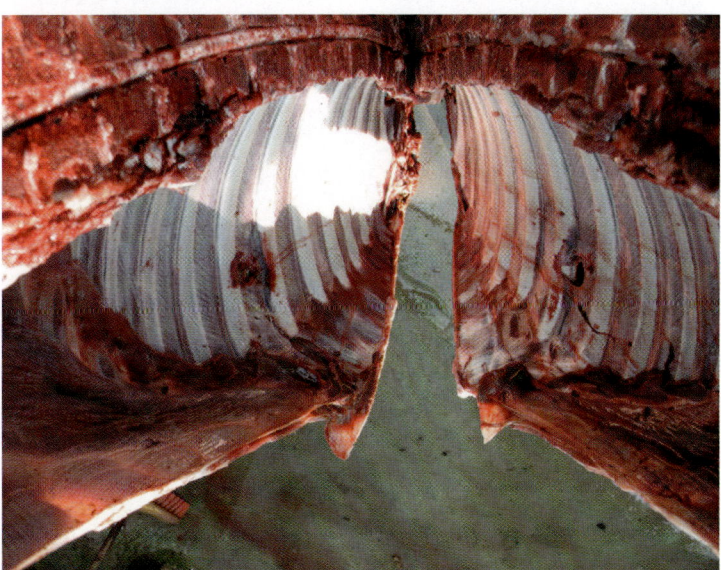

I prefer a **double lung through-and-through** for no wasted meat. A 125yd kudu cow I shot for the camp dinner table. I didn't find that **.45-70 Swift 350gr**, but never expected to. To me, a recovered bullet is evidence of sub-optimal performance. I want *exit* wounds. They make tracking much easier.

heavy-for-caliber bullets
200gr .30 • 250gr .338 • 300gr .375 • 400gr .416 • 500gr .458
(all Swift A-Frame except for Hornady .458)

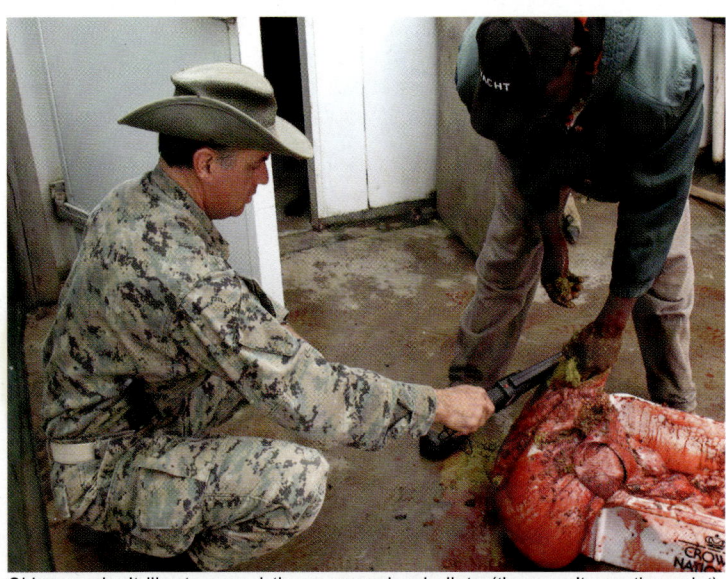

Skinners don't like to spend time recovering bullets (they can't see the point). A **hand-held metal detector** makes the chore easy, even in a kudu stomach. On the Internet for less than $100. (I left the **Pro-Scan II** with my PH as a gift.)

From behind the background rock pile I was glassing a waterbuck herd and my peripheral vision caught this **duiker ram**. It took me nearly a minute to *slooooowly* shift positions, and exchange binos for my Winchester Model 70.

.30-06 was overkill, but what isn't on a 20yd duiker? The **200gr TSX** sailed through without much meat damage. Tough/heavy bullets are best.

You never know what you'll encounter in the bush, or how! Hunting is a daily excitement, even without firing a shot.

My farthest shot over three safaris: about 400yds at a running baboon. I missed him by less than 3" according to my PH. I wouldn't have tried such a shot on game, but baboon are considered pests. Rifle is a **.308 Savage Scout with 3-12x Burris BallisticPlex handgun scope**—a very capable package with which I'd *lots* of bolt time using 15¢/rd surplus FMJ. (That bargain ammo is long gone thanks to hindered importation and the rapidly sinking dollar.)

TANZANIA SELOUS GAME RESERVE

Just after shooting my first African game animal, a face-on hartebeest in the Selous at 96yds. Having never tried them, I never got the hang of those **shooting sticks** back in 2005. Most PHs use them, so practice at home before Africa, and you'll shoot much better in the field.

Construct your own with three 6' bamboo poles, tied together with a vacuum cleaner belt (Eureka, size F&G).

Scope is **Burris 1¾-5x20mm**. A decent $225 DG optic (now made with 32mm objective).

The Lichtenstein variety of **hartebeest** is hunted only in Tanzania. A homely antelope, they are fleet of foot and good eating. It wasn't high on my list, but game was sparse in our concession and it was prudent not to pass him up on Day 4 out of seven. Rifle is **Winchester Model 70 Express in .416 Rem** with 400gr Hornadys (which expanded/shed weight too much for my taste).

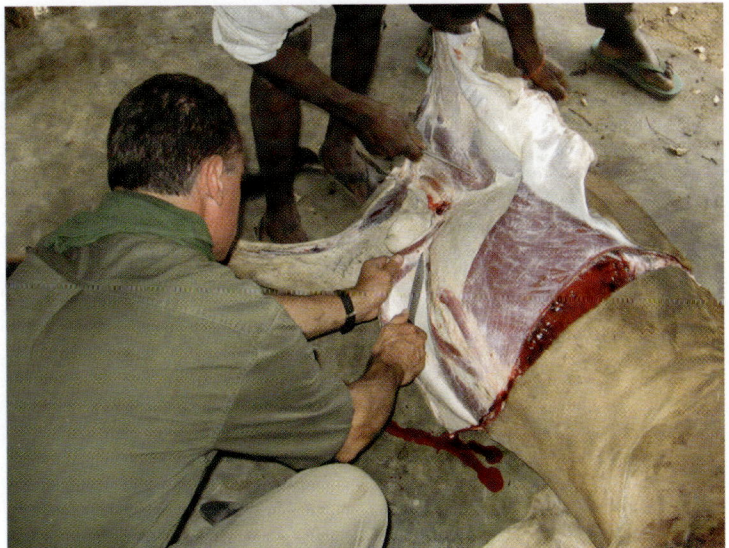

Since he was my first trophy, I decided to have him shoulder mounted (something not often done for hartebeest). Helping to skin your animals is a treat, and a vital part of the safari experience. The knife is an old favorite: my versatile **5½" Mad Dog Arizona Hunter** which I always take to Africa.

The Selous rains were late, so local watering holes (*korongas*) were unusually full. Game was harder to find because they didn't have to travel far for water.

Tasco 7x50s were a bit large, so the following years I carried smaller binos such as Fuji 8x24s, Zeiss 8x30s, and **Shepherd 8x42s** (my favorite).

A client's common view: the head tracker carries the shooting sticks as PH Craig Lang (holding an ashbag to test the wind) glasses a possible buffalo bull.

PH Craig Lang had put down a charging elephant at 5yds—*the day before* I and my hunting partner arrived for our 2x1 safari. Back home, "Jack" bizarrely claimed that *he* had shot the elephant because Lang "*panicked.*" Belatedly, I learned that my "friend" was a pathological liar, convicted serial thief, and combat vet fraud. (Moral: Smoke out the sociopaths beforehand.)

This aged **buffalo cow** had been mired in the mud for days. The Tanzanian game scout refused to put her down, leaving her for the inevitable hyaenas. African natives rarely share Western sentimentalities about wildlife suffering. The **Camelbak 100oz Mule** has been great gear for all three safaris.

This **young lioness** was gored by one of the two buffalo her pride had killed in what was a horrific fight (which also claimed a hyaena). She took three days to die, and it was forbidden for even the PH to intervene. I wanted to salvage her teeth, but could not have brought such back without a CITES permit.

Pony-sized, the Tanzanian subspecies of **Burchell's zebra** have no shadow stripes typical of the southern variety. A 400gr/.416 soft at 80yds/250° angle just behind the shoulder was quite effective. They are *very* tough animals, and .338-.458 is not too much gun.   (.308/.30-06 with 200gr is a fair minimum.)

.416 Rem Mag bullets:

400gr Barnes TSX
400gr Swift A-Frame
350gr Barnes TSX
350gr Swift A-Frame (loaded)

The 400gr TSX seats far too deeply for this case, and why use a 350gr TSX over the **400gr A-Frame**?

3.600"
O.A.L.

A typical East African safari tent. They are almost luxurious in comfort. Shower and flush toilet are behind bamboo screening. I wouldn't mind at all a 28-day hunt with my tent as home. The camps have 3 client tents, take 20 men two weeks to build, and are generally used for two seasons.

Comfortable quarters indeed, and I never slept better. Laundry was done daily, and pressed to perfection with a coal iron. A hardworking 4kW Honda generator powered lighting for the entire camp. Lights-out was at 11PM, not that I could usually stay awake reading until then.

Our barman Alberto could have worked in any quality hotel. Beer, wine, and liquor was included in the daily rate (though some clients do abuse it). Enjoying drinks by the fire after a long day is a memorable part of a safari.

Every charter plane is met by the local village children. They never grow tired of the activity and especially enjoy the propwash of takeoff.

A great assortment of jewelry on a Zanzibar beach table. Prices are very good, and beautiful necklaces were $5-10. Bring your lady back some unique gifts.

Tanzania is famous for intricately carved ebony art. This example is from one solid piece, selling for only $50. A very desirable curio, but heavy, so make sure it doesn't put your bag overweight.

Sadly, I didn't have the room for this one. All the more reason to return to East Africa!

Truly stunning artwork of a Masai clan, all carved from a 7' tall ebony trunk. Considering the incredible craftsmanship, asking price was a reasonable $7,300. (In Aspen it would fetch *15 times* that.) Freight cost would be high, as this carving weighed well over 1000lbs. (And how to *pack* the thing?)

It may still be at Mwenge carvers' market in Dar. If you buy it, let me know!

KRUGER NATIONAL PARK

Animals in the Kruger Park may be blasé, but they *do* bite. Stay in your car!

Lions often chase giraffe over Kruger tarmac roads, where they lose footing. Here were two lionesses, some cubs, and a well-maned lion all taking turns. This is the kind of scene that the Kruger Park is famous for. The KNP is worth spending several days in, but reserve your camp cabins early.

[Hyaenas] *come to collect scraps from meals tossed over the fence by some irresponsible* [Park] *visitors. These people do not realize that in the process . . .* [the hyaenas] *become extremely dangerous beggars.*

(Note: In other words, they turn into welfare liberals.)

Ultimately, these problem animals will have to be destroyed as they become a threat to human lives.

(We, however, encourage our own dangerous beggars!)

Locust wings. African nature is everywhere, if you have the eyes to see it.

Not a wide spread of horns, but his superb boss is practically a helmet. Seen just off the highway outside the Kruger Park.

These two old *dugga* boys had massive bosses like great domes of concrete. I'd encountered nothing like them in Tanzania two years before!

Even a monitor (sort of like our iguana) made an appearance in the Kruger. They can viciously whip their tails about, so beware.

You will daily see several species together, especially at the watering holes. (Baboon were also present here.) A drive-thru zoo!

It's probably better to visit the Kruger Park *before* your first hunt, to help train your game eye—however, you may be disappointed that your ranch animals are not so easily visible! They understand *"the advantage of not being seen."* (Monty Python reference unavoidable.)

Hippos in the Kruger just north of Oliphants camp. You don't want to get between them and their water as the morning sun begins to bake their hide!

Fairly typical scene in the Kruger, seen from a bridge nearby. 400yds off to the right was a lioness patiently eyeing a nervous herd of impala.

Since 2005 Tanzania, I've probably shot my one and last zebra. Now, I enjoy just watching them too much. This Kruger Park herd numbered about 60. Notice the typical shadow stripes of the southern Burchelli.

A waterbuck calf is about as cute as it gets. Notice the rump ring, which had to be the inspiration for cartoonist Gary Larson's "*Bummer of a birthmark!*" quip.

THE CRUELTY OF POACHING

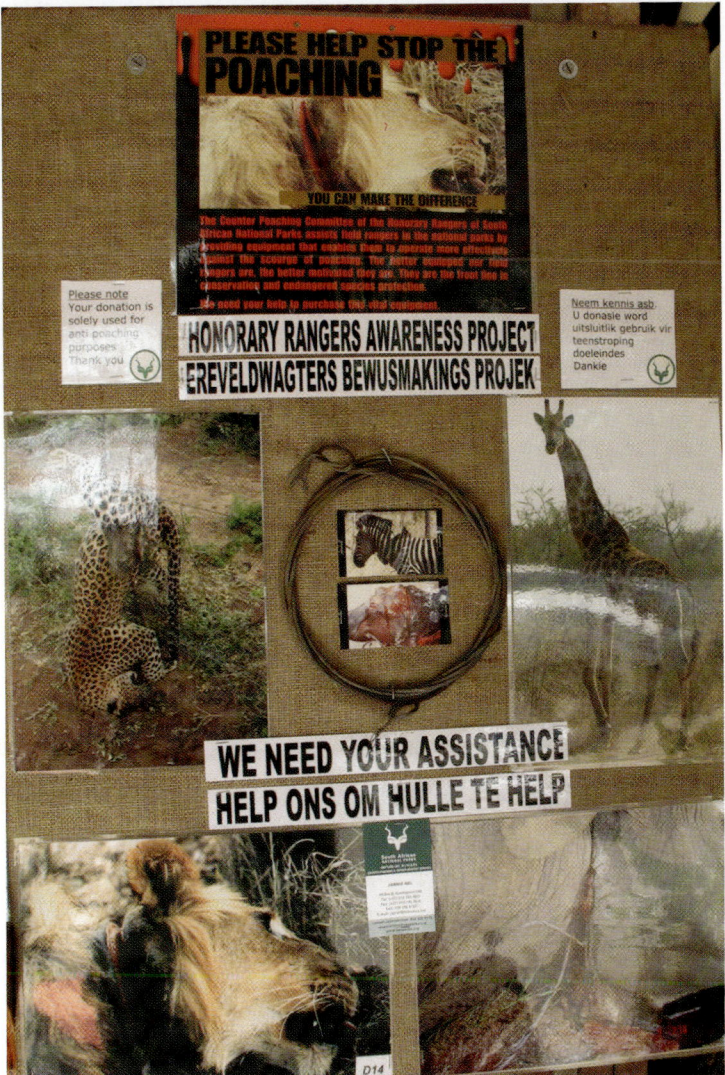

Poaching in South Africa (including in the Kruger Park) is sadly on the rise. Please drop some money in the donation bin to help fight this.

Poaching is a deeply *cultural* issue stemming from a misguided feeling of entitlement and a lack of property right history amongst the native blacks. They don't believe that anybody can *own* animals, even on a private ranch stocked by game auctions.

Poachers set this brushfire in typical retaliation for one of their mates getting caught the week before (to be fined only R500/$70). Nearly 10% of this 6000 acre ranch was burned. (Across the highway is a tribal trust land of a *million* acres, which the natives have totally denuded of all its game.)

While it used to be "*shoot, shovel, shut up*", poachers can no longer be dealt harshly with by ranchers in the new South Africa. (By contrast, they are shot on sight in Tanzania's Selous game preserve.)

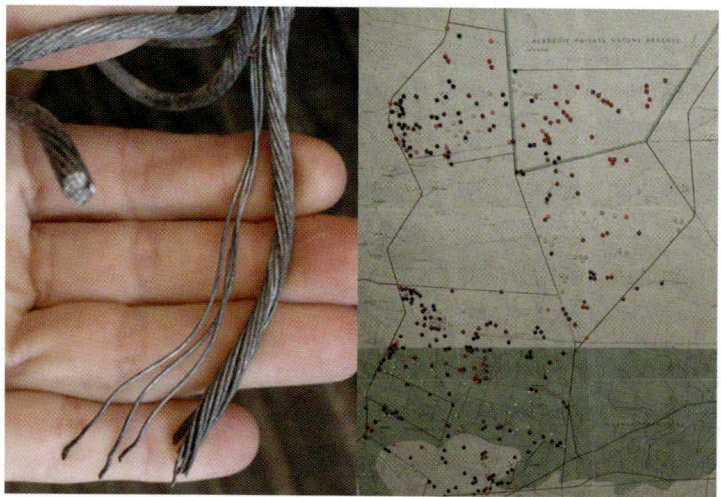

A poacher's snare of aircraft cable. These are indiscriminately cruel to all animals. What gets caught dies horribly, and most are never eaten by the poacher, anyway. It's all quite a senseless waste.

Maps from just one anti-poaching operation near the Kruger. Poaching is rarely stopped, but it can be made to move on elsewhere.

A RANCH *NOT* TO HUNT ON

Helping out on another property, I experienced a tragic example of a game ranch which did *not* provide "fair chase" conditions. 1000 acres was not large enough (note the overgrazing), and the animals had little prey refuge from the many tower blinds. As these continually terrified giraffe, eland, and wildebeest ran about the fenced perimeter in a panic, many were wounded—some of them by multiple shooters. Just heart-breaking. It was like WW2 Berlin zoo animals stampeding down the *Kurfürstendamm* during an Allied air raid.

This nice impala ram was probably wounded from a shooting tower, and never properly followed-up. You have a responsibility to hunt ethically, *always*. The right shot on the right animal *will* present itself, so be patient.

SWAZILAND AND KwaZULU NATAL

A beautiful river near the southern border of Swaziland. I found the country to be a real pleasure, and significantly different from surrounding South Africa. Racial tensions in Swaziland are not so pronounced as *apartheid* was not imposed there, and very few whites live in this autonomous kingdom.

Photo surreptitiously taken at a Swaziland border station. Why they used a Savage Scout .308 is a mystery, when an AK47 is much more fitting.

The folks at Savage Arms were quite flummoxed by this. (Notice the "left-hand" version.) I doubt that this rifle was actually confiscated; they likely used a random photo.

A typically nice toll highway in South Africa. Try to remember the motto of the well-dressed Socialist: *Keep left—look right!* It takes a few days to get the hang of it. (Have good maps, a pre-paid cell phone, and lots of local contacts if you plan to hire a car. Don't drive at night; things can get weird.) After a month in hunting camp, I spent two weeks and 2000 miles touring the country. Most folks were astonished to see an American driving about (since we normally just fly in to hunt, seeing nothing but airports and bushveld). South Africa is stunningly diverse, and well worth a lengthy exploration.

An impressive lodge hotel in Zululand overlooking the Valley of the Kings.

The remains of Ft. Victoria (called *Ft. Mthonjaneni* by the Zulu), built by Clarke's columns in August 1879 and garrisoned by three companies as 58th Regimental HQ. It was abandoned three weeks later after the war was lost.

A fine memorial to the Zulu kings. Their home sites and battlegrounds can be seen from this ridge. The Zulu are extremely proud of their warrior heritage, so be careful not to disrespect them. They gave the British their greatest military defeat between the American Revolution and the fall of Singapore. Although KwaZuluNatal (KZN) is a province, it is very independent-minded.

BACK ON THE SOUTH AFRICAN GAME RANCH

PH Mark Ivy is quite the professor on single malt Scotch, and took me on a world tour. A most memorable evening—for research, of course. Every game ranch will have a nicely stocked bar, packed with nostalgic relics. (Bring something special from America for their collection.)

"Mumps" (for his huge cheeks) and I became great friends. He was an absolute fiend for biltong, though.

There's nothing like a camp cat to round out your safari.

Ostrich eggs are the size of grapefruit, and equivalent to 20 chicken eggs. They are frequently stolen by poachers, who sell them. Each egg will fetch R50 ($7) apiece, equaling 10 hours of minimum wage. (No wonder some people steal rather than work.) If you buy a souvenir empty egg, do so only at a reputable shop, or in the Kruger Park.

Did you know that **German Shorthair Pointers** can hatch ostrich eggs? It does take longer, however.

Gemsbok for sale. Game auctions—frequently held for ranchers to replenish breeding stock—are a very interesting slice of South African culture if you can attend one.

This **fly larvae** was found in the nose of my wildebeest cow. Such nasal pests are a reason for the wildes' notorious snorting and snuffing.

Not classically dressed for **wingshooting**, but only results matter. My o/u 12ga is a fine Japanese copy of the excellent Winchester 101, which a friend pointed out to me at a gun show for only $350. This was the first time I'd hunted with it, and with pointer dogs. Great fun! If you haven't your own, shotguns are available to rent, and shells are reasonably priced. Birds are only $1-2 each.

If your camp offers wingshooting, don't pass it up. It's a great diversion from game hunting, and the camp will nicely prepare your francolin and guinea fowl. If limited by weight to only two long guns, forsake the second rifle for a 12ga, as you'll miss having it (I did in 2007; no loaner shotgun fit me well).

Have a tracker carry your rifle, since you'll likely encounter game.

"*Savage and stark*" (Capstick), **gemsbok** are notoriously fierce when wounded, so approach with great caution. Not indigenous to most game ranches, but they do well there. (Finishing shot photos from the 2006 video of my hunt.)

My 39" **gemsbok** was the largest bull ever taken on that ranch. He had eluded us for several mornings, keeping past 300yds or more. Though just 1" off Rowland Ward, the *experience* for me trumped the tape measure. Hunting should be an inner-directed joy untethered to the arbitrary record books.

The **blue wildebeest** is called "*the poor man's buffalo*" for its similar habits and fun to hunt. "*Queer, fiery, eccentric*" according to Theodore Roosevelt. They are very tough animals, and you must hit them well with ample caliber/bullet. Wounded, they can go for *miles*. Both of mine were one-shot kills with a .308.

Black wildebeest (white-tailed gnu) are 40% smaller, with very different horns. They were nearly extinct by 1948, but have made a comeback on private game ranches. Their name gnu comes from the Hottentot *ga-nu* for "snort."

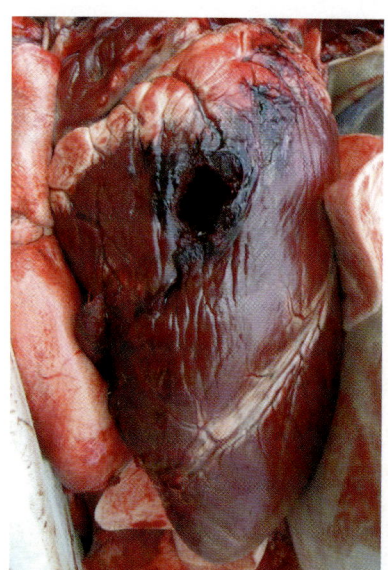

"*Aim so low that you begin to feel uncomfortable*," PH Mark Ivy advised, and I center-punched the wildebeest's heart at 100yd/0°. He still ran 50yds on residual hydraulic pressure.

This shot and its 100yd belly crawl to get into position rates as one of my most memorable hunts. It was textbook in every way, and balanced out some elsewhere mediocre shooting.

Few hunters make 100% perfect shots, so don't be too hard on yourself if you flub it. Keep a cheerful attitude and you'll soon bounce back.

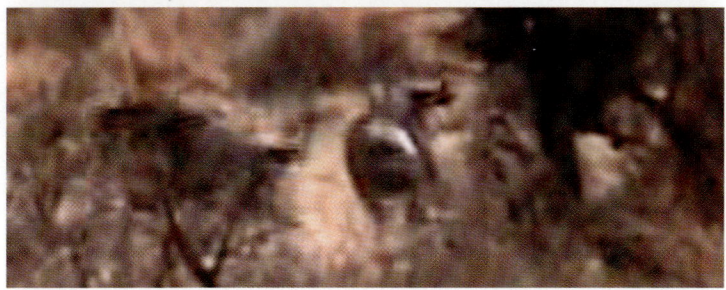

Herd animals clump together, making safe shots difficult (especially with reliably exiting bullets). I had to wait for the center **wildebeest cow** (top photo) to stand clear of others before I took her with my .308. The loud *Kugelschlag* and the wonky way she ran off confirmed a solid high-heart/lung hit. She made only 50yds before dropping. Wildebeest are great to practice on before your Cape buffalo, and nearly as much fun.

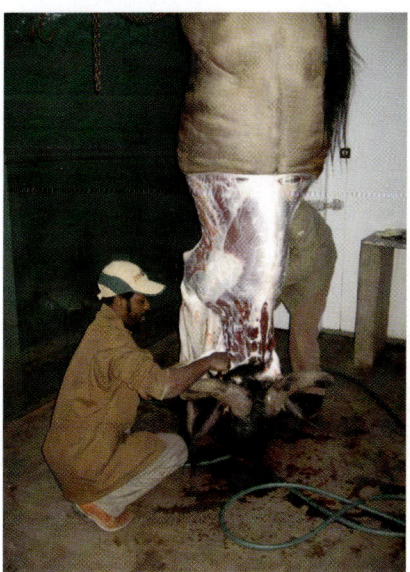

John is skinning my **wildebeest** for a shoulder mount. The skill of my camp staff is very high, and this bull was hanging in the cool room within an hour.

Shoulder mounts are much more expensive in taxidermy, shipment, and customs duties, so save such for very special trophies.

Wildebeest makes *such* a nice flatskin that a Euro mount is often preferable to shoulder.

Just after breakfast, tracker Herbert saw a **warthog** behind the lodge *kopje*. We clambered up, and I took the walking tusker from sitting/looped-up at 125yds, 90° angle, 20° declination. (Photo and inset are from the 25 frames/second digital video. Note steenbok ewe at upper right.)

As the shot broke while leading him, he paused, placing the bullet 3" too far forward in the shoulder. He still dropped in his tracks. The finishing spine shot after his death spasm was unnecessary, but I wanted to be sure. Two shots/two hits in 4 seconds, with **.308 Savage Scout** bolt rackings completed inside a second of each shot. (They called me "*Belt-fed*" after that. Over 1000rds of FMJ practice made my bolt manipulation utterly reflexive.)

My first bushbuck, a nice 14" ram. Very fierce when wounded—shoot carefully! My modern "pre-64" **Win M70 .30-06** has a very durable CeraKote finish. With **200gr Barnes TSX or Swift A-Frame**, it is ideal at sportsmanlike ranges: 100yd eland, 200yd zebra/wildebeest/gemsbok, and 300yd kudu/waterbuck.

I prefer **USMC digital camo** (green or desert, depending on dryness of foliage) over civilian hunting clothes. More rugged and better concealing.

By contrast, the **US Army's ACU** is effective only in certain urban terrain. An ideal clothing choice when hunting kudu from Granny's sofa.

A very old 52½" **kudu**, which PH Mark Ivy said wouldn't have lived through the next hunting season. Very wide spread, and lots of ivory on the tips. If we all look very happy and relieved, it's because we *were*. After I winged him the previous afternoon, it took us from 7AM to 2PM the next day to finally get him. The final 500yds he led half the team on their hands and knees through brambles a rabbit would shy from. A very sly old fellow, and amazingly tough.

As if kudu horns grow around a mandrel! The purpose is martial: he can see *through* the holes when he lowers his rack during a fight.

In gratitude for following-up on my kudu, I took the camp out to a restaurant dinner and drinks. A rare treat for the native staff, and they dressed in their best threads. (One nearby table did not appreciate our mixed racial company, so I glowered at them until they left.)

Bushpig are great fun to hunt, and superb eating (especially their ribs). Very aggressive when cornered, so shoot them well! Nigel Ivy (likely a future PH) got this one with his uncle's .308 Mauser and **180gr Barnes TSX**.

There's nothing like a kudu **filet cooked in the bush**! Insist on lunches like this.

Also, having *one* cold beer at midday is generally OK with PHs, as meatime beer is considered a "*tipple*" in Africa.

Ask your PH first, however, as some prefer their clients not to have *any* alcohol at all during hunting hours. This is a sensible rule, so don't take it personally.

A decent **steenbok ram**, certainly "*representative of the species.*" These small solitary antelope are quite challenging to hunt, and most delicious.

The excellent **3-10x40mm Shepherd 310-P2 scope** in Leupold Quick Release rings was perfect for Africa. The inset photo is a facsimile of the 18" circles ranging reticle subtending at 300, 400, 500, and 600yds—not that an ethical hunter should attempt first shots past 300yds. Windage/elevation tick marks are in useful minute-of-angle increments (1MOA @100yds = 1.047"). The Shepherd also features one-shot zeroing, still unique in the industry.

South Africans call their BBQs a *braai*, which is held in a round firepit *lapa*. Great food and conversation abound there. These were amongst my favorite times in Africa. The *braai* is a South African tradition, and it's difficult to eat any better elsewhere! Ask your outfitter to host one for you.

Zebra "sushi" sliced transparently thin. A lodge favorite, devoured instantly.

Retailing for about $7/lb, **biltong** is a continent-wide currency, tradeable to anyone. Shopping malls have "Biltong Huts." Your PH will include some biltong in your daily rate, but gluttons like me must purchase extra rations. I bought 13lbs of it for my two-week roadtrip. Due to USDA restrictions you cannot bring *any* of it back, but rest assured that I was still chewing on my last bite when going through US Customs.

"*You are not shooting to kill. You are shooting to make immortal the thing you shoot. To kill just anything is a sin. To kill something that will be dead soon, but is so fine as to give you pleasure for years, is wonderful.*"
— PH Harry Selby

❖ 9

BUFFALO BULLETS, CALIBERS, & RIFLES

> *No one but he who has partaken thereof can understand the keen delight of hunting in lonely lands. For him it is the joy of the horse well-ridden and the rifle well-held; for him the long days of toil and hardship, resolutely endured, and crowned at the end with triumph.*
> — Theodore Roosevelt

Since I was going after buffalo, I needed to find myself at least a .375 H&H Magnum, which is the minimum legal caliber across Africa. At a small gun show I spied a man carrying a CZ Brno ZKK 602 bolt action in .375. With McMillan stock, rings, dies, and some ammo he wanted just $700. I couldn't extract my wallet fast enough. My first African rifle! Controlled feed, Mauser-type extractor, fixed ejector, and double square bridge forged steel receiver with integral scope bases.

While very pleased with my Brno, after research I began to sour on the .375 for buffalo.

CALIBER vs. CALIBER
some thought on the .375 H&H?

A 300gr .375 bullet at 2550fps *is* a DG caliber, but with little excess power margin:

> What are a .375's normal chores? Just about anything, at any time. The .375 will not reach out over the short-grass plains like a smaller-caliber, higher-velocity cartridge will — but it will do the job in a pinch, albeit with a good deal more punch than is needed on the

smaller African antelopes. It will also drop buffalo and even elephant with deadly efficiency, given reasonable shot placement. It will not do this as effectively as something over .40 caliber, but it will do it....

The beauty about the .375 is that you never know exactly what you might run into next in Africa. With a .375, you are ready for anything, if not exactly perfectly armed for anything.

The lower .40s offer a significant edge over the .375 on dangerous game. They won't make up for sloppy bullet placement any more than anything else, but they will stop a charge much more reliably.

There is a big difference between hitting a buffalo with a .375 and hitting one with the .416. And there's an equally big difference between a .416 and a .470, .500, 458 Lott or .460 Weatherby — provided the shot placement is equally good.

— Craig Boddington, *Safari Rifles* (1990), p. 59, 70, 291

I recommend nothing lighter for buffalo than a .375 H&H Magnum with a good, tough 300-grain controlled-expansion bullet like a Partition, Swift A-Frame, Barnes X or Winchester Fail Safe. Provided the bullet is placed nice and low in the shoulder for the heart and perhaps the adjoining lung area, buffalo can be killed relatively easily, shot for shot, with a .375 without a problem.

Still, I would prefer to use a considerably heavier rifle on buffalo, as they can be extremely dangerous once they are wounded. I therefore consider a .375 magnum to be the minimal practical caliber, and am far happier with something heavier. I'm delighted with . . . the .416s and I have found all of them — Remington, Rigby, Dakota, Weatherby, etc. — wonderful for buffalo.

— Geoff Broom, *A Life On Safari* (2004), p. 232

Hair raising escapades with charging buffalo and rampaging elephants seem to go hand in hand with the .375. The only conclusion I can draw from this is that **it doesn't get the job done**.

— Jim Carmichael

When circumstances are perfect, [the .375 H&H] is just fine [for Cape buffalo]. But sometimes circumstances are not perfect.

— Jeff Cooper, *C Stories* (2004), p. 241

Cooper's further thoughts about the .375 also stuck with me:

1) For Africa it's too much on 90% of game, and not quite enough on the remaining 10%.

2) A .375 on Cape buffalo is like using a 9mm on people. Most of the time it will be satisfactory . . . most of the time.

Hmmmm. Well, I don't carry a 9mm for self-defense, so that got me thinking. If I weren't planning on buff, then for a one-gun African hunt the .375 is superb (and it's the minimum caliber allowed on lions and buffalo, should you need to shoot one). And if I could guarantee a superb first shot placement on an undisturbed buff, then the .375 would do just fine. But, dangerous game *is* dangerous game, and I read of just too many buffalo wounded with a .375. If your first shot doesn't put him down, then you must track what has become quite literally a second type of animal — *i.e.*, a very cheesed-off and adrenalized beast full of rage and murder. Trouble is . . . you're still using the same cartridge for your follow-up shots as you did for your *first* shot. The buffalo has become more formidable, but your ammo hasn't changed to keep up.

So, even though the .375 H&H is a wonderfully versatile cartridge for Africa and North America (*i.e.*, moose, big bears), I wanted more confidence in my buffalo rifle. Such a gun must be capable of delivering, if necessary, a charge-stopping blow to halt that "second" animal in his tracks. Hence, a 400gr at 2400fps (*i.e.*, .416 Rigby ballistics) was the minimum for *me*, with a 500gr at 2300fps (*i.e.*, .458 Lott ballistics) being the practical maximum (for one who will not hunt elephant, and thus doesn't need a .500 or 6000+fpe).

If a .375 is about max for you, then practice until you shoot it *perfectly* and it will likely be fine on buff.

> *You're not a professional and won't need the same things out of a rifle as he will. Sure, there's an edge to the bigger calibers in the types of eyeball-to-eyeball things he'll get into but if his client were using a [.375] rifle he could shoot well and delivered his shot properly, there wouldn't be a hairy confrontation in the first place.*
> —Peter Capstick, *Safari: The Last Adventure* (1984), p. 97

Use a *very* high quality 300gr soft, such as a A-Square Dead Tough or Swift A-Frame. Such bullets, well placed, will make the .375 do its job. (North Fork and Barnes TSX are also great bullets, but may require compressed loads in the H&H case.)

However, if the .375 is *still* too much gun for reliable shot placement, then you've no option but the 9.3x62mm in Zim. If *that* still too stout, then Cape buffalo is out of your league as there is nothing less you can legally use in Africa (nor would any sane hunter *want* to).

.375 H&H versus .416 (Rigby and Remington)

Though I've read of too many .375 problems on buffalo, such do *not* seem to occur with a .416. The historic body of anecdotal experience points to the .416/400gr/2400fps as the *reliable* minimum on DG (especially for charge stopping).

"*But the .416 Rem needs compressed loads for 400gr!*" some would retort. With an all copper Barnes TSX, yes, but not with Swift A-Frames. You can stay under 97% load densities and still get 400gr/2400fps (or 350gr/2600fps).

"*But the .416 Rem has insufficient case taper and sticks!*" Well, its .025" taper is much less than the .375's whopping .065", but .025" has been shown sufficient taper for reliable feeding and extraction. In fact, .022" seems the practical minimum. (Weatherby's .020" is not enough, and those cases do stick.)

The .375 has been hailed for decades as the best "one gun" for Africa (though not a brilliant choice for DG). But that was *then*. Today, we have superb 350/400gr bullets for the .416s, and there remains no compelling reason (other than less recoil) to stick with a .375. The below table shows 200yd zero data from Swift A-Frames:

	SD	BC	100yd	200yd	300yd	100yd PI	SPI	Royce KoV
.375 270gr	.274	.325	+2.1"	2749fpe	- 8.9"	91	72	82
.375 300gr	.305	.349	+2.6"	2777fpe	-11.0"	97	69	83
.416 350gr	.289	.321	+2.5"	3362fpe	-10.5"	90	103	97
.416 400gr	.330	.367	+2.9"	3420fpe	-12.0"	100	100	100

Compared to the 300gr/.375/2550fps, the 350gr/.416/2600fps shoots flatter, has 17% higher RoyceKoV at 100yds (*i.e.*, 97 vs. a mere 83), and 21% more energy at 200yds. From the *same* parent case, in the *same* action. (It gives up only 7PI.)

The **350gr/.416 TSX** seats shorter than 300gr/.375 TSX, but with nearly identical BCs (.345 versus .357). Even only on plains game, the 350gr/.416 tops the 300gr/.375.

Since the **400gr/.416/2400fps** will still shoot 2" as flat as a 300gr/.375/2550fps out to 300yds (the farthest you'll shoot, anyway), the only advantage of the .375 is *slightly* less recoil, and better ammo availability. *If* you can comfortably shoot a .375, then a 350gr/.416 might not be too much, so give it a try.

Use 400gr A-Frame for DG, and 350gr TSX for plains game. The .416 is a much better "one gun" than the .375.

.416 versus .458

Some (such as Jeff Cooper) *pooh-pooh* anything less than a .458/500gr at 2400fps on buffalo. While I agree with Cooper's take on the .375 being occasionally marginal on buff, I think the .416 is as reliable on buff as the .40S&W is on people.

Praised by such notables as Harry Selby (who carried one for 50 years as a PH), Jack O'Connor, Geoff Broom, and many others, the .416/400gr at 2400fps is well-proven on *all* dangerous game. Even John "Pondoro" Taylor (whose .458/500gr at 2400fps for *elephant* Cooper latched onto as a *buffalo* minimum) candidly admitted that:

> For all-round work amongst dangerous game, both thick-skinned and thin-skinned, there is no better magazine rifle than Rigby's .416.
>
> — John Taylor, *Big Game and Big Game Rifles*

Most PHs and experienced DG hunters like the .416/400gr, but Terry Wieland greatly prefers the .458 Lott, even in 400gr:

> The [.458] Lott with a 400-grain bullet will do anything the [.416] Remington will do out to any range at which you might want to shoot such a bullet,...
>
> — Terry Wieland, *Dangerous Game Rifles* (2006), pp. 150-151

While he asserts that test-box penetration differences are "*minimal*" (his bullet types and data are not referenced), it seems incredible that a 74 vs. 100 PI would not evidence itself:

	SD	ME	PI	SPI	RoyceKoV
.416 400gr	.330	5117	100	100	100
.458 400gr	.272	5578	74	132	103

> ...and [the .458 Lott] will do so...with no case-sticking problems at all (allegedly inherent in the .416 Rem).

What .416 Rem case-sticking problems? Wieland admits:

> . . . I have never heard of a .416 Remington bolt jamming from high pressures. (p. 182)

Regarding taper, the .458 Lott has .032" — a good number but only .007" more than a .416 Rem (which also has the unmentioned feeding advantage of a smaller diameter bullet.).

Between the .416/400gr and the .458/500gr for DG:

> Is it a life-threatening difference? **Probably not.** (p. 184)

So, to recap Wieland, the .416 Rem is *not* known for case sticking and its 400gr bullet *is* the practical DG equal to the .458/500gr. The .416 Rem took the best punch its greatest detractor could throw, and remained firmly standing. (His subchapter heading "*The .416s and Their Ilk*" points to a personal bias despite his own begrudging admission within.)

While a .458/500gr at 2400fps does give an extra 1000fpe and greater cross sectional area which is comforting for that rare charging buff, most PHs are quite comfortable with a .416 and today's excellent bullets. So was I. **A .458 is nice but I don't believe it *vital* for buff.** I'd have bought any available .458 Lott, but I was by no means undergunned with a .416 Rem.

While a .458 Lott 450/500gr flies like a .416 350/400gr, those heavier bullets cross the recoil threshold for most hunters, and generally without proportional increase in effect. **Bigger is better only if you can shoot it well.** (Even Wieland loads down to 2250fps.) Since shot placement is the most important factor (followed by bullet design, and thus penetration) the important fact is that many hunters will more easily shoot a .416. **In my opinion, a .416 offers the best balance between power and controlability.** You just don't read of anecdotal inadequacies from well handled .416s.

The .375 is a bit light on buffalo, and the .458 is a bit heavy in recoil for most hunters. **The .416 is "just right."** Its 400gr/2400fps is proven DG medicine, and its 350gr/2600fps shoots about as flat as a .308 200gr/2500fps (*i.e.* usable out to 350yds with 19.5" drop). Unless you've tested a .458 Lott and are comfortable with the recoil, the .416 is all the gun you need for buffalo, and it will give you more confidence than any .375.

For a 7- or 10-day buffalo/misc. hunt, a .416 will serve nicely as your one rifle for all game.

what's the deal with belted cases?

First, you must understand the internal dimension of headspace. It is the distance between the bolt face and some case body reference ("datum point") that abuts the chamber. The cartridge must be of sufficiently tight fit within the chamber so not to come apart (or even stretch unduly), yet not too tight that a fired case will not extract easily. Headspace is a highly critical dimension which cannot vary more than about .008" (*i.e.*, just two sheets of paper).

Before belted cases, headspace was either from the rim or the shoulder. Since rimmed cases do not feed flawlessly from repeaters, those rifles require shouldered cases. This is fine if there is enough case body diameter to provide an ample shoulder, but what if the bullet is nearly as wide as the case?

An answer was to add a belt for headspace control. The .375 H&H Magnum (of 1912) was the first. Some magnum cases have sufficient shoulder for headspacing, but the belted case quickly became visually synonymous with "magnum," so the belt stayed. What many riflemen (including myself) don't like about belted cases is that feeding can be fussy (not what you want in a DG rifle), and handloading them is more tedious.

Nonbelted advantages are: better bore alignment, increased powder capacity, more consistent and uniform burn rate, and improved functioning and headspacing capabilities.

To avoid having to settle for a belted case, one must search for a case of slightly larger diameter — i.e., enough body to provide a usable shoulder. (Dakota recognizes this by using the .416 Rigby case for their .450 Dakota. Nothing else, not even the .404 Jeffery, has ample case diameter for .458 bullets.)

.375 calibers

There are several: .376 Steyr, .375 H&H, .375 Weatherby, .375 Dakota, .375 Ruger, .375 Rem Ultra Mag, and .378 Weatherby. The first five are 70-96 RoyceKoV. Only the .378 Weatherby exceeds a 100 RoyceKoV, at 103. As you can see, piling on velocity to 300gr .375s is not the answer, especially when bullets will shatter at DG ranges <100yds. This bullet hasn't the mass or frontal area of .416/400gr or .458/500gr.

.375 bullets

300gr is the best *common* choice. (270gr SD is only .274.) If I had no choice but a .375, I'd use only an A-Frame or TSX. (The very heavy 350gr/380gr bullets show much promise.)

(.1359" cross sectional area)	.305	.356	.386 sec. density
Swift A-Frame	300gr		
Barnes TSX	300gr		
A-Square Triad	300gr		
North Fork	300gr		
Norma		350gr	
Rhino (www.rhinobullets.co.za/tests.htm)			380gr

.376 Steyr (270gr/2500fps = 3900fpe)

For DG caliber legal minimums, the shortened 9.3x64 was necked up to .375. As the .375 H&H is only *just* DG adequate, this round should have always been a .358 (as in my idea for the ".360 Cooper"). OK for cats, but not for buff with a mere 78 PI, 62 SPI, and 70 RoyceKoV. This is no better than the old 9.3x62.

Its only rifle is the .376 Steyr Scout and that action was designed for only 2700fpe — *not 3900fpe*. I've seen one whose barrel sleeve separated ¼", creating an unfixable problem. The rifle and round just aren't up to the job, sorry.

.375 H&H (270gr/2750fps = 4535fpe, 300/2550 = 4331fpe)

The Grand Old Man of .375s, dating back to 1912. It's the .30-06 of medium cartridges, and available about anywhere.

.375 Weatherby
.375 Dakota/Ruger (300/2650 = 4471fpe)

Weatherby: The earliest .375 competitor to the H&H, adding 100fps. Discontinued for its megabrother, the .378.

Dakota/Ruger: The only beltless standard-action length .375s (which helps to avoid short cycling the bolt), these were done right. They may eventually eclipse the .375 H&H, primarily because rifle manufacturers don't have to come out with a magnum action. (Savage, Remington, Kimber, etc. will probably offer rifles in .375 Ruger.)

The .375 Ruger holds 6gr more water than the .375 H&H, but I don't care for its extremely minimal .017" taper and high pressures (the recipe for extraction problems).

.375 RUM (270gr/2900fps = 5043fpe, 300/2750 = 5039fpe)

A beltless magnum-length, with gratuitous velocity.

.378 Weatherby
9.53 Lazerroni (300gr/2850 = 5412fpe)

Recoil is just *vicious*. Unsuitable for <200yd hunting as the bullet is still 2500+fps and will likely break up or deform. A 500yd elk rifle for people who cannot stalk within 300yds.

If a .305SD 300gr soft at 2500fps is not sufficient, then piling on 100-400fps more velocity (which will break up) is not the solution. What DG needs is *not* a faster 300gr .375, but a larger caliber with more mass. Go .416, even it's only a 350gr.

.416 calibers

The .416 caliber is a *great* compromise between knockdown power, flat trajectory, and manageable recoil. A .375 is a bit light for some buffalo, and a .458 a bit much for some shooters. Thus, the .416 "medium heavy" is a fine choice for many hunters. When backed up by your PH (and even a buddy), I'd not feel at disadvantage with one during a charge.

Don't bother with the uncommon .400 Pondoro/ASDPM (a .409), the .404 Jeffery (a .423), or the belted .400 H&H.

.416 bullets

The 400gr A-Frame (with excellent .330SD) is the DG choice, if your case capacity can throw it 2400fps without pressure issues. If not, then try the superb 370gr North Fork or 350gr A-Frame. (While the 350gr TSX at 2525fps is a decent choice, it's a 101% load and I prefer a higher SD than .289.) Nosler Partition is OK, but the below are better bullets.

(.1359" cross sectional area)	.289	.305	.330 sectional density
Swift A-Frame	350gr		400gr
Barnes TSX	350gr		400gr
A-Square Triad			400gr
North Fork		370gr	

.404 Dakota   (400gr/2400fps = 5117fpe)

A necked up, shortened .404 Jeffery case which gives proper .416 Rigby ballistics, yet from a standard-length case.

If you've a strong Mauser 98 action in standard length and wish to build up a buffalo rifle, the .404 Dakota is a valid choice. Beltless, yet with ample shoulder for good headspace control. The rim diameter of .544" isn't too large for boltface and feed rail gunsmithing. Its only real disadvantage is compressed powder loading, which can lead to overpressure in hot climates.

.416 Rigby   (400gr/2400fps = 5117fpe)

A superb non-belted case from 1912 with well-proven African ballistics. (For example, my Selous PH had to drop a charging cow elephant at 5yds the morning before my arrival, and a 400gr Hornady solid did just that. If he wasn't sold on the .416 Rigby before, he certainly is *now*.)

Immortalized in Robert Ruark's *Horn of the Hunter*, the renowned PH Harry Selby's .416 Rigby became Africa's most famous rifle (and caliber). Harry carried his Mauser 98 for nearly fifty years (his double rifle was run over by a lorry back in 1949, so he bought the only big-bore then available in Nairobi). It killed everything: elephant, rhino, buffalo, lion, and leopard. Harry liked it so much, he never went back to doubles. (It was recently sold to a private buyer.)

Taylor highly praised the .416 Rigby:

> You certainly could not get a better or more reliable magazine rifle for general work against dangerous animals. It's a great killer. . . . There's a certainly about it that gives one great confidence.
> **I cannot speak too highly of the .416.**
> — John Taylor, *African Rifles and Cartridges* (1948), p. 103

For a while, the .416 Rigby nearly died out. Kynoch made the last batch of brass back in 1968, and none else was available until B.E.L.L. began making cases in the mid-1980s. Federal now makes ammo, and Norma, RWS, and Lapua sell cases.

pros:
Superb ballistics from a low-pressure round (44,000psi) not given to sticky extraction. Excellent shoulder headspacing without a belted case. Widely used/available in Africa (though at $17 per *round* at Dar's only gun store). Nostalgic. It shoots as flat as a .375 out to 300. Factory rifles from Ruger and CZ.

cons:
Huge case head diameter (.590") will sacrifice 1rd mag capacity. Designed for Cordite, the large shell is inefficient for 400gr bullets. Its sharp 45° shoulder wears out more quickly.

final comments:
Had my 602 Brno been in .416 Rigby, I'd have happily left it alone. If you buy a new CZ 550 Magnum, consider this caliber. Rebarreling my .375 H&H, however, would have also required gunsmithing of the bolt face and feed rails.

.416 Rem Magnum (400gr/2400fps = 5117fpe)
Remington's 8mm Mag (derived from .375 H&H) blown out to .416, nearly identical to its .416 Hoffman wildcat father.

pros:
.416 Rigby ballistics (400gr at 2400fps) in an efficient case. Well proven and liked by PHs. Factory chambered rifles (Blaser, Remington, Ruger, Winchester, CZ, Ed Brown). Widely available ammo.

cons:
Belted case. 10,000 more psi than the .416 Rigby, and thus more subject (though I wouldn't say "prone") to sticky extraction (not even its antagonist Wieland has heard of such). Older ammo can decompress in storage by pushing out its bullets, so do inspect all rounds before taking to the field.

final comments:
I very nearly chose this cartridge for my Brno rebarreling as no further gunsmithing was required, and it is popular/available in Africa. A friend used a 21" Blaser in .416 Rem as his one gun in Tanzania, and killed everything quite well with it over his 21 days.

To avoid powder compression go with the **400gr A-Frame** and 77.5gr of IMR4895 (95% case density), or 79.0gr of RL-15 (97% case density). Varget is also a good choice.

The 350gr Barnes TSX takes up as much case as the 400gr A-Frame, but what's the point since the heavier bullet has a higher SD, and will likely retain at least 87.5% of its weight? The 400gr TSX's length requires a compressed load to approach 2400fps, so this is *not* the bullet for .416 Rem. (see photo)

.416 Dakota (400gr/2550fps = 5777fpe)

Derived from the .404 Jeffery case. (Imagine a necked-up .375 RUM.) Requires a 3.65" magnum action. Has 15% more capacity than .416 Rem in a non-belted case. A very nice round, but Dakota discontinued it (usurped by their shorter .404 Dakota which fits in .30-06 actions). www.superiorammo stills loads for it. The new .400 H&H is a similar beltless round.

.416 Weatherby (400gr/2700fps = 6477fpe)
.416 (10.57) Lazzeroni Meteor (400gr/2730fps = 6621fpe)

If you think you need 6500fpe, then get a .458. Boosting a 400gr .416 bullet to 2700fps is the wrong way to go. Softpoints will more tend to break up, and solids will simply zip right through. For more energy, increase the bullet's *mass* (and frontal area, too), *not* its velocity. Yes, they shoot flatter than a .338 Win, but you stalk within 75yds of buff, not pop them from 250. Finally, the 26" barrel and horrific blast from the muzzle brake combine to create an all-around excessive package.

.458 calibers

Certainly, against any dangerous game more energy is better . . . but where does one *stop*? If a 6000fpe .458 Lott is better than a 5100fpe .416 Rigby, then isn't a 8300fpe .500 A-Square preferable still? Or a 10,000fpe .577 Tyrannosaur?

Where does one *stop*? I'll *tell* you where. It stops just where defensive handgun calibers stop: **When you can no longer shoot it *well*.** If you can shoot a .40S&W as well as a 9mm, then pack a .40. If you can shoot a .416 as well as a .375, then carry a .416. But if a .458 gives rise to flinching, then it's too much gun for you. This is why most PHs recommend their clients bring a scoped .375: not for the ballistics, but because it's the *most* rifle that *most* clients can shoot *well*. (And don't forget that the PH is backing up the .375, usually with at least a .416.)

> Every rifle and cartridge combination has its own threshold that can be identified only by shooting it, but it is worthwhile to . . . keep your standard load just below it. It is much easier on the rifle, it reduces the chance of a malfunction such as a stuck bolt, and it allows for more precise shooting.
> — Terry Wieland, *Dangerous Game Rifles* (2006), p. 308

I've fired the .375 H&H, .416 Rigby, .416 Rem Mag, .450 Nitro Express #2, .460 G&A, .500 Jeffery, and others. Recoil (being 80% mental) doesn't much bother me. So if I can just as easily shoot a .458 in Africa as a .416, why not take a .458? With good bullets placed well, I doubt that buffalo would know the difference between a .416 or a .458 Lott. (I read of one buff requiring *ten* good hits from a *.460 Weatherby* to finally go down, and another needing *fifteen* from a *.470 Nitro*, so sometimes it just ain't the cartridge!) Nonetheless, I seriously considered a .458 of some type for my Brno.

.458 bullets

The ideal is the 500gr with its outstanding .341SD. (There is even a 600gr/.409SD for elephant.) Be sure your case can send 500gr at least 2250fps without compressed loads.

(.1647" cross sectional area)	.272	.307	.317	.341 sectional density
Swift A-Frame	400gr	450gr		500gr
Barnes TSX		450gr		500gr
A-Square Triad			465gr	500gr
North Fork	400gr	450gr		

choosing amongst the .458s
These are the ideal parameters, but you can't have all five:

	nonbelted	noncompressed	500gr/2300	3.60" max OAL	4rd
.458 Win				✔	✔
.460 G&A	✔		✔	✔	✔
.458 Lott			✔	✔	✔
.450 Dakota	✔	✔	✔		
.460 Wea		✔	✔		

.45-70 (and .450 Marlin)   (350gr/1900fps = 2806fpe)
This is *not* a viable DG cartridge, even with an A-Frame. If the .458 Win is marginal, then guess what 600fps *less* will do. Even the blazing hot commercial load of 460gr/1800fps for 3310fpe is just not buffalo energy. Besides, an easily short-stroked lever-action is no DG rifle. Avoid, avoid, *avoid!*

.458 Win Mag   (500gr/2040fps = 4621fpe)
The design parameter was to equal .450 Nitro Express ballistics of 500gr/2150fps. The 500gr (with highly compressed loading of 101-110%) is at *best* a 4900fpe cartridge (and usually only 4600fpe), which is bettered by the .416/400gr at 2400fps (offering deeper penetration and much flatter trajectory). *Not* a great choice for dangerous game. (The late Finn Aagaard liked it, but the excellence of the man made up for the caliber.)

2400fps is the "magic" MV for good PI, and the .458 Win/500gr gives 2100 tops. Hitting at 2600fps (as with a .460 Weatherby) is not critical, but hitting at 2300fps vs. 1900fps *is*. **That 400fps is the difference between .30-06 and .30-30.** I deem the .458 Win "the .30-30 of the .458s."

A-Square's 465gr (.317SD) at 2250fps is the best compromise in weight vs. velocity for this round. Also, good is the 450gr A-Frame. If handloading, *avoid all ball powders* (which tend to cake up in hot weather, risking squib loads). Compressed loads can decompress over time, so check often!

Ammo is widely available in Africa (most PHs will have a spare box), and it can be used in a .458 Lott (which is what you should prefer anyway). If you have no logistical choice, then handload 450gr A-Frames (2260fps with 71.5gr of H-322 @ 98%) or 465gr A-Squares. Avoid compression, and thus the long Barnes TSX. Use a 24" barrel to squinch all possible velocity. Stalk *very* close with this round, as its MV is less than the 100yd impact velocity of a .458 Lott. Gee.

.460 G&A (500gr/2300fps = 5875fpe, from 22"bbl)
This is the .404 Jeffery case necked up to .458 by Tom Siatos, and popularized by Jeff Cooper's Brno ZKK 602 "Baby" (which I had the honor to fire in October 2006 at the TR Reunion just after his death).

pros:
Excellent, proven terminal ballistics on dangerous game from a manageable magnum beltless case with no reduction in magazine capacity. Pac-Nor has barrels.

cons:
It's necked up too much, leaving a very narrow shoulder (and thus poor headspace control, according to even its loudest champion Jeff Cooper). Tedious to handload (using a .50 die to initially remove all case taper). Remains a wildcat with no factory ammo or rifle support, and has been deservedly overshadowed by the .458 Lott. G&A = Gone&Away.

.450 Ackley (500gr/2300fps = 5875fpe)
A necked-up .375 which *can* fire .458 Win and Lott (though forming a shoulder). Very similar to the .458 Lott, but with a slight shoulder for a parallel neck in order to provide uniform neck tension on the bullet. (The .458 Lott merely tapers to the mouth.) Pac-Nor had barrels for my Brno, but the .458 Lott now enjoys superior factory gun/ammo support.

A fine cartridge, but the .458 Lott has clearly edged past.

.458 Lott (500gr/2300fps = 5875fpe, from a 22"bbl)
(465gr/2400fps = 5949fpe)
Another necked-up .375, which has eclipsed the Ackley. The .458 Lott was standardized by A-Square, who produces both rifles and ammo in the caliber, as well as brass and bullets.

pros:
Excellent, proven ballistics on dangerous game from a manageable magnum case. Straight-walled, it can safely fire the shorter .458 Win (like a .38 Special in a .357 Mag). Very popular amongst PHs. Factory support in both rifles (Ruger, CZ) and ammo (A-Square, Hornady). Long case life.

"Economical cost, versatility, and convenience" according to Terry Wieland, its greatest fan, as well as:

The .458 Lott will handle anything from elephant down to dik-dik, given the right bullet,...
 ...with bullets available in every configuration, in weights from 300 to 600 grains, it is a handloader's dream cartridge when teamed with H4198. ...If I wanted to hunt the world and own only one rifle, this would be it.
— "Covering all the bases with an all-around battery"

cons:
Belted case. 500gr/2400fps requires compressed powder charges, which risks overpressure/sticky extraction in very hot weather. Straight wall case is a bit tedious to handload, and it doesn't provide optimal neck tension.

final comments:
Generally a fine choice, and probably the best belted .458. It's certainly becoming the most popular. If you've an M1917 or P14 Enfield, then rebarreling/gunsmithing to the .458 Lott will give you a very capable African rifle. If your .458 Win action will handle a 3.65" OAL cartridge, then rechamber/refit for Lott. Load 500gr to 2250-2350fps for more tolerable recoil.

You really can't go wrong with this round. It's not perfect like the .450 Dakota, but it's *very* good. And it's *available*.

.450 Dakota/.450 Rigby   (500gr/2450fps = 6663fpe)
The .416 Rigby necked up to .458. CZ chambers for it. (The Dakota has a less sharp shoulder, which is my preference.)

pros:
Superb DG ballistics from a low-pressure round not given to sticky extraction. Can easily throw 600gr without pressure issues. Non-belted cases with excellent shoulder headspacing.

cons:
Mag capacity reduced by one round. Expensive cases. Barrels not yet common (you can order a custom reamer for your barrelmaker). Requires a longer/heavier magnum action.

final comments:
Although acceptable .458s can be had from .375 H&H and .404 Jeffery cases, you're stuck with either a belt (.458 Lott) or a skimpy shoulder (.460 G&A). To avoid both requires a .416 Rigby case — it's just that simple. If I'd had the time for the necessary gunsmithing, I'd have rebarreled my Brno in .450

Dakota. It's perfect for buffalo and elephant (and a better choice than the .458 Lott, which will do).

If you've a rifle already in .416 Rigby, then no action gunsmithing will be necessary if you ever want to rebarrel.

.460 Weatherby   (500gr/2580fps = 7389fpe)

If the .450 Dakota isn't man enough caliber for you, then try *this* behemoth. Very useful for knocking freight trains off the tracks and that sort of thing. Yes, African game is tough, but you're not hunting *Stegosaurus* over there.

Besides, you'd have to own a push-feed Weatherby rifle for this known sticker of a case. Not wise for a DG gun.

.475 calibers

There aren't many for bolt-actions. Only three.

.475 bullets

These enjoy 8% more sectional area than the .458, yet with very good .317SD. Superb choices in 500gr, plus the fun of shooting handgun bullets of 275, 325, and 400gr for practice.

(.1772" cross sectional area)	.317 sectional density
Swift A-Frame	500gr
Barnes TSX	500gr
A-Square Triad	500gr

.470 Capstick   (500gr/2400fps = 6397fpe)

This is the .375 case maxed out to its largest practical bullet diameter. Developed by A-Square's Col. Art Alphin and named after author Peter Hathaway Capstick, this excellent round throws a .475/500gr at the magical 2400fps (though with compressed loads and 55,000+psi pressures). It's not straight-walled to the mouth like the .458 Lott, but rather provides an actual parallel neck for superior tension on the bullet (thus avoiding a heavy crimp).

But for the belted case, minimal .014" taper, and high-pressure, I like the .470 Capstick very much. Both rounds have the same case and pressure issues, but the .470 has better neck tension and throws a bigger (8%) bullet at the same velocity. CZ once chambered their *de luxe* grade gun in this superb cartridge, which makes the utter most of the .375 parent case.

.470 AR   (500gr/2300fps = 5875fpe)
A necked up .375 RUM. Load to 2200fps for mild pressures, as 500gr can't be thrown without compression at 2400fps from even a .404 Jeffery case.

.470 Mbogo   (500gr/2500fps = 6941fpe)
Until June 2007 I'd gotten myself pretty excited about my wildcat idea of a necked up .416 Rigby. It would provide better headspace control than the .505 Van Horn (and with higher sectional density, .317 vs. .294 — and flatter trajectory, BC of .321 vs. .283). Its PI is 100, for a 177 SPI and a 139 RoyceKoV. And the .475 has 8% more frontal area than a .458. Quite suitable for elephant, and a real buffalo stomper. It would be to the .470 Capstick what the .450 Dakota is to the .458 Lott — *i.e.*, a beltless case without pressure issues of the 55,000psi .375 H&H case. I called it the .475 Ruark after author Robert C. Ruark, who used a .470 N.E. in *Horn of the Hunter*.

Too late. It's just been done, and done well: .470 Mbogo. My .475 Ruark had .025" of taper and a 30° shoulder, vs. their .015" taper and 35°. The .470 Mbogo holds 9gr more water than a .460 Weatherby. 500gr/2500fps is easily reached with RL-15 and no compression.

It's already very successfully killed several buffalo, and performance was superb. *Yes!* In my view, this is the *best* all around DG cartridge, and with 275-500gr versatility. I am wistful about my .475 Ruark, but glad that somebody has already taken this forward. www.470mbogo.com

.500 calibers (.505 and .510)

There are .505 Van Horn (a 525gr necked-up Rigby), .505 Gibbs (525gr at 2300fps), the .500 Jeffery (570gr/.510 at 2300fps), .495 A-Square (570gr at 2420fps, the best designed of the .500s), and the .500 A-Square (600gr at 2500fps).

Renowned heavy rifle maker Ryan Breeding mentioned to me at SCI 2007 that real buffalo killing power becomes evident in the .50s (vs. the .458s over the .416s). This is something to keep in mind if you've the budget for a .500 and plan on *often* hunting buff. (Personally, I'll "make do" with the .470 Mbogo.)

Most of us, however, will have to suffice with a .375-.458 (which are also much more versatile on lesser game).

the RoyceKoV (DG)

There are many ballistic minimums for buffalo: a .375 caliber (for sufficient wound channel diameter), a muzzle energy of 4500fpe (bullet weight minimum is embedded in this), a muzzle velocity of 2400fps and .300+SD. If any of these fall below minimum (such as MV in the case of 500gr/.458 Win), then killing power suffers.

Shock must be balanced against penetration. The 500gr/.458 Win has about 9% better SPI than the .416 Rigby, but 23% less penetration, and the field prefers the .416 Rigby. SPI without sufficient penetration will not reach the vitals, and penetration without sufficient SPI will not destroy the vitals.

To portray the balance between SPI and penetration, we'll again use my RoyceKoV, but with a different constant for DG. Same calculation as the plains game index, but using the .416 Rigby 400gr/2400fps as the *reliable* first shot minimum on undisturbed buffalo. Also, since most DG are shot *within* 100yds, ME will suffice since differences in BC do not appreciably affect the rankings within 100yds, and certainly not within 50yds.

The Royce PI is calculated by dividing the muzzle energy (ME, muzzle or downrange) with cross sectional area (SA), then multiplying its quotient by sectional density (SD), then dividing with 124. (This assumes no bullet expansion, deformation, or path variance.)

The Royce SPI is calculated by multiplying KE by the SA of the bullet, then dividing with 6.95. SPI is very useful as a *rough* guide, but remember that bullet performance remains paramount.

KE kinetic energy = (V^2/450,240)bullet weight in grains
SD sectional density = (gr/7000)/D^2
SA cross sectional area = πr^2
PI Penetration Index = ((ME/SA)SD)/124
SPI Shock Power Index = ME(SA)/6.95
RoyceKoV (DG) = (PI+SPI)/2

While there are several cartridges with PIs in the 70s (.376 Steyr, .458 Win, .470 N.E., .505 Gibbs), these operate at the very low end of penetration. Go to something with 90+ PI.

cartridge	gr.	SD	SA	MV	ME	Royce PI	Royce SPI	Royce KoV
.45-70 Marlin	325	.221	.1647	2050	3033	33	72	53
.45-70 Marlin	460	.313	.1647	1800	3310	51	78	65
9.3x62	286	.305	.1052	2360	3538	83	53	68
.376 Steyr	270	.274	.1104	2550	3900	78	62	70
.375 H&H	270	.274	.1104	2750	4535	91	72	82
.375 H&H	300	.305	.1104	2550	4331	97	69	83
.416 Rem 21"	370	.305	.1359	2360	4577	83	89	86
9.3x64	286	.305	.1052	2650	4461	104	68	86
.375 Rugr/Wea	270	.274	.1104	2840	4835	97	77	87
.375 Rugr/Wea	300	.305	.1104	2660	4713	106	75	90
.375 RUM	270	.274	.1104	2900	5043	101	80	91
.458 Win	500	.341	.1647	2040	4620	77	109	93
.375 RUM	300	.305	.1104	2750	5039	112	80	96
.416 Rig/Rem	350	.289	.1359	2600	5235	90	103	97
.458 Win	450	.307	.1647	2250	5060	76	120	98
.458 Win	465	.317	.1647	2220	5088	78	121	100
.416 Rig/Rem	**400**	**.330**	**.1359**	**2400**	**5115**	**100**	**100**	**100**
.470 N.E.	500	.317	.1772	2150	5133	74	131	102
.458 Lott	400	.272	.1647	2500	5553	74	132	103
.378 Wea	300	.305	.1104	2850	5412	121	86	103
.458 Lott	450	.307	.1647	2425	5877	88	139	114
.458 Lott	465	.317	.1647	2400	5947	92	141	117
.458 Lott	500	.341	.1647	2300	5875	100	139	120
.505 Gibbs	525	.294	.2003	2300	6166	73	178	126
.416 Wea	400	.330	.1359	2700	6477	127	127	127
.470 Capstick	500	.317	.1772	2400	6394	92	163	128
.450 Dakota	500	.341	.1647	2400	6394	109	152	131
.505 Van Horn	525	.294	.2003	2400	6716	80	194	137
.470 Mbogo	500	.317	.1772	2500	6941	100	177	139
.500 Jeffery	570	.313	.2043	2300	6697	83	197	140
.460 Wea	500	.341	.1647	2580	7389	123	175	149
.500 A-Square	600	.343	.2003	2470	8130	112	234	173

This table is not Gospel, but merely a *guide*.
PIs are not necessarily linearly effective.
The lower the PI, the closer you should stalk.
Sectional density of the *impacted* bullet is what really matters.

There is *quite* a bit of information embedded within the RoyceKoV: cross sectional area, muzzle energy, and penetration (derives from ample velocity and SD). And the yardstick of all this is the classic ballistics of the .416 Rigby as a proven standard praised by African professionals for nearly a century. Meaning, any RoyceKoV in excess of 100 is gravy for most buffalo, and extra insurance for those really tough ones.

The .375 H&H is too often marginal for buff, and with a RoyceKoV of 83 there's no mystery why. Go .416/400gr instead.

The .505 Gibbs is an example of a good, though inefficient round. An MV of 2300fps is respectable, but not quite enough to push that large .2003 inch^2 bullet with .294 SD clear through. Its RoyceKoV of 126 is great, but with a modest 73 PI. Huge cross sectional area is nice, but *not* at expense of ample penetration. (Same issue for the .458 Win and .470 N.E. with their 74-78 PIs. You've better choices available.)

Between the .458 Lott and the .470 Capstick, the larger .475 bullet (which has a higher MV and SA) slightly outshines the .458 bullet (which penetrates marginally better). But since the .458 Lott is becoming the .458 standard and is widely available, its 120 RoyceKoV is no excuse to pass on this excellent round for .470 Capstick's RoyceKoV of 128. Commonality can be a significant factor.

The .460 Weatherby — considered a most unpleasant caliber to shoot — is a prime example of overkill. Most hunters would develop quite a flinch, causing poor shot placement. (So, what's the point of a 149 RoyceKoV?) If you're not recoil-averse and want a .500 for DG and runaway freight trains, the .500 A-Square (600gr/2470fps) is your answer.

The beltless .450 Dakota is superbly balanced and really drives those 500gr bullets home. (The 600gr — *.409*SD! — is great for elephants.) This or the .470 Mbogo is the round of choice if you are going to do a *lot* of buffalo hunting, as 5-10% of buffs will charge. Meaning, you'll need to hunt 10-20 buffs to encounter a problem. And when you do, you'll be *very* glad that you had 100-109 PI and 131-139 RoyceKoV.

PROPER BULLETS

The bullet is the least expensive, most important part of your hunt. Everything you've got in that hunt — airfare, guides, licenses — rides on that projectile.
    — Bill Hober, President/CEO Swift Bullet Company

Bullets kill by tissue destruction. They do not kill by shock.
    — Finn Aagaard, as told to Terry Wieland in 1990

I'm assuming you've chosen some flavor of .416 or .458 for your buffalo (which is sufficiently flat shooting for all lesser game out to 250yds). Now, it's time to settle on the right bullet. Wieland made the good point that your bullet should hold together to penetrate a buffalo skull at full muzzle velocity. To save your own life, you may have to rely on exactly such a shot.

exit wound, or stopping just short of the far hide?

To some, exit wounds are wasted energy, while others prefer their increased blood loss (and spoor for tracking).

I'll repeat myself from Chapter 8: if the bullet has nicely expanded *and* reached the far hide, then all energy available to the vitals *was already expended on them*, so no useful energy was "lost" by creating an exit wound.

The only time to avoid an exit wound is in a thick herd with risk of wounding a second animal after perforating the first. Ask your PH about the herds in your game area.

solids

...I still insist on using only solid bullets on wounded buffalo. A brain shot is the only effective stopper of a determined charge. For this, [only] a solid can be relied on to fully penetrate the heavy bone surrounding the brain.

— Robin Hurt, Foreword, Wieland's *Dangerous Game Rifles*

Solids are designed to penetrate straight through anything in its path: shoulders, chest, etc. They do not expand. They do not break up. They are used to follow-up on wounded DG. Their only function is to penetrate in a straight line.

If I may add one technical observation it is this: a very strong case can be made for using only solids on all African game. You can then take a shot from any angle if you know anatomy and the solid bullet will not break up, nor expand and slow up. It will continue straight on its course toward the vital organ you intend it to pierce. Shooting by anatomy from any angle with solids is the deadliest and most merciful way to hunt. But first the hunter must learn the anatomy of his animals properly. Then, until he is really "checked out" he should see each animal skinned and butchered and trace the paths and results of this shots. Eventually he will be like a surgeon except that he will be armed with the lightning rapier of the long-reaching solid instead of a scalpel. Then he should try to take his shots closer and closer: for the pleasure of the stalk and to be able to apply his surgery the better.

— Ernest Hemingway, foreword to *Man and Beast in Africa*

There are bimetal solids (*i.e.*, with a lead core, such as the Woodleigh). A-Square (a leaded naval bronze with perfect nose for reliable feeding) would be my choice.

Monolithics (made of just one metal, such as a bronze alloy). Given the same weight, monolithics are longer than lead core bullets, so verify reliable magazine feeding. I like Barnes.

A high velocity solid striking heavy bone *will* deform, if only slightly.

soft-nose

Now *this* is where the difference lies! Softs vary greatly, and there are only a few which I can heartily recommend. First of all, you should choose only a *bonded lead core* bullet for buffalo. Bullets without a bonded core do not hold together well, and are unsuitable for buffalo. My choice would be the Swift A-Frame. Also great is the Barnes TSX, a copper solid which expands moderately without the weight shedding.

I wish I'd used something other than Hornady's bonded 400gr in my .416 Rem. While they nicely killed my hartebeest and zebra (with good penetration), I felt their weight retention was too low at 82.3% and 88.9%. I suspect that they would have broken up on buffalo. (One hunter used the *older* Hornady soft on his buff, and spined it from a lucky scapula deflection. The bullet exploded and only two jacket shards were found.)

Too much expansion will decrease penetration, and you risk not reaching the vitals (especially on a raking shot). Ideally, you want to penetrate the full width or length of the animal (and through the opposite hide, if no risk of wounding a second animal). That's maximum trauma to the vitals.

Since a soft is recommended for your buff's first shot (followed by solids), it is paramount that you choose the best. I'd heard for years good things about Woodleighs, but they expand excessively above 2500fps. Trophy Bonded Bear Claws are good, but not highly accurate in all rifles due to their solid copper shank (without grooves), and quality control has recently suffered. The new Hornadys are reputed to be quite good. Nosler Partitions in .375-.458 are OK, but I think the best currently available bullets are:

A-Square Dead Tough
Swift A-Frame
Barnes TSX
North Fork

A-Square Dead Tough (www.a-squarecompany.com)

This company takes a *very* scientific approach to their bullet design, especially regarding overexpansion's tendency to cause erratic wound channels. If the petals extend too far, rotational velocity (*i.e.*, angular momentum) is decreased and the bullet becomes unstable.

Your buffalo bullet should *not* expand past the front third of itself. (My Hornadys peeled back to the base, and measured 1" in diameter for 2.5x expansion. Anything >2x is a poor trade-off.) This keeps the retained weight where it should be: at the rear, to conserve angular momentum (as an engine's flywheel).

Dead Toughs have a soldered core and typically retain 89% to 98.5% of weight; they are found in their animals nose-forward after *lots* of penetration. And they are designed to expand no more than 1.6x (which is the best overall multiple for a balanced range of BBC.). Impact velocity of 1500-2900fps.

These bullets are probably tops for controlled expansion at all velocity ranges per bullet. They expand reliably at lower velocities, yet will not break up easily in the *über*Magnums. Available from MidwayUSA and Cabela's.

Swift A-Frame (www.swiftbullets.com)

Sort of a stouter Nosler Partition, these are *very* well regarded by professionals, and Craig Boddington often uses them. They hold up beautifully.

One of their .423/400gr A-Frame's stopped a buffalo head-on at 25yds, going from chest to rumen pouch (the first part of the stomach). Recovered weight was 381gr (95%) with a mushroom diameter of .782" (1.96x original). With a BBC of 48.5, that is almost perfectly balanced performance.

I've never heard of or read a bad report about A-Frames.

Barnes TSX (www.barnesbullets.com)

> Because of the X-bullet's unique qualities, the matching of case, bullet weight, and velocity becomes critical to good terminal performance. If this is achieved, however, the Triple-Shock-X gives fine performance.
>
> — Terry Wieland, *Dangerous Game Rifles* (2006), p. 231

Great performance is typical of the TSX. Their terminal ballistics are extremely consistent, rarely breaking off a petal and thus retaining near 100% of weight. Even if all four petals are lost, 85% weight retention is assured. Also, if lead ever becomes a universal environmental pariah, then Barnes is way ahead of the game. Impact velocity range is 1600-2600fps.

A friend of mine used 270gr .375s in Namibia. Most retained 99-100% of weight, scoring 42-48 BBCs. Ranges were 20-275yds. (He wished for slightly more penetration, but that was the trade-off using 270gr vs. 300gr.)

So, what's the *trade-off* in all-copper Barnes TSX bullets?

For compression-vulnerable calibers (*e.g.*, .416 Rem, .458 Win, .458 Lott), the TSX is too long (even in 90% weight). For example, a 450gr TSX is as long as a 500gr A-Frame, and thus seats just as deeply. While some cases such as the .416 Rigby can accommodate this, .375 H&H parent cases cannot. (See photo diagram.) The .458 Win is worse still and really should be loaded at most with 450gr A-Frames or 465gr Dead Toughs.

Even if a 500gr A-Frame were to keep only 90% of its weight (unlikely) and thus weigh what a 450gr TSX *began* with, it nonetheless struck the animal with 50gr more mass. The energy of that shedded 50gr was spent in the animal, so what have you lost as long as penetration and track did not suffer?

Also, why give up *sectional density* if you don't *have* to? These TSX/A-Frame caliber pairs have identical seating depth:

cartridge	gr.	SD	bullet	MV	ME	Royce PI	SPI	Royce KoV
.416 Rem	350	.289	TSX	2600	5235	90	103	97
.416 Rem	400	.330	A-Frame	2400	5115	100	100	100
.458 Lott	450	.307	TSX	2425	5877	88	139	114
.458 Lott	500	.341	A-Frame	2300	5875	100	139	120

The TSX PIs are 10-12% less, and its RoyceKoVs are 3-6% less. This is not insignificant, especially if little-to-nothing is gained in TSX bullet performance over the A-Frame.

Now, if all lead-core bullets lost their noses like Nosler Partitions and ended up with only 70% weight retention, *then* a stronger argument for the TSX could be made. However, some softs such as the A-Frame are *so* good at holding together and expanding uniformly that they largely negate the argument for

100% copper bullets. And, as already explained, certain cases *need* the greater density of lead-core bullets to avoid compression and to leave ⅛" magazine gap for best feeding.

Now, if you want a lighter bullet load for thin-skin game, you'll enjoy superior BCs vs. the same weight in lead-core bullets (the positive flip-side to long copper bullets), faster velocities, flatter shooting, and clean killing. Say, for wildebeest or eland, a 350gr TSX .416 or a 450gr TSX .458 Lott would be an excellent load. But for DG in those calibers, you need a dense lead-core bullet that doesn't seat so deeply, yet has the highest SD. Yes, a 350gr TSX .416 Rem at 2525fps *will* nicely kill buffalo; I'm not alleging otherwise. But, for *that* caliber, a 400gr A-Frame is a better choice. More mass, and with a much higher SD. Such simply *has* to kill better.

Also, if you've a .416 Rigby or .450 Dakota, *then* you can gracefully load full weight TSX bullets to benefit from their top SDs, superior BCs, *and* the fine performance that Barnes offers. For such calibers, TSX would be my choice.

The North Forks are all 90% weight bullets, so you won't be able to enjoy the unsurpassed BC of a 100% weight copper bullet (as in the TSX) from those Dakota and Rigby cases with ample room for such long bullets.

North Fork (www.northforkbullets.com)

A Wyoming company that makes very fine bonded-core softs. Basically, there is just enough of a lead core to mushroom, but no more than needed. (Once the maximum diameter is reached, why tolerate a bullet which keeps petaling?) As in the Barnes TSX, the shank is grooved to reduce galling and provide a sealing effect on bore size variance.

Their weights may seem curious (.416/370gr, .458/450gr) but this is because North Forks sacrifice about 10% in weight for added velocity since they require 2200-2500fps impact velocity for ample penetration. (All of the hot mags at 100yds are still above 2500fps, by the way.) Retention is 95-99+%.

These bullets are an excellent example in the *balance* of several vital factors: weight, penetration, and wound channel. (A friend was very pleased with his .416 Rem 370gr/2360fps, though I think the North Fork better suited for higher MVs. Past 60yds, his bullet has dropped below the 2200fps optimum expansion threshold.)

final thoughts

> ...for dangerous game one should use the heaviest bullet that is normal for the caliber: 300 grains in .375, 400 in .416, 500 in .458. By using a heavier bullet, you will automatically reduce velocity and the possibility of overexpansion. You will also guarantee maximum penetration.
> — Terry Wieland, *Dangerous Game Rifles* (2006), p. 242

Swift, North Fork, and Barnes TSX all expand up to 2x with superb weight retention. The Dead Tough expands no more than 1.6x because A-Square places more emphasis on conserving angular momentum (for the best straight-line penetration). Handload your .416 or .458 with any of the above and you won't be able to blame your bullet. *Any* of them will perform superbly if you do *your* part. Some books you *must* buy:

Rifle Bullets for the Hunter	www.riflebullets.net
Any Shot You Want	www.a-squarecompany.com
Dangerous Game Rifles	www.countrysportpress.com

RIFLES OTHER THAN BOLT-ACTIONS

doubles

> I prefer a double rifle for my own use because I know that if I get into trouble, it is going to be at very close quarters. That second shot has gotten me out of trouble on more occasions than I care to think about. . . . My experience of charges has always been at very short range — often under five yards (which is too close for a second shot from a bolt gun).
> — Robin Hurt, Foreword to *Dangerous Game Rifles* (2006)

Craig Boddington's *Safari Rifles* is the place to start for your research. His 1990 prices are naturally outdated, but the general information remains thorough. Wieland's *Dangerous Game Rifles* is a new and useful addition to the subject.

Doubles are really best suited for elephant hunting, and not necessary for buffalo (unless you hunt them as does PH Mark Sullivan). While a .470 Nitro Express is certainly nostalgic, a good one will begin at $10,000. For 20% of that you can have a perfectly good bolt gun (with scope), *and* more versatility for the one- and two-rifle hunts. If you've the money and inclination for a double, go for it!

singles
These have no logical place for dangerous game, especially those shot in close cover. Great for mountain sheep, but nearly suicidal for DG!

levers
A poor choice for several indisputable reasons: weak primary extraction, easily damaged magazine tubes, very difficult to clear malfunctions, and they are simply unavailable in sufficiently powerful calibers.

A 400gr A-Frame is cannelured incorrectly for the .45-70, which eliminates this fine bullet. Besides, a *hot* .45-70 can get within only 400fps of factory .458 Win loads, and the .458 Win is only just adequate for buffalo as it is. My friend Rich Lucibella hunted Zim buffalo with a .450 Marlin and managed to survive, but I don't recommend taunting the odds like that.

autoloaders (Browning, Remington, Winchester)
Worse than levers because of their added complexity, and none are manufactured in DG calibers. Forbidden in the RSA.

conclusion
For the vast majority of African hunters, a bolt-action rifle (preferably scoped) is the only practical and affordable choice. It's what most PHs use (unless they can afford a double).

BOLT-ACTION BUFFALO RIFLES

This is easy. The dangerous game (DG) requirements (strength, ruggedness, reliability) are clear; the choices (Mauser 98 type actions) few.

forged steel receiver, controlled feed, claw extractor, fixed ejector.
Period.

That rules out the: Rem 700, Savage, Browning A-Bolt, SAKOs, Ruger M77 (investment cast), Weatherby (2rd mag, finicky feeding, sticky extraction), and the "post-64" push-feed Win M70. Yes, you could take a push-feed Rem to Africa and most likely come back alive, but controlled-feed is more reliable and will not double feed if you short-stroke the bolt. My friend Kevin "Mad Dog" McClung (whom I respect as a rifleman, hunter, and gunsmith) typically spelled it out well:

What do I want in a DG rifle?

1) Bolt action, controlled feed, claw extractor, fixed ejector. Extra recoil lug on barrel. Full length bedded stock. Recoil lug integral on action. (No twist off lug washers on my heavy recoiling high torque DG rifle, thank you!!)

Suitable actions include: Winchester pre-64 Model 70, Dakota 76, P14/P17 (and Remington 30, 30S, and 720), Mauser 98 (and CZ).

2) Suitable caliber, .416 Rem Mag or Rigby at a minimum, prefer .450 Dakota or 500/.450 Dakota. Both of these cases are essentially .416 Rigby blown out to larger diameter...

3) Barrel length cut to minimum acceptable for caliber and desired accuracy. 20" minimum, 24" max. Medium taper. Fluting optional.

4) Weight no more than 10 pounds.

5) Composite (not injection molded) or laminate hardwood stock.

6) Full time iron sights with tritium insert in front post. I use the NECG Adjustable Express rear and banded ramp front with interchangeable posts. Warne mounts for Schmidt & Bender 1.5-6x Illuminated Reticle scope with QD rings.

7) Large readily accessible truncated cone shape bolt knob with long bolt handle.

8) Four position sling with flush swivel mounts.

9) .8" Pachmayr Decelerator pad.

10) MD Labs ST2 coating on all metal parts. Super corrosion resistant, twice the Taber abrasion resistance of black T, and self lubricating.
Options: Leopard light mount on forend. interchangeable recoil pads for winter/summer weight clothing.

With the exception of the large caliber callouts mentioned above, the preceding is how I build pretty much ALL of my rifles. Optics or irons may vary a bit on the smaller caliber hunting rifles, but otherwise, that's how they need to be for me. YMMV, but you'll be sorry if it does.

your viable choices of DG rifles

If you stick within the below list, you won't go wrong. Deviate, and you're just begging for trouble.

A-Square Hannibal

Using the robust M1917 Enfield action, they will make a very high quality DG rifle in nearly any caliber you choose (I'd go .450 Dakota), and for a reasonable price. An excellent value.

Ed Brown Express (www.edbrown.com)
Very high quality rifles up to .458 Lott. Controlled-feed, 24" Shilen barrel, 4+1rds, McMillan stock. About $3750.

Brno 602 (.375 H&H, .416 Rigby)
All the basics, though a bit rough. I liked mine and nearly rebarreled it from .375.

602s have reverse-style M70 safeties (correctable with a mod from J. Wisner, 146 Curtis Hill Road, Chehalis, WA 98532). Some safety mods have been known to fail, just so you know in advance. PH Alan Lowe was killed during an elephant charge, presumably because his safety mod failed him.

CZ 550 Magnum (.375H&H, .416 Rigby, .458 Lott, .470 Cap)
This is the modern version of the Brno 602 with a few improvements. Quite affordable at $875. Their Classic is offered in .404 Jeffery, .450 Rigby (*Yes!*), and .505 Gibbs.

Choose the laminated stock for extra strength. The integral base is very nice, but the CZ rings are pretty rough (go Talley instead).

Dakota 76
A custom-made pre-64 M70 of wonderous quality. Worth saving up for such a dream rifle. .450 Dakota is my choice.

Empire Rifles
Gorgeous quality Mauser action rifles.

Mauser M98 in 9.3x64
Although a .366, it's a great .375*esqe* caliber that will generally do the job. Legal for Zim buff. Well-proven in Africa.

Ruger M77 Mark II Magnum (.416 Rigby, .458 Lott)
A nicely featured rifle for Africa, but they are known to have extraction/ejection issues. They are also *noticeably* heavier than Win M70s because of investment cast steel receivers (which, ounce for ounce, are weaker and heavier than forged steel receivers).

While I've never heard of a Ruger M77 action suffering from catastrophic failure, because of its extra weight, poor balance, and my lesser confidence in cast steel receivers, I don't own any M77s. For a dangerous-game rifle, I will not take unnecessary chances, especially when forged steel receiver rifles are readily available for the same money. (See the chapter appendix for more from an expert in steel and forging.)

U.S. M1917 or P14 Enfield

Very strong military actions for *any* DG caliber, and with a superb safety. An excellent choice as the heart of your custom heavy rifle. While the safety is sound, it is 2-position only and doesn't allow safe unloading of the magazine.

If you ever see a good, tight action (Winchester or Remington only, no Eddystone) for sale at a gun show, snap it up. (Remington also made three commercial models, the 30, 30S, and 720, all of which are suitable for a DG rifle.)

Whitworth Mark X

These are very reasonably priced rifles in .375 and .458. The 2-position safety isn't ideal, and I've heard of feeding issues, but for $500 you've some money left over for twiddling a fussy gun. Not a top choice, but viable if on an extreme budget.

Winchester Model 70 pre-64

Absolutely gorgeous rifles, but you'll pay at least $2000 for a nice one, if not $2500+. Unfortunately, the only African calibers it was ever made in were .375 H&H (just adequate) and .458 Win Mag (action is too short for .458 Lott rebarreling).

Winchester Model 70 Classic Super Express (.416 Rem)

A good balance between quality and price. It has a longer mag body than the pre-64. These are very good rifles for the money, and more nicely finished than the CZ 550 Magnum. The wood stock must be pillar-bedded, else it will likely split. Tighten up any bolt shroud play.

recoil

> *There is the answer to the recoil bug-bear — forget about it. Given a well-balanced weapon that fits you, just concentrate on putting your bullets where you want them and leave your rifle to take care of its own recoil.*
> — John Taylor, *African Rifles and Cartridges* (1948), p. 319

As Jeff Cooper often wrote, recoil is 80% *mental*. Practice with light loads at first and work up to field loads. (After you're zeroed, leave the bench, which accentuates felt recoil.) If recoil is still unbearable then you've a few options.

weight

The easiest and cheapest way to reduce felt recoil is by having a sufficiently heavy rifle. While a .308 pared down to 7½ pounds is desirable, you'd want a heavier .416/.458. Your buffalo rifle will (and should) weigh 9-11lbs. (I prefer 9½-10lbs.)

muzzle brakes

Yes, they will reduce felt recoil by 20-30%, but at the expense of hideous muzzle blast and overpressure. PHs hate them, and some safari outfitters will not let you use them.

Coil Chek stocks from A-Square

An oversized buttstock and recoil pad which spreads out the recoil energy. Very effective, though they feel blocky.

Even a normal stock properly fitted to you will greatly reduce felt recoil.

mercury counter-recoil tubes

By spreading out the recoil energy over time, they transform a violent, sharp shove to a more gentle push. Reduces felt recoil by 15-25%. Standard in CZ .500 rifles.

barrel band front sling swivel

Front sling swivel studs mounted on the stock will often tear your finger on heavy rifles.

barrel length (22"-24")

A friend has a 21" Blaser in .416 Rem which throws a 370gr North Fork at 2360fps for 4577fpe. This works out to 83 PI, 89 SPI, and 86 RoyceKoV, which is only slightly better than a .375/300gr and its 83 RoyceKoV. A very handy rifle, but with an excessively short barrel that reduced energy to .375 H&H levels. While he hunted well with it, he'd traded full .416 Rem power for handiness. (The Blaser's action is short enough that a 23" barrel wouldn't have been unwieldy.)

Since a .416/400gr has less mass than a .458/500gr, it needs every bit of its 2400fps. Each inch less than 24" reduces MV by 25fps. The new Win M70 has a 23½" tube, which is a fine compromise between MV and handiness.

So, for .416" choose a barrel 23"-24". For .458: 22"-23". Balance is also a factor so consider barrel length/thickness.

iron sights

A *must* for any DG rifle. Optics are not necessary for a dedicated heavy (*i.e.*, one not used on lighter/farther game), but iron sights are a must. Train with irons first! Buffalo are large targets, and during a charge front posts are much quicker than reticles. McClung recommends NECG Adjustable Express rear and banded ramp front with interchangable posts. (Remember to verify the correct raised leaf *before* taking a shot, or settle for just a 100yd leaf and dispense with the others. Keep It Simple.)

scopes

> *If there is a better dangerous game scope than the Leupold Vari-X III 1.5-5x, I have yet to see it. It is a compact scope with a one-inch tube, it has a good, simple, duplex reticle, and it sits low on the rifle. It is durable to a fault.*
> — Terry Wieland, *Dangerous Game Rifles* (2006), p. 294

I tend to agree, though I had to scope my .416 elsewith. Leupold also offers their superb VZ-7 1½-6x24mm (30mm tube), including a year membership in either SCI, BC, or RW. (That same $1700 could buy a Schmidt & Bender illuminated 1½-6x42mm.) I'll soon discuss scopes in greater length. Be careful not to overtighten the rings, especially the forward one which surrounds the objective lens elements.

stocks

For strength, choose (as in the CZ 550 Magnum) laminated wood over walnut. Such will be about as strong as synthetic, but nicer looking. Check it very carefully inside for cracks! Also, make sure that the recoil lug is properly bedded, and that the tang is stress relieved (no recoil should be transferred to the stock there). Synthetic stocks are very strong, but lack the classic warmth of wood.

trigger

> [A bad] *trigger's like the last turn of the key opening a sardine can.*
> — Ernest Hemingway, *Green Hills of Africa*, p. 102

A 2½-4lb crisp trigger is one of the most conducive elements to accuracy, especially from field positions. A horrible trigger can be tolerated on the bench, but will ruin offhand shots (which are likely in Africa). Win M70 triggers are simple to adjust.

SO, WHAT *DID* I TAKE TO AFRICA?

Just as I was about to send off my Brno 602 for a .416 Dakota rebarreling, I learned of a local guy who had several safari rifles for sale. Since a buyer was interested in my Brno, I had the chance to get into a completely different rifle if I found something I liked.

And I did. A Winchester Model 70 Classic Super Express (*i.e.*, the modern "pre-64" with controlled feed). Forged steel receiver. Its barrel had been cryo treated (luxurious and unnecessary for a 200yd rifle). It had a lovely trigger job breaking at a glass-rod crisp 40oz. And it had an AO tritium front sight dot with Express rear. The walnut was very handsome. It shouldered well and felt right. The owner assured me that it was quite a tackdriver. (<2MOA is unnecessary from a buffalo rifle, but never hurts.) The price was fair, and less than what I would have into my rebarreled Brno (after adding iron sights).

The only issue? I wasn't wild about the caliber: .416 Rem. Great ballistics, commonality, etc., but it had that belted case and 55,000psi loading. Although I had never actually *heard* of any feeding or extraction trouble in the field from a .416 Rem (or the .458 Lott, also belted), the possibility of such remained a splinter in my mind.

OK, time to weigh the theoretical against the *practical*. About then I recalled what my friend McClung had once posted:

> I realize that the .416 Rem is a belted case which I initially objected to, but after speaking with some trusted associates that have hunted DG (dangerous game) in Africa with it I am confident that it will serve as well as can be expected, and I can do it at a cost that I can more nearly afford without the wife and kids leaving for greener pastures...

This was after he reluctantly postponed his plans to have made up a buffalo rifle in .505 Van Horn (a necked-up .416 Rigby).

It *was* a good rifle. The action was slick. It needed nothing but optics and a sling. The caliber had the ballistics I wanted. I had access to plenty of .416 cast bullets and .375 H&H cases to neck-up and fireform for cheap practice ammo. (And, if ever I just couldn't stand the belted case, I could rechamber it to .416 Dakota.) It went home with me.

It proved very accurate and reliable in Africa, and I never once regretted choosing it. Having shot a zebra and hartebeest with it, I'm now very fond of *Mr. Selous.* It will certainly return to Africa with me for buffalo.

I basically arrived at Mad Dog's same conclusion. While I'd have preferred a rifle originally in .416 Rigby, the .416 Rem remains a good cartridge, its belted case notwithstanding. Occasionally, real-world considerations of time and money overshadow largely theoretical ideals. This can be a tough call for the purist, but it's one you may have to make, quickly.

I will say this, however. Since I plan to *often* go back to Africa for buff throughout my life, I will someday treat myself to a custom Dakota 76 in .470 with an illuminated 1½-6x Schmidt & Bender (God's choice of scopes!). The .416 Rem will then be relegated as a loaner rifle for any friend who hasn't yet his own.

my M70's modifications
sling
Simpler is better; less is more. I used an OD nylon 1¼" web sling in polymer Brute swivels from Outdoor Connection. The system was strong, quiet, lightweight, comfortable, inexpensive, and looked good. What more could you want?

Had I time to modify the stock, I'd have added some flush-mount Pachmayrs with a Ching Sling (which has a second loop for your support bicep to lock into, adding much to your stability) as found on the Steyr Scout.

Though I prefer African carry (weak side, muzzle down), I found such ironically unused while in Africa due to the frequent high grass. I used American carry (strong side, muzzle up) fairly often, but how I usually carried my Winchester Model 70 was horizontally by its barrel, with the stock resting on my shoulder. This is how our PH carried his slingless .416 Rigby, and I found it the most comfortable. Safe muzzle control is generally possible, though not perfect — an adjunct to carrying rifles in the field amongst others.

Keep your rifle on safety, check it often, and do not trust them! (My 3-position safety was knocked into the middle position on three occasions by tree limbs.)

heatshrink tubing on the bolt knob

The modern M70 classic is instantly distinguishable from the older pre-64 by a knurled band around the bolt knob. Functionally unnecessary, and after a half-hour of dryfire bolt work my hand began to develop a blister. This would not do. So, I had the idea of adding a piece of black heatshrink to the knob and ¾" of the bolt handle, and it applied very nicely. No more blistering, and my bolt work became even quicker. It held up great in the bush. I recommend this mod for *all* M70 Classics.

magazine spring

The spring had a funky elbow to it which I suspected caused an intermittent last round feeding malfunction during vigorous dryfire practice with dummies. A new replacement spring (which *still* had that elbow) seemed to solve the trouble. Though I never had any feeding problems in Africa, I am just not 100% confident of the factory spring. (I even tried a mag spring from Ruger's M77 Safari, but it nosed up the follower above the rails.) Get a superior spring from J. Wisner, 146 Curtis Hill Road, Chehalis, WA 98532. (He also sells forged steel extractors for the Model 70.)

scoping the Win M70 Classic Super Express

This presented more hassle than imagined because of how Winchester shortened the rear receiver bridge of their standard action (to make room for a magnum-length cartridge). The rear base is thus necessarily shorter, and has .330" hole centers. All this combined to limit which scopes could be mounted (due to turret towers and belled lens housings).

In all, I put together a very good optics/mount package for just $300, which served me well. I could have spent more money on the scope, but for what practical advantage?

bases (Talley matte; $24)

Requiring QD (quick detach) rings, I first considered Leupold's Quick-Release System (which I have on my M70 Classic .30-06). Double-lever cammed rings remove in seconds without tools, and hold their zero. But, it was not to be, as no scope I wanted would *quite* fit where the rings ended up. So, I had to look elsewhere.

My only other choice was Talley, which are of renowned quality. Though I despise vertically-split rings (a chore to install), the Talley bases would allow the scopes I had in mind.

Their rear base properly oriented with the wider boss in front (as the larger shoulder to absorb recoil) unfortunately overhung the action by ¼". While not critical, such *might* hang up a speed reload. So, I reversed the rear base, which allowed for perfectly flush mounting on the rear bridge. I gave up a bit of shoulder strength for the rear ring, but since the front base was oriented properly I thought the system as a whole was sufficient.

rings (Talley 1" matte low QD; $108)

Very high quality rings with big throwlevers. The matte blue blended nicely with the rifle and scope finishes. They were trued up slightly in a lathe, and I installed the scope with black silicon (a Mad Dog tip).

I had one occasion to remove the scope when following up at night on a possibly wounded buffalo, and the QD feature was most appreciated!

scopes and magnification

Although most buffalo (and the other odd game you may encounter) can be well shot with iron sights, a low-powered scope will improve most shooting by at least 25% (especially older hunters). Magnification should be 1-2x/low and 4-7x/high. 2x is the highest of the minimum appropriate for a DG rifle, but at least 4x is preferred on the high end to be useful. You should prefer a Leupold for its hig-quality:medium-price ratio:

1-4x	Leupold VX-II 1-4x20mm	$300
1½-5x	Leupold VX-III 1½-5x20mm	$400
1¾-5x	Burris 1¾-5x32mm	$250
	Burris Fullfield II 1¾-5x28mm	$300
1¾-6x	Leupold VX-III 1¾-6x32mm	$400
2-7x	Leupold VX-I 2-7x33mm	$199
	Leupold European-30 2-7x33mm	$400

Although you won't likely be shooting in extremely low light conditions, I do prefer an objective lens larger than a mere 20-24mm. For the extra 2oz., it's worth it to me.

Leupold VX-III 1¾-6x32mm (#55024)

One of the best scopes for your DG rifle. Only 11.3oz, rugged, with a nearly perfect magnification range, and a 32mm objective. The extra $200 above a VX-I is worth it. Choose the heavy duplex reticle. (This scope needs the German #4!)

Leupold European-30 2-7x33mm (#54120)

This is a new 30mm tube scope, and what I might have chosen in 2005 for my .416 Rem. The German #4 is similar to the Burris 3P#4, and would be my choice. Weight is 11.7oz.

Burris 1¾-5x20mm (#200088; 3P#4 reticle)

I chose this because it was one of the few which could be mounted on my M70 (even with Talleys). I preferred a larger objective than 20mm, and Burris apparently agrees as they replaced it with a 32mm model (#200708).

A primary reason I chose the Burris was for the superb **3P#4 reticle**, which was just the ticket for DG. (Leupold's German #4 wasn't offered in the scope I'd wanted.) Very quick acquisition, yet with great sighting precision. A great reticle for buffalo, as well as everything else.

Although a fixed-power scope would have sufficed, twice I bumped up the magnification of my Burris to 5x while on the shooting sticks to verify which animal my PH was pointing out. (My face-on hartebeest at 96yds I shot while on 3x, to give me a bit more sighting precision on its narrow chest.) So, variable power *does* have its place, even on a DG rifle. Gone are the days of inherent fragility, and I had ample confidence in my scope.

My Burris 1¾-5x20mm scope held perfect zero, never fogged up or broke, and gave excellent service during my safari. It was a great value for the $200, and its 32mm replacement (#200708) from www.natchezss.com would be a good choice.

scope caps

I've mixed results with the see-through flip-open caps from Butler Creek. An objective lens cap lost its lens, and another kept flipping open through the bush. Do take *something* to protect your lenses, even if it is a rubber Bikini cover. Actual snapshots are rare; you'll have time to remove it.

scope price vs. quality

Only a rich man can afford a cheap scope.
After all, when the scope breaks, he can afford another hunt.
— old Schmidt & Bender ad

Must you buy a $1500 German glass for your buffalo rifle? No, but it sure couldn't hurt. While there is *nothing wrong* with a good Burris or Leupold, there *is* a palpable extra peace of mind that comes with owning the very best. If you've some extra coin to throw on your equipment, then check out a Kahles 1-4x, or a 1½-6x from either Swarovski or Schmidt & Bender. While our $200-400 American scopes made by Burris and Leupold are very nice, there's just something about a $1500 German glass.

Is the Euro glass four to eight times the quality as it is in price? No way. Not even twice the quality. The qualitative increase is the difference between 99.5% and 90%. You'll never miss your animal because of an 90% American scope. Never. However, it is pure *joy* to own an example of something that is just about *perfect* in its class. Whether or not this is worth an additional $1000+ over a perfectly fine Leupold is up to you.

on buying the best, even if you *"can't afford"* it

Even if you *don't* have the spare coin, I would still urge you to choose *something* in your world that matters, and go whole hog. You can live in a shack and drive a beater, but have at least *one* untarnished jewel in your life. Most of what we own and do is alloyed with baser metals. Have *one* thing that is of the *finest* quality. It will stand out like a quasar, reminding yourself that you are a unique human being — the only one of your kind ever issued. You have DNA, fingerprints, tastes, talents, and experience nobody else ever had, or ever *will* have. You are special. Even if you cannot treat yourself royally as often as you'd like, have one thing in your life that *shines*. Have one thing in your life that requires no excuses, no equivocation.

Even if a CZ 550 Magnum is the best you can afford, consider topping it off with a Schmidt & Bender. You will grin like a boy every time you shoulder that rifle.

Life Is *Short*. Don't forget to spoil yourself. You'll never miss that extra $1000 you spent on a German glass. What will remain, what will *abide* for decades is the joy you receive — day in and day out — from that something *truly* special. You don't have to own the best of *everything*. Just *one* thing. www.schmidtbender.com (Check out their 1.5-6x42mm.)

LAST WORD

If you have a reliable forged-steel M98-type action in some variant of .416/400gr or .458/500gr making 2300-2500fps with bullets from Swift, North Fork, Barnes, or A-Square, topped with a Leupold 1¾-6x32mm scope in Talley rings — you are properly armed for African dangerous game.

The rest is up to *you*. It won't be the fault of your rifle, scope, caliber, or bullet. That understood, forget about all the lingering debate over rifles. Now, go *practice* with it!

AT THE RANGE

softs and solids

Generally, the primary hunter's rifle will be fielded with a soft in the chamber, solids in the mag. (Other hunters will all have solids, as back up.) Assuming 2-3 rounds to confirm zero, and that most of your animals are killed with one-shot stops, you will shoot about 50% more softs than solids.

The softs:solids ratio should be about 5:3. Remember that 50rds is the U.S. Customs maximum to bring back.

cycle *all* rounds in your rifle *before* Africa!

My hunting "friend" provided the handloads, and 4 rounds in 40 had bulged cases and wouldn't chamber. (At least I found out *before* the field, not during.) Murphy is alive and well, and you must do everything you can to neutralize him. Double check everything. (And don't hunt with a *nutcase*.)

testfire your handloads

All rifles are enigmas and you must develop *firsthand* knowledge of an ammo's reliability and accuracy. Make sure that your softs and solids print within 1MOA of each other.

range ballistics

Earlier I wrote that the .416/400gr at 2400fps shoots about as flat as the .375/300gr at 2550fps. Well, so does the .458/500gr. Zero for 100yds at +3" and you'll be right on at 200yds (with a drop of 12" at 300yds).

cartridge	gr.	MV	ME	0yds	100yds	200yds	300yds
.30-06	180	2700	2913	-1.50"	+2.39"	ZERO	-10.64"
.338 Win	250	2700	4046	-1.50"	+2.28"	ZERO	- 9.82"
.375 H&H	300	2550	4331	-1.50"	+2.70"	ZERO	-11.72"
.416 Rig/Rem	400	2400	5115	-1.50"	+3.02"	ZERO	-12.95"
.416 Wea	400	2700	6477	-1.50"	+2.00"	ZERO	- 8.50"
.458 Win	465	2220	5088	-1.50"	+3.57"	ZERO	-14.69"
.458 Lott	465	2400	5947	-1.50"	+2.99"	ZERO	-12.46"
.450 Dakota	500	2400	6394	-1.50"	+2.87"	ZERO	-11.59"
.470 Capstick	500	2400	6394	-1.50"	+2.91"	ZERO	-11.88"
.470 Mbogo	500	2500	6941	-1.50"	+2.65"	ZERO	-11.03"
.460 Wea	500	2580	7389	-1.50"	+2.00"	ZERO	- 9.00"
.505 Gibbs	525	2300	6166	-1.50"	+3.61"	ZERO	-14.18"

Since most animals will be shot within 250yds (if not 150yds), your heavy rifle is sufficiently flat shooting to suffice as your one gun if you zero for 200yds.

If you have time before the hunt to get exact dope at 25yd intervals out to 300yds, it's worth the effort. However, if you do not, there's no reason to panic. **With a 200yd zero, forget all about bullet drop between 0-225yds and hold *dead on*.** You will strike within a 4" radius (because 4" is the bullet's max ordinate at about 130yds) of your aiming point, and that's plenty tight enough for anything but very small game (*e.g.*, warthog, impala, etc.). Go for a *lung* shot if you can, because it's a much larger target area than the shoulder/heart.

Peter Capstick zeroed for 100yds, knowing that 200yd and 300yd drops were roughly 6" and 24" (two feet), which he found easy to remember. Not a bad system, either.

Your caliber should be capable of breaking a shoulder and damaging *both* lungs of your animal. Your rifle must be <2MOA for adequate precision. And, finally, you must not get into more rifle than you can reliably and comfortably use well.

"Whatever your choice, for whatever reasons, competence and familiarity count for far more than minor points of technical superiority."

So, don't get *too* hung-up on calibers or rifles. A great shooter with a battered .375 will outperform a mediocre shooter with a new .470 Mbogo. Don't fall for that silly American trait of trying to buy competence through expensive equipment and 3000fps magnums. As a gun author once quipped, "*There are plenty of all-purpose calibers. Where are all the all-purpose hunters?*"

Competence you don't buy, you *earn* through training and practice.

You are the most important variable, not whether or not you take a .458 or a .416 or a .375 — or if it's a Barnes or a Swift. **Any decent caliber/bullet will do . . . if *you* will do!**

A Few Words about Cast Steel Rifle Receivers

by Kevin McClung
MD Labs Senior Engineer
Copyright 15 January 2007. All Rights Reserved.

My good friend Ken Royce has asked me to add my two cents regarding the "cast receiver" issue. Profligate spender that I am, he is getting far more than two cents worth. The subject merits no less, as it relates to the safety and survivability of the dangerous game hunter.

The thesis here is that cast steel receivers are inherently less desirable in a Dangerous Game Rifle (DGR) than a properly heat treated forged billet machined steel receiver. *Why?* Because the cast receivers are *not* as durable or reliable due to the process they are created with: Vacuum Casting.

In a DGR, reliability is *everything*.

The problem with cast high carbon steel (as opposed to cast titanium or aluminum alloy) is that the carbides precipitate in dendrites, rather than being evenly distributed throughout the steel as in forged material. The forging distributes the carbides properly and homogeneously, and develops suitable grain structure and direction, rather than the amorphous matrix and dendritic crystalline structures found in cast steel.

If the cast receiver manufacturers were forging after casting, hey, no problem ... but that costs more money — money they are apparently unwilling to spend to make a better product. They are quite content to make a product that is simply adequate for the uneducated.

Material properties of steel vs. titanium is an apples and oranges comparison, perhaps even an apple and potato type comparison. Titanium and carbon steel are as different in basic properties as any two metals can be. Despite their tendency to produce homogeneous structures during casting, even (vacuum) cast titanium and aluminum alloy structures require suitable heat treat to assure the desired properties are developed after casting.

Investment cast steel makes great paperweights, but it lacks suitable strength to weight ratio to be ideal for much else. In point of fact, no one has used plain Jane cast carbon steel for heavy gun barrels since the 1880s, when truly large scale forging technology came into being. **The cast receiver manufacturers are *not* using cast steel in their rifle barrels**, just the low pressure pistol barrels. All of their high pressure barrel applications are done in forged steel. (That should tell you something!)

Actually, you *could* make a bolt action rifle receiver out of 7075 T6-51 billet *aluminum,* given the forces involved. Steyr already did this with the Scout, and others have done so with .223 and .308 caliber AR clones. It *does* make for a lightweight rifle, *but* the repeated bolt cycling, pressure spikes and such will eventually fatigue the breech face of the bolt gun.

Then, it *cracks.* *You* do not get to choose *when* it cracks. *Murphy* does.

Durability is the issue.
You pay a *price* for the weight loss.

Ask yourself: How *reliable* should a Dangerous Game rifle *be?*

Ask yourself: How *reliable* do you want *your* Dangerous Game rifle to be?

The problem here is that to derive suitable strength without adding unnecessary bulk, the carbides must be evenly distributed throughout the steel. Carbide dendrites have the problem of making a fernlike lattice of extremely hard and very brittle material in the matrix of the alloy. As a result the knives, receivers or other items made this way tend to have very low modulus numbers. In other words, they lack springiness despite the soft, spongy nature of the matrix of metal alloy surrounding the dendrites.

When these carbides precipitate out into veins (dendrites) each of them becomes a potential fracture line in the steel.

They have the dubious advantage of adding a "saw tooth" type structure to the steel at the edge of cast steel knives, but the ability of the steel to withstand any wear, shock, prying, or other robust usage goes out the window. **Carbide dendrites are built in *failure paths*.** The dendrites are considerably more brittle than the surrounding steel, and offer a fernlike failure path for stresses to propagate brittle stress cracks.

Carbon steel or martensitic stainless that has been cast is technically no longer properly alloyed, anyway. The segregation of the (formerly) alloying constituents means that it doesn't actually meet the specs for that alloy anymore. Sure, all of the stuff is still in there, but it isn't distributed properly. There are those that may argue that point, but I'll stand by it.

Fact: The cast receiver manufacturers use vacuum casting. Vacuum does *not* align grain structure, so far as the metallurgy goes. Neither vacuum nor centrifugal casting distributes carbides properly.

Fact: Forging *does* align grain structure and properly distributes the carbides in the alloy.

Fact: Casting carbon steel and martensitic stainless produces carbide dendrites. These dendrites weaken the structure (as compared to a forged structure) by precipitating carbides in a fernlike lattice.

Fact: Casting steel is merely a way to save time and money in obtaining a net or near net shape. Its sole benefit is LOW COST to net shape. The penalty for the cost saving is less strength, ounce per ounce, than a forged part.

Fact: Serious high performance applications require that cast steel ingots are roll forged to sheet, plate or billet; or are hammer forged to near net shape after casting to develop ultimate attributes for a given alloy. This is true in everything from mild steel used in car bodies to structural steel used in aircraft and automatic weapons. Manufacturers of cast receivers skip all of that troublesome "middle part" where the best attributes are developed.

Fact: This is not to say that investment cast frames and parts are not adequate for many functions, even in weaponry. But, merely "adequate" in the eyes of the manufacturer is often less than wholly desirable for the end user who may be betting his life on the gear.

It is simply my choice to use a superior part with superior attributes of strength and durability, *especially* when they are commonly available at *competitive* prices.

I would also point out that were investment casting high strength steel to net shape a desirable method of making a *truly* superior firearm, this process has been available for over 200 years now and has never once been used to produce an American military shoulder firearm of significant caliber, nor has it been applied with notable success to high strength cutlery or edged tools.

There are many cast steel axes available, and they are invariably inferior to forged axes of identical pattern. Even Krupp's famous *cast Stahl* was subsequently hammer or roll forged to obtain best attributes.

Ruger's steel castings are not, in my opinion, better or worse than any other steel casting used in firearms. They *are*, however, inherently weaker, ounce per ounce, than forged steel receivers of proper construction and heat treat.

That's right: *casting is casting.* Nothing magic about it.

Here's another clue to the investment cast receiver inferiority: Check out the May 2005 *American Rifleman*. In it you will find a glowing puff piece on Ruger's Gold Label SXS 12 bore. They show a cutaway of the cast receiver, and all of the internals, which are also cast, except for the springs. Compare the general appearance of the "high end" Ruger internals to, say, those of a nice old Winchester Model 21, or, for that matter, a Remington 870 Wingmaster. (*Note* that the Ruger Gold Label SXS *barrels* are *not* made from castings. Even low pressure stuff like shotgun barrels require a better steel quality than offered in castings, especially in thinner barrels. They do use castings for the locking lugs though. *Ugh.*)

Ruger gets away with cast steel to near net shape and machined handgun barrels in their semi-autos, but their big bore guns use roll forged bar stock for barrels. If their cast stuff was "just as strong", why are they not using it for *everything*? They could sure save more money that way.

Also, in the same magazine, you will see an ad for the Sako 75, another weapon with an investment cast receiver. Note the excremental quality of the integral scope mount lugs atop the receiver. These have always been integral on Sako, but the new cast versions are rounded off on the ends and edges and look awful.

The old ones were precision machined. Also note the "as cast" surfaces inside the Ruger, and on the tail end of the Sako. The casual user never sees these surfaces, so the manufacturers don't bother to finish them. Orange peel-looking at best, and at worst, indicative of voids and other impurities.

A lot cheaper to make, though. In fact, the May 2005 *American Rifleman* article subtly points this out.

So, in closing, I would strongly recommend that you take the above data into account prior to betting your life on a weapon with a cast steel receiver.

After all, Murphy loves to go hunting...

Copyright Kevin McClung, 15 January 2007.
All Rights Reserved.
Printed with permission.

(Royce Note: Since market prices of forged steel receiver rifles are not any higher than cast steel receiver rifles, there is no *monetary* incentive to choosing cast steel. Thus, what incentive remains at *all*?)

❖ 10

SAFE GUN HANDLING

Smokeless powder firearms have been around for over 100 years. Americans own about 300 million guns. One would think safe gun handling to be the norm these days. It's not, for basically two reasons: lack of proper training (do you know the Four Rules?), and lack of peer pressure regarding gun safety (in which the chronically unsafe should be hounded).

Your PH guides hunters of all ages, experiences, and origins, and what makes him more nervous than a wounded leopard in tall grass is an jittery hunter behind him waving muzzle about with finger on the trigger. There is no excuse for such behavior! There are two basic gun safety rules for Africa:

Never board a vehicle with a chambered gun.

Never hand a gun-bearer a chambered gun.

Your PH will eagle-eye you for the first couple of days, but don't take it personally. He's only protecting his last remaining eardrum from getting blown out by your "unloaded" rifle.

THE FOUR BASIC SAFETY RULES

There is no such thing as an "accidental discharge." There is a cause for every action, and **guns do not "go off" by themselves.** They must be loaded and fired by a human. When the shooter is untrained or careless — *then* occurs an ND (negligent discharge). And such can happen to the experienced.

There are only Four Rules to learn and live. You'd have to blow two of them simultaneously to cause a tragedy.

Rule 1
All guns are always loaded.
   In your mind, there is no such thing as an "unloaded" gun. You *never* handle a gun differently because it's "unloaded."
   Whenever you pick up a gun — even if you're alone and the only one handling it; even if you personally just disassembled — *check the magazine and chamber.* You could have forgotten loading it, or somebody could have handled it without your knowledge. Have *firsthand* knowledge of its condition *every* time you pick up a gun! Make this a *perfect* habit, which you will later unthinkingly perform even if you are drousy, disoriented, injured, or distracted.

Rule 2
Never let your muzzle cover anything you don't want to destroy.
   Never wave your muzzle past body parts, man or housepet. If somebody can see even a *crescent* of your muzzle, then you're being unsafe. (If a muzzle waver is indignant with your objections because his rifle is "unloaded" then demand that he instantly aim at his own foot and pull the trigger.)

Rule 3
Keep your finger off the trigger until your sights are on the target.
   Violations of Rule 3 account for 80% of gun mishaps, as people have a sympathetic muscle response when they trip or are surprised. Resting your finger on the trigger is the hardest habit to break. Your trigger finger should feel "at home" indexed straight along "armrest" of the stock or fully across the trigger guard.
   Fingers on triggers shows extremely sloppy gun handling. (When you see this, ask him what he's about to kill since he's obviously prepared to shoot *something.* Shame works.)

Rule 4
Be sure of your target and what's beyond it.
   One fellow, untrained and nervous, shot a suspected intruder hiding in the closet. It was his 16 y/o stepdaughter, skipping school. This was no "accident" — this was *negligence.*
   Rule 4 is vital when hunting. Could that bull be a cow? If your 200gr Barnes sails through, will it hit another animal?

the short version
Always ask yourself: *Where's my trigger finger? Where's my muzzle?* Keep these safe and nobody dies.

negative reinforcement
Safety violations should be *rarely* made, and *only* in the initial training.

One of General Patton's principles was that mistakes should be *paid for* instantly. Does a hot stove ever postpone burning you? Similarly, gun safety violations should be safely "painful." Make a pact with your family and shooting buddies that anybody caught violating *any* Rule immediately coughs up a $20 bill. Unsafe handling should be instantly painful to the guilty, before it's fatally painful to a *perforee*.

The life you save may be... your *own*.

in hunting camp
If anybody is unsafe (including the PH, as the Four Rules are not yet widely practiced in Africa), *speak up*! Safety is everyone's concern, so don't be shy. Refuse to hunt with somebody dangerous, no matter the embarrassment.

GUN SAFETY AND CHILDREN

Thanks to safety programs like the NRA's Eddie Eagle, negligent fatalities of children 0-14 y/o have fallen from 550 in 1975 to 200 in 1995. Though even one is too many, 200 is nearly zero considering the 40,000,000 gunowning homes. With the exception of toddlers, I believe in gunproofing children, *not* childproofing guns (which can't be reasonably done to readily accessible defensive guns). With proper safety education, guns are no more risky in your household than are gas stoves, solvents, or steak knives. Do the following:

demonstrate the destructive power of guns to children
They need to see firsthand how powerful guns are, instead of having false impressions made through TV. Shoot a can of soda or a watermelon with a high-velocity hollowpoint.

no toy guns allowed
Toy guns which are "safe" to point at others create very stubborn bad habits. Guns are serious tools requiring awesome

responsibility, and toy guns only dilute this vital issue. Take your children shooting often, and they'll never want toy guns.

if a gun is unexpectedly found, don't touch it
The child should know to leave it alone and tell an adult. Praise the child effusively for doing this.

family guns are *always* available for inspection
Eliminate the "forbidden fruit" syndrome of your guns. Face it, kids love to snoop around when their parents are away. I did, and you did. (The hideous taste of that dictionary-sized bar of chocolate always perplexed me.) Therefore, let's make the desk drawer .38 and the closet shotgun no big deal.

Make an absolute promise to your children that, *with your supervision*, they may look at and handle *any* of the family guns *at any time, if they ask first*. You promise that you will drop what you're doing, day or night, and handle the gun together. **You will do this cheerfully, *without fail*.**

Never break a promise to a child.

Once children are a little older and have proven their safe handling and responsibility, they may handle and/or shoot their guns without your supervision, but with prior permission. (In some States, children must have on their person your written permission, or they must be accompanied by you.)

Once they're in, say, junior high school, they may use their own guns as freely as their bicycles.

Once they're 18, take them to a good shooting school.

SafetyOn—a fantastic interactive teaching CD

For more instruction on the basics on gun functioning, care, handling, safety, defense, etc. — get this amazing CD which uses 3D and virtual reality. (www.SafetyOn.com)

CONDITION OF WEAPON

Knowing these Conditions will not only help you understand firearms, but they're necessary for common communication (instead of saying *"loaded"* or *"unloaded"*). There are four variables involved (chamber, magazine, hammer, and safety), and these Conditions elegantly cover their relationships.

Zero
Loaded chamber. Cocked hammer or striker. Safety disengaged (*off*). (This would *only* be used during live fire.)

One
Loaded chamber. Cocked hammer or striker. Safety engaged (*on*). (How handguns should reside in their holsters. *"Cocked and locked."*)

Two (mostly handgun applicable)
Loaded chamber. Hammer down. Safety off.

Three
Empty chamber. Loaded magazine in gun.
(Fine for home storage.)

Four
Empty chamber. Empty/no magazine. (Long-term storage Condition.)

MALFUNCTIONS

Quit saying *"My gun jammed!"* First of all, jam is found only on toast. Equipment either functions or it *malfunctions*. Secondly, we need to be specific; what *kind* of malfunction? The firing cycle of any firearm is simple and sequential:

feed	(inserting a round from the magazine into the chamber)
fire	(mechanical action causing ignition of round)
extract	(removal of case from the chamber)
eject	(removal of case from the entire firearm)

Failures can occur at any phase, and fixing them must be ingrained into your subconscious to be performed *automatically* without conscious thought. The more reliable your weapon, the more you must practice malfunction drills.

failure to feed (also called a Class 1 malfunction)
Usually the shooter short-stroked the bolt, a common thing when going to a longer throw magnum action after years of short or standard action experience. You can reduce risk of this with *lots* of practice, or by choosing one of the magnums in *standard* length, such as the .404 Dakota.

Sometimes it is the fault of the magazine (empty, fussy floorplate, or weak spring), or the ammo (case deformed).

failure to fire (also called a Class 2 malfunction)
Assuming no failure to feed, this is either an ammo or gun problem. Sometimes it's just a dirty or faulty gun (weak striker spring or broken striker). Usually it's bad ammo (bad, high, inverted, or missing primer). When under attack by an animal, do a *Rack-Bang.* When not under time pressure, eject the round after waiting out a potential hangfire for 30 seconds.

If an abnormal sound or sensation was felt upon the trigger pull, *cease firing* as it probably was a **squib load**. This is when a less-than-full-powder round was fired by the primer, often lodging the bullet mid-barrel. Check your barrel!

failure to extract (also called a Class 3 malfunction)
Sometimes a case sticks in the chamber, or a case rim rips off, or an extractor breaks. Have a broken case extractor with you, as well as a spare extractor, could salvage your hunt.

failure to eject
Bolts with internal ejectors (Savage, Browning, Remington, post-64 Win 70, etc.) can be prone to this (due to weakened spring, worn/crudded/frozen solid ejector), whereas you *rarely* see such with Mauser fixed ejectors.

A failure to eject can lead to a double feed where a round remains in the chamber with a second round pressed hard from behind (which doesn't often happen in controlled-feed actions).

This is all the more reason to insist on a rifle with robust extraction and ejection: the Mauser 98-type action. For dangerous game, this is vital.

FINAL THOUGHTS

It is completely *your* responsibility to become thoroughly skilled and safe with your rifle. If taking both light and heavy rifles, I'd urge that they be Winchester Model 70s as they operate exactly the same.

If you must *borrow* something for Africa, spend ample time behind it (especially if its safety is different, or the bolt throw longer). You'll need 300+ repetitions of dry-fire to begin to ingrain your muscle memory.

❖ 11

SOUTH AFRICA PEOPLE & CUSTOMS

understanding South African English

British English, but with African slang (often Zulu, etc.).

ablutions	bathroom activities
bakkie	("bucky") small pickup truck less than one ton
bioscope	movie theater
bonnet	hood of a car
boot	the trunk
borehole	well for water
braai	outdoor BBQ, a national pastime
caravan	trailer
chemist	pharmacy
chips	french fries
cubbyhole	glovebox
dam	reservoir
Dankie	Thank you in Afrikaans (don't use in Zululand) *Baie dankie* ("Buy a donkey") is thank you very much.
dodgy	an unreliable or hinky person or situation
donkey boiler	wood-fired water heater (electric is a *geyser*)
dustbin	(also *rubbish bin*) trash can
Eish!	exclamation meaning from *Darn!* to *Sh*t!* to *F*ck!*
flask	Thermos bottle
garage	service station with mechanic
geyser	electric hot water heater (wood is a *boiler*)
hectic	a crazy time
hire	to rent (as in a car)
holiday	vacation
Howzit?	How's it going?
Izit?	Really? Is that so?

Ja	Yes (Afrikaans)
jersey	sweater
knickers	ladies underwear
kopje/koppie	rocky dome
Kreepy Krauly	swimming pool cleaner (these enrage elephants)
lapa	where a *braai* is held, usually a round terrace with firepit
lekker	("laka") nice, pretty, great, enjoyable
lift	elevator
loo	bathroom
lounge	living room
Madiba	"Old Man" respectful universal nickname for Mandela
mozzie	mosquito
mustard sauce	a blend of mustard and mayo (take your own mustard!)
nappies	diapers
now, just	very soon (between 5-30 minutes) to soon (few hours)
now, now	almost immediately (within 1-5 minutes) to very soon
oke	("oak") a guy or bloke
paraffin	kerosene
pavement	sidewalk
petrol	gasoline
plaster	Bandaid
pudding	any sweet desert
puncture	flat tire (a *slow puncture* is an HIV positive person)
queue	(v.) to wait in line, (n.) the line in which one waits
robot	traffic light
rondavel	small round cottage or even hut
rubbish	trash
serviette	napkin
Shame!	Pity! Too bad!
SMS	to text message on your cell phone
spanner	wrench
spoor	track or sign of animal
starters	appetizers
sticky tape	Scotch tape
sundowner	evening cocktail on the veranda or by the firepit
take-away	to go order, take out
takkies	tennis shoes
TIA	This Is Africa (when things are badly snagged up)
tomato sauce	ketchup
torch	flashlight
trolley	cart (grocery, bagage, etc.)
veranda	porch
windscreen	windshield

hunting slang and terms

representative of the species   not a bad trophy but not a great one, yet deserving of congratulations

monster   a huge ram or bull, unquestionably Rowland Ward and SCI

South African races

The country is not called "the Rainbow Nation" without reason. There is no such thing as a "typical" South African.

Blacks (37.2m or 79.4%)

Those of purely African descent may be divided into two main groups, the Nguni (Zulu, Xhosa, Swazi, and Ndebele) and the Sotho (North Sotho, South Sotho, and Tswana). The northeastern Shangaan-Tsonga and Venda are different.

Whites (4.4m or 9.3%)

There are Afrikaans (descendents of the original Dutch settlers of 1600s), English (1800s settlers and occupation), and others (Portuguese, French, German, Italians, etc.).

Since the ANC took the government reins, about a million whites have left the country for the UK and Australia (Perth).

Coloured (4.1m or 8.8%)

Interracial people of Dutch and San mix. They are renowned for their humor and wine making.

Asian (1.1m or 2.5%)

Primarily Indian, first brought out to the Natal in 1860. Well established through all of South Africa.

the San

These are the Bushmen, the first inhabitants of South Africa. Racially distinct, being generally lighter in complexion with almost Mongoloid features. The quintessential hunter-gatherer, with a unique language. Bushmen are excellent game trackers. (Watch the movie *The Gods Must Be Crazy*.)

South African etiquette

Etiquette is a vital part of daily living in the multiracial South Africa, especially with its *apartheid* history. Things are quite tense between the races below the surface level, which is why everybody tries to keep the surface level extremely polite. Pay attention to all of that when you're there, and play along.

You will grease things along your way, and impress everyone as not the typical boorish American.

greetings

These are more ornate than what Americans are used to. Even on cell phones a mere *Hello* won't suffice; there has to be a:

Hello, how are you?
Hello, well, thank you, how are you?
Fine, thank you.

This verbal ritual is important amongst black South Africans, and *must* be completed before getting down to business. (When in Rome . . .) Be *sure* to adhere to it when speaking to *any* government official; the courtesy will go a long way for you.

Also, you'll notice more cheery intonation in South African English, sounding almost overdone to our ears.

black South African handshake

It's a three-part deal: conventional, then sliding to fingers pointing upwards, then back to conventional. They'll show you.

dress and clothing

Rural areas are still conservative, so tank tops and "muscle shirts" may be frowned upon.

City people often dress smartly; very casual attire is not appreciated. Neither is going to town in your dusty safari garb. Dress up a bit with nice slacks and a button-down shirt.

their loud voices

This is common, even in normal conversation.

punctuality

South Africa is not like Switzerland about this. Within 15-30 minutes is considered punctual. *You* be on time, even though the other party probably will *not*. *TIA*, remember? Things are often going haywire in Africa, and it is amazing that the place works as well as it does.

hospitality

South African hospitality is like nothing you've ever seen outside the Deep South USA. You will likely be invited to the locals' homes, and *they mean it*. In fact, if you do not visit them when passing through, they may even be rather hurt about it. Even if you're the hotel type, try to accept some invitations.

I stayed in seven different homes there, most of them friends and relatives of my PH and his wife. Everyone was simply lovely and gracious, and it made for a great trip.

as a guest
A bottle of wine is always a hit, especially if you've brought over a nice Red from California. Biltong from your hunting camp is always welcome, as it's the national snack of South Africa. If invited to a *braai* bring cold beer.

when meeting tribal leaders, or the elderly
Show perfunctory respect, but don't kiss rump, either.

drinking
South Africans drink with great gusto. At their *braais* they can get pretty funny/sloppy, but not to the point of fraternity-level inebriation. So, be prepared to hang loose and enjoy the good times, but don't get out of control.

driving
People being passed will usually pull over even to the far shoulder. The overtaker then flashes his hazard lights twice as a *Thank you!*, replied by the overtakee with a flash of his high beams. I was astonished at the consistency of this ritual, but it's part of the exaggerated courtesy used to oil race relations.

tipping (7 Rand = $1 in 2007)
Good restaurant service should be tipped 10%. (The American 15-20% is quite extravagant there.)

There are only full-service petrol stations in the RSA, and the pump "jockies" are pleasant and efficient. Tip them R1-3.

For the small oddjob, remember that the national minimum wage is R5.10/hour, so a R5 tip (70 cents to you) is an hour's wage to them. Mostly, 2-4 Rand will do.

Sometimes, however, it's good to be *very* generous. When SA had canceled my connecting domestic flight for a later one, giving me less than an hour to make my USA flight, they arranged for airport staff to run me through the whole gauntlet (usually taking at least 2 hours). Ran through we *did*. He got me to the head of the line in three crucial places, and personally loaded my rifle case onboard. I palmed him a well-deserved R50 note, which was like $40 to an American airport employee.

food

I'm partial to game, and South Africans enjoy kudu and eland as we enjoy our steaks. You won't see much pork there, but if warthog or bushpig is available it's quite the treat. Some of the veggies are unique, such as pumpkin and water lilies. If you've never before tried chutney, here's your chance. The breads are very good, and usually home baked.

Pick an outfitter whose clients rave about how the game is served. (Avoid any camp which cuts corners by serving *chicken*.)

pap (maize porridge)

Universal amongst blacks and whites, served at any meal.

fettkoek

Hard to explain, but it's sort of a bread taco/pita thing filled with rice, meat, veggies, and chutney. Delicious!

beer and wine

Outstanding! ***Urbock*** is my favorite beer (hard to find), but *Windhoek* or *Castle* or *Hansa* are fine, too.

A cheap table wine (R30/$4.50 for 1.5liter) was surprisingly good. Any medium-priced red wine will be quite nice, but your hosts can advise you further.

prices

Very little will seem expensive to an American. Petrol and groceries are about the same, but much else is cheaper. I got an excellent shampoo and style for only R60 ($9). Fixing a flat tire at *SupaQuick* was only R16 ($2). Prepaid cell minutes are R1 (14 cents), and a new SIM card R10 ($1.50). A domestic flight roundtrip to Joburg was only R800 ($115). A bar or restaurant beer is usually R5-8 (about $1), and meals aren't exorbitant (unless you're in Joburg).

Car rentals are a bit steep (compact $35/day). Ammo is *not* cheaper and neither are electronics, binos, knives, etc. If you make any significant purchases, keep your receipts and get a VAT refund at the airport before you fly home.

communication
cell phones
They are *ubiquitous*. Coverage is the best in Africa, and you can get cheap prepaid phones anywhere. (I heard that some natives spend up to 30% of their income on airtime.)

I had one during a six-week trip there (thanks AM!), and given how haywire things can go in Africa, I consider a cell phone a *must* for any hunter (especially if you're traveling on your own afterwards).

Ask your outfitter to get you a prepaid *before* you land (delivered to you at the airport through your rifle permit liaison) so you can give the number out before you fly to South Africa. It's also very handy to have it upon arrival in Joburg in case your domestic connection is screwy (count on that!).

internet
WiFi is not yet that common, but most hotels will have it. Internet cafes can be found in most larger towns. Service is not as fast as at home, and do expect to pay R40-60/hour. Not all web proxies will work with an African IP address (since many online scams originate from Nigeria and South Africa).

GPS
Commonly used by the Land Rover crowd. If you're driving about on your own, download the RSA maps. I'm an Olde School map guy, but sometimes wished for a GPS.

radio and TV
Radio stations abound, and are great fun to listen to.
TV I didn't watch once, so I'm not the guy to ask.

political hot potatoes
land reform
Any land acquired by whites after 1914 can be formally claimed by blacks alleging ancestral dispossession. My PH was forced to sell to the local tribe his family ranch (purchased by his English great-grandfather just after WWI). Fortunately for Mark, he got a pretty good price and was allowed to retain ownership of all his game. Now, he is in partnership with the tribe for his safari outfitting, and it's one of the rare working arrangements. Without the onsite experience of the white

former owners, these confiscated properties inexorably lose their income generating capacity.

"Land reform" is most upsetting to generational white farmers. Many white farmers see South Africa slowly drifting towards Zimbabwe-type confiscation, especially since all the Scandanavian funds donated for land claims have been frittered away by graft and corruption. A large avocado farm in Tzaneen purchased in 1913 (and presumably inviolate) is under dispute now.

The current wave of "land reform" is subsiding, but if envy takes increasing hold of politics it will be an easy thing to amend 1919 for 1949. Stay tuned.

theft

Stealing is rampant in South Africa. Keep your valuables secured and your bags locked at all times.

My PH runs a very harmonious camp and treats his staff extremely well (to the point of being chided for it by his white PH colleagues). Nevertheless, they steal from him. His wife had R900 taken from her purse, tools and utensils are routinely lifted, and processed meat in the butchery has to be watched like a hawk. Leave some biltong unattended and it'll be gone almost instantly. *And this is in a good camp!*

It's a *cultural* thing, as whites are believed to "owe" the blacks. Game purchased at an auction and trucked in to the ranch? To the poacher it was always *his* people's. There is no such thing there as the sanctity of private property, which spells disaster in the long run.

violent crime

Annually, there are 20,000 murders and 55,000 reported rapes. Carjacking gangs use AK47s. Nocturnal mobs terrorize the beaches and cities. Muggings occur in broad daylight. South Africa is dangerously violent if you're in the wrong place at the wrong time. Whites live in gated communities and farms behind 7000 volts of 6' electrified fence. They dash into town, quickly do their business, and then try to get home before dark.

I once missed a turnoff and drove on for a few miles out of town into a small village whose street was teaming with people. While in the middle of the day, I felt a significantly hostile buzz. Their faces were pretty easy to read: *What is he doing here?*

There is vast black animosity just below the surface and it springs up without notice. I predict rocky times ahead.

police corruption
Crime is rising for basically two reasons: the police (now generally black staffed) won't vigorously fight it, and citizens are hamstrung from defending themselves. If a PH is too rough with a poacher, the poacher walks and sues. (One poacher actually threw rocks at an armed Nature Conservancy officer who'd come to arrest him! He was fined only R500, about $70.)

HIV/AIDS
In Swaziland 40% are HIV infected, and South Africa is close behind. Several million will die in the next few years. I passed by a small local cemetery and counted over a dozen recent burials. AIDS is *rampant*.

After a decade of intense public education, *everyone* in South Africa understands that AIDS is a *behavioral* disease generally *preventable* with condoms (which are freely available). It doesn't matter. People who live in what I call "the eternal present" will not inconvenience themselves in the slightest for some theoretical future gain. Tomorrow is not guaranteed, so why sacrifice anything to it? (Especially if one could die from AIDS! Talk about a vicious circle.)

One tracker (whose girlfriend died from AIDS, and is himself showing some early symptoms), commented that using a condom is like trying to drink a bottle of water with the cap still on. AIDS amongst black Africans is a social and cultural certainty because of a gaping lack of time horizons.

Vaccines? Forget about them. AIDS is now documented as being able to mutate *from carrier to receiver*. (Imagine a lock that changed its combination every time it was opened.) AIDS is extremely complex, and its rapid mutation defies a vaccine.

Promiscuous behavior won't change, no universal vaccine can be found, so people will continue to die. Black Africa is busy depopulating itself and will look *very* different 20 years from now. In the meantime, a dying and envious people could politically wring the nation dry with a wave of socialistic theft.

illegal immigration
Millions are swarming in, from Zimbabwe and Mozambique, primarily. They will work for less wages than any South African, and are overtaxing government programs and health care facilities. (Americans living in the Southwest can certainly empathize.)

OUTLOOK FOR SOUTH AFRICA

Very *dodgy*. While the country is hard at work and its economy booming, the graft, corruption, theft, and increasingly socialistic politics are hobbling what could be a very fine country. Most whites are very gloomy about the future, and many of them plan to leave sooner than later. Without the educated managerial and professional class, South Africa will very quickly slide (as in Zimbabwe).

However, that there has been no civil war since the 1994 elections is amazing. People *are* trying to get along and forge some unity, and a black middle class *is* now emerging, but all this will remain a long uphill battle.

In summary, things weren't too bad in 2007, so I'd go hunting ASAP. Things could be much worse in five years, and certainly in 10. Get your safari in *now*. Do not wait.

METRIC CONVERSIONS

length
1 inch	=	25.4 millimeters (mm)	1 mm	=	0.03937 inch
1 inch	=	2.54 centimeters (cm)	1 cm	=	0.39 inch
1 foot	=	0.305 meter (m)	1 m	=	3.28 feet
1 yard	=	0.9144 meter (m)	1 m	=	1.094 yards
1 mile	=	1.61 kilometer (km)	1 km	=	0.6214 mile

area
1 acre	=	0.405 hectare (ha)	1 ha	=	2.47 acres
1 mile^2	=	2.59 km^2	1 km^2	=	0.3861 mile^2

weight
1 ounce	=	0.0296 liter (l)	1 l	=	33.8 ounces
1 quart	=	0.946 liter (l)	1 l	=	1.057 quarts
1 grain	=	0.06481 grams (g)	1 g	=	15.43 grains
1 ounce	=	28 grams (g)	1 g	=	0.035 ounce
1 pound	=	0.454 kilogram (kg)	1 kg	=	2.2 pounds

energy and velocity
1 ft. lb	=	1.356 joule (j)	1 j	=	0.7376 fpe
1 fps	=	0.305 meters per sec	1 mps	=	3.28 fps

temperature   C° x 1.8 + 32 = F°   (F° - 32) / 1.8 = C°

C	-20	-15	-10	-5	0	5	10	15	20	25	30	35	40	45°	C
F	4	5	14	23	32	41	50	59	68	77	86	95	104	113°	F

✦ 12
ANIMALS

names for the sexes ("buck" and "doe" not used in Africa)

ram	ewe	(all smaller than nyala)
bull	ewe	(nyala only)
bull	cow	(all larger than nyala)

female animals without/with horns; species herding?

hornless	with horns	gregarious?
kudu		yes
waterbuck		yes
nyala		yes
impala		yes
rhebuck		yes
bushbuck		no
reedbuck		no
steenbok		no
klipspringer		no
duiker, grey		no
grysbok		no
dik-dik		no
	eland	yes
	buffalo	yes
	wildebeest	yes
	gemsbok	yes
	sable	yes
	hartebeest	yes
	roan	yes
	blesbok/bontebok	yes
	tsessebe	yes
	springbok	yes
	duiker, blue and red	no

(Interesting that most horned ewe/cow species are also gregarious and herd.)

savanna/woodland diet of animals

grazers	←both→	browsers	carnivores
white rhino	Grant's gazelle	elephant	lion
waterbuck	impala	giraffe	hyena (3 species)
zebra	springbok	nyala	cheetah
roan	Thom. gazelle	bushbuck	caracal
gemsbok	klipspringer	gerenuk	African wild dog
topi	steenbok	duiker, grey	jackal (3 species)
hartebeest	eland	kudu	serval
wildebeest		black rhino	bat-eared fox
tsessebe			mongoose
warthog			genet (2 species)
reedbuck			

This is not the book for any exhaustive description of African game. There are many of those, most of them written by very experienced hunters, PHs, and wildlife experts. See the chapter Resources for a helpful list. I've encountered many during my (so far) 50 days in the bush over the course of three hunts, but not nearly everything. (Yet to see are such classic critters as hyena, springbok, cheetah, and leopard.)

For a very quick and thorough visual introduction to game, visit the Kruger National Park for 2-3 days. (Book early, especially over weekends and holidays.) While the animals are blasé, they *do* bite. (Don't expect, however, to enjoy such casual behavior during your hunt on the game ranch!)

For the following animals, after their scientific names, Afrikaans and Swahili names are usually given.

pachyderms

Rhinos belong in this section, but not in this book. If you have the money to hunt rhino, then you don't need me!

elephant (*Loxodonta africana*)   Afrikaans olifant   tembo
4-5 tons, 25mph, 22 month gestation, 1-2 young, 70yr lifespan

Capstick: "*14,000 pounds of screeching murder*"

African and Indian elephants are the last survivors of 352 species of the order *Proboscidea*, which once roamed all continents but Australia and Antarctica. (North America once had great mastodons and wooly mammoths.)

They live in a closely knit matriachal society, with an old wise cow (even post-menopausal) as the leader. Highly social, showing an odd fascination with their dead (bodies are covered with branches, or greeted; old bones are carefully investigated and even carried about).

6mph is a 10 minute mile, and elephants can do that *all day long*. Can *you*? They can run 15-20mph, and catch a fleeing human. (A sprinter's 10 second 100yd dash is 20.5mph.) Everything about elephants is large scale: a ton of inch-thick hide, a 600lb skull, a 50lb heart, and a 13lb brain. Their trunk (with 50,000+ muscles) is incredibly versatile: it can uproot trees yet pluck a single blade of grass. Females come into estrus only 2-6 days every 3-5 years.

They are very vocal, though 75% of their sounds are too low (at 14 Hertz) for us to hear, yet allows them to remain in contact up to 6 miles. (One part of a call sounds like water sloshing within a pipe.) They trumpet when trying to scare you off, but their charges are usually ears back and silent (which is all the more terrifying, according to one PH who had to stop a charging old cow). Their highly veined ears cool the blood by 5°.

They are active 16-20 hours a day, eat over 300lbs of forage, and drink over 25gal of water. Since they like lush leaves, their foraging is quite destructive of trees. They can feed higher than even giraffe.

KNP elephants go on an annual drunk with fermented *marula* fruit, with varying effects (just like people). Some just stand around in a stupor, while others turn quite vile and aggressive, smashing cars and stomping on park rangers.

Nearly every day we would encounter elephants, and it was always a thrill to see them in their own habitat. I'd ridden on elephants in India years ago, but to see African elephants in the pristine Selous was most special!

Since they have no natural enemies other than man, they must be systematically culled. They have bred up in protected areas and one may hunt them, though a costly proposition. (The KNP has 2-3x as many elephants as it can support. Instead of being culled by rangers, they could be sold to game ranches. This would help fund conservation efforts.)

Rifle: .416 400gr/2400fps at least. Your caliber must have a very high PI value, sufficient to penetrate the skull!

buffalo

While there are four species, the primary one hunted is:

Cape buffalo (*Syncercus caffer caffer*) buffel mbogo nyati
1300+lbs, 35mph top speed, 330 day gestation, 1 young, 25yr lifespan

Capstick: *"just too mean to die"*
Ruark: *"He looked at me as if I owed him money."*

Although placid if undisturbed, they are ferocious when angered. ("*Syncercus caffer*" means "joined-horned infidel") If wounded, you'll wish you had a field howitzer because they can really soak up the lead. One Afrikaans hunter remarked, "*Jy kan nooit seker wees dat 'n buffel dood is voordat sy biltong nie breekdroog is nie.*" ("You can't be sure that a buffalo is dead until its biltong is so dry that it snaps.")

They form large herds later in the season to search for water, and they feed on long grass. Masailand buff have the thickest boss. They graze 8-10 hours/day, but are sensitive to heat, so you'll most likely see them early mornings and at dusk.

Only two herds with shootable bulls were seen in the Selous, and on the first and last days. Days 2-6 were empty of old *dugga* boys. Later in the season that improved, I heard.

The closest encounter with a live buffalo I had in the Selous was an ancient cow hopelessly mired in the mud just 20' away. She was at that point just ticking hyena bait. We implored our game scout to put her down and save her the misery, but being young and green he refused.

In the Kruger, I saw many buffalo—some just 10-20' away.

Rifle: Depending on country, 9.3x62, 9.3x75R, or .375 is legal minimum, but use a .416 or .458 if you can shoot it well.

carnivores

Interestingly, there is very little prey overlap between the different predators, which reduces hunting overpressure. Even when a common animal such as impala is hunted, hyena take the newborn and cats take the adults.

lion (*Panthera leo leo*) leeu simba
440lbs, 50mph top speed, 110 day gestation, 3-4 young, 15yr lifespan

Ruark: *"Every hunter wants his first lion, and possibly his second because he is shooting at a symbol. After that you couldn't bribe him to shoot another lion unless it was in his lap."*

While there are bigger, stronger, faster, and more clever animals in Africa, the lion is quite a formidable package. It's not called "king of the beasts" without reason. They will feed every 3-4 days (usually on impala, wildebeest, zebra, and gemsbok), and eat as much as 110lbs at a sitting. Lionesses hunt in packs and do most of the killing. Most PHs don't much care for lionesses because (being fully protected by law) they become bold and confident from never having been hunted. Also, they train their cubs to hunt on domestic cattle.

Lions hunt as a team: the lionesses sneak up from downwind and form a hunting crescent within 200yds. About dusk, the male will move upwind to provide his scent, then roar to scare off the prey towards his ladies. Nice trick.

I saw only one Selous lion, a young lioness which had died the previous day from wounds sustained during a buffalo kill. It must have been quite a battle, for the KIA included her, two cow buffs, and a hyena. It had taken her a couple of days to die, and she did so lying on her left side under a fallen tree branch. Days later we came back and the hyenas had drug her off 150yds and consumed nearly all but the head (which still looked intact). The skull (or even the teeth) would have been a superb bring-back, if only it had been legal.

In Kruger Park you will see many lion, some of them feeding on kills nearby. (A favorite tactic on giraffe is to run them across a paved road where they lose their footing.)

Rifle: A .375 is the minimum gun for lion, with softs. A .416 or .458 is significantly better, according to Boddington (who's never seen a one-shot lion kill from a .375 H&H).

leopard (*Panthera pardus*) luiperd chui
150lbs, 100day gestation, 1-3 young, 15-20yr lifespan

Capstick: "*He always gleams, a perfect shimmering sheath, a mantle of magnificence over steel muscles as smoothly swirling as the tail of of a trout pool.*"

These are Africa's most secretive creatures, and quite solitary. (They only meet to mate, and then part.) They dispatch their prey quickly, severing the jugular or neck in one clean bite. Pound for pound they are strong enough to haul up trees for safekeeping their dead prey (impalas primarily, and at least one a baby elephant!). (Curiously, vultures will not touch a leopard's larder.) They are rarely active by day, and stalk/ambush hunt by night. Very aggressive when cornered, and they will attack instantly. If you botch yours, odds are 50:50 that he'll wound one of your hunting party in return.

Their cunning is legendary: they have been seen rolling in buffalo dung to disguise their scent, or leaping across dirt tracks to avoid leaving sign. They will repeatedly circle and cross over their own spoor to confuse dogs. Highly versatile in climate (deserts to mountains) and feeding (bats, fish, hyrax, birds).

Though seldom seen, they are not endangered at an estimated one animal per square kilometer. It's nearly impossible to rifle hunt them to extinction. Even when trapped, they (unlike everything else) stay calm and often pry their paw out. Their sound was described by Peter Turnball-Kemp as "*a harsh rasping, . . . as the uneven sawing sound produced by inexpert handling of a two-handed crosscut saw.*" That sound can be eerily replicated with a cardboard box, a long piece of string, and some candle wax.

They are usually baited and shot from a hide at 40yds. Sometimes they are hunted with dogs. (This means the dogs do all the actual hunting, and the hunter kills a treed leopard.)

Rifle: .308 and up, with light/fast softs and a 42+mm scope. For wounded leopards many PHs prefer 10ga shotguns with 00 buck. An attached light is a must.

african civet (*Civettictis civetta*)   siwet   fungo

I saw this beautiful spotted feline crossing a Selous road one evening. They are as large as a terrier, and stockily built. Like a skunk, they can spray a blinding musk.

caracal (*Felis caracal*)   rooikat   simba mangu

Very similar to a lynx with long, black-tipped ears (its name, in Turkish). Solitary nocturnal hunters which can vertically jump 10' to swat a bird. A very striking cat. While leading some biltong hunters for a kudu cow, we flushed a caracal focused on guinea fowl. He bounded away like a streak.

African wild cat (*Felis silvestris*)   vaalboskat   kimburu

Similar to a house tabby, often interbred. Still, it is a wild animal; Rowland Ward recognizes them. Unlike the small spotted cat, they are easily tamed and become affectionate.

hyaena, spotted (*Crocuta crocuta*) gevlekte hiëna fisi
Ruark: "*A hyena's giggle is date night in the female ward of a madhouse.*"
Fascinating animals, capable in packs of taking even lions and buffalo by running them down at 40mph (which they can maintain for two miles). Overnight they can cover 40 miles. They crunch bone for its nutritious marrow, hence white feces.
Females are 15% heavier and more aggressive (due to high levels of testosterone, manifesting in a pseudo-penis). Their clans are matriarchal and highly complicated, and males are submissive and groveling (the original "metrosexual").
I saw only a decomposed one, though heard them at camp every night as they visited our skinning shed's gut piles. Their *whooo-oop*, giggles, and snickers evoke all that is Africa.

spiral horned antelope
eland (*Taurotragus oryx*) eland pofu
1600-2000lbs, 270 day gestation, 1 young, 15yr lifespan
Masai: "*God's cattle*"
Gentle giants of the antelope world (and not aggressive even when wounded), but larger than cattle. They are all-around feeders which browse in winter and graze in summer. Can go without water for long periods. When walking they often make a clicking sound (from their hooves, not their carpal bones). Their famous "eland trot" is 10mph. That's a 6 minute mile, *all day long*. While after impala, I stalked up to a large eland herd within 30yds and enjoyed watching them for nearly half an hour.
Eland have been successfully raised as domestic meat and dairy stock in the Ukraine and in the former Rhodesia. A game ranch owner once had a pet cow eland called "Belinda" who was very protective of "her man."
Rifle: at *very* minimum 200gr .30-06. A .338 is preferred for shots past 50yds, and/or heavy cover. Be sure to aim up the *leg* vs. down from the dewlap. A quartering away shot is preferred, to avoid that massive shoulder.
My Transvaal PH remarked that at least *one-third* of all eland shot are lost. Have a powerful caliber and tough bullet, and place your shot well. (And be prepared for a long follow-up!)

kudu (*Tragelaphus strepsiceros*)   koedoe   tandala
575lbs, 230 day gestation, 1 young, 15year lifespan

    Capstick: *"sly, tricky, and smart — a man's trophy"*

    Very large and elegant antelope, their beautiful spiral horns are especially prized by hunters. They are essentially browsers, somewhat territorial, and very shy (avoiding open ground). Strong sexual dimorphism. Known for their astonishing leaping power, and can clear a 6' fence from a standing start. They are not, however, fast or graceful runners. When startled, they have a very loud hoarse bark. They drink at midday to avoid the morning/evening predators.

    Rifle: .308 and up. They have a "glass jaw" like a moose and are not as bullet-resistant as gemsbok. Even elk are tougher. Beware, however, of *kudu vudu*, as their majestic appearance has a powerful effect on the newbie. (This I know!)

nyala (*Tragelaphus angasii*)
up to 230lbs, 180 day gestation, 1 young, 15 year lifespan

    Zulu: *"the shifty one"*

    Beautiful, expensive ($3000), and rather uncommon. They stay in shady thickets and are difficult to hunt. Unlike bushbuck, they browse *and* graze. Nyala would be quite the treat for your third safari. I was fortunate to help staff a nyala hunt in 2007, though the hunter missed two of them (only from supported positions could he shoot well).

    Rifle: A .308 is plenty.

bushbuck (*Tragelaphus scriptus*)   bosbok   pongo
up to 200lbs, 180 day gestation, 1 young, 13 year lifespan

    Not a fast runner, they prefer to hide, and are territorial. Very aggressive against predators (they've been known to kill even leopards) and human hunters. They rest during the day amidst the densest cover. Their camouflage has the effect of shafts of soft sunlight. Sort of a "poor-man's nyala." They sometimes hang out with baboons for their sentinel system.

    A 21-day-hunt animal in Tanzania and very shy, we walked past the calmest and biggest one our PH had ever seen. He must have known that we couldn't touch him as he looked at us with about as much fear as a cow gaping at a freeway. Craig logged in the GPS coordinates of that 17-incher for the next guy.

In 2007, John (a tracker) and I were driving to the bushcamp lodge to check on a water leak. Though I wasn't hunting that morning, I routinely took my .30-06. As we rounded a curve I spotted an animal's shadow under a tree and noticed horns. Bushbuck! And he was a decent-sized one, too. I piled out before we'd even come to a full stop, and took that nice 14" ram. Not a 15½" Rowland Ward, but that didn't bother me in the least. Bushbuck are pretty rare, and it's always a treat to find one.

Rifle: A .308 is plenty.

ringed horned antelope
Roosevelt sable (*Hippotragus niger rooseveltî*) palapala
500lbs, 270 day gestation, 1 young

Ruark: "*my nomination for nobility, strength, and beauty*"
Capstick: "*bold, savage, and noble, . . . as gleaming, glossy, grackle-purple as waxed anthracite, with a harlequin two-toned face colouring more like war paint than markings*"

Thoroughly stunning, elegant animals. $1800 on a 21-day Tanzania hunt. Best place to hunt them is the Selous. Highly territorial (thus easier to hunt than kudu), especially at waterholes where they can displace other antelope, zebra, and even buffalo cows.

Our Selous camp's previous hunters had killed one just hours before my arrival, so I got to inspect him closely. In the field we walked into a stealthy herd of about eight, making me wish that I was on a 21-day hunt.

Rifle: .308 or .30-06, 180/200gr would be my minimum.

gemsbok (*Oryx gazella*) gemsbok choroa
500lbs, 264 day gestation, 1 young

Capstick: "*savage and stark*"

A very hardy desert antelope able to live without free water. The only rumimant with horns at birth. Its neck and nasal passages have an intricate cooling system of many extra veins, and its fur is hollow and bristly for extra insulation. Territorial, and very aggressive when surprised, cornered, or wounded. (They're called the "desert warrior.") Gregarious, and often in herds. Their distinctive black band helps to break up body shape, and reminds me of such lines painted on battleships. Gemsbok may be responsible for the unicorn legend, for when broadside they appear to be one-horned.

Not indigenous to most RSA game ranches, but they still thrive there. They are very challenging to hunt, given their keen eyesight, wariness, and endurance. Long shots typical, especially if hunted in their native Namibia. Can be difficult to sex, as they all have horns. Most animals make some quirky mistake that seals their fate (such as running elk stopping at a human's whistle). Not so with gemsbok, according to PH Mark. A spooked herd will take off, never slowing down and never looking back. Along with wildebeest and eland, hunt gemsbok in the morning, giving yourself all day to follow-up if necessary.

I hunted a very big bull for several mornings, but he would always keep 300+yds of distance, his horns gleaming in the sun like sabers. I finally caught up to him, and when I did it was a surprise for the both of us. A 40yd snapshot broke his shoulder and anchored him. He did not go down easily, a tribute to that very tough old beast. (He is the bull on this book's back cover.)

Rifle: .308 (200gr) and larger calibers.

waterbuck (*Kobus ellipsiprymnus*)   waterbok   kuru
575lbs, 280 day gestation, 1 young

With its white ring on the rump, waterbuck had to be the inspiration of Gary Larson's cartoon "*Bummer of a birthmark!*" Coats are shaggy and coarse, which is expected from an animal that hangs about in reed beds and marshes. Not marathon runners, and fairly easy to hunt (makes a fine trophy). Musky smelling (thus generally avoided by predators), but the meat can be prepared to taste much better than its reputation, even to the equal of kudu (I kid thee not). The trick is not touching the meat with your skinning hand.

I'd like a nice trophy bull, as they are beautiful animals. They are good practice to hunt before your kudu.

Rifle: A .308 is plenty, as waterbuck are not hardy.

blesbok (*Damaliscus dorcas phillipsi*)   blesbok

A subspecies of the nearly extinct bontebok (now breeding up on private ranches), but not quite as brilliant in color. Another one of cartoonist Gary Larson's favorite critters.

The ranch had a small herd of seven blesbok, and Mark kindly gave me to permission to hunt any of the ewes. He described the general area where they were most often seen, and off I went with my .30-06 Win 70. Working upwind for a mile toward their favored locale, I stalked up to a large kudu bull who barked in surprise and ran off. Not hunting kudu then, this was great fun and made my morning. I gave the area a few minutes to settle down from the indignant kudu, adjusted my track slightly to veer off from his and resumed my patient trek upwind.

I prefer to hunt solo no later than mid morning, while the tree shadows are long, in which I pause every 50yds or so. As I quietly move from shadow to shadow, I constantly pan full left to right, viewing new gaps between the terrain for animals. Simply moving forward 20 feet can uncover game previously behind cover. (This, of course, also works in reverse as they can now see you.) With this technique, I've come up within mere feet of duiker, steenbok, eland, and once even flushed a caracal nearly within arm's length.

Spotting movement, I slowly crouched down and used my excellent Shepherd 8x42s. Several animals were milling around, about 100yds ahead. Though impala-sized, they were not quite impala-colored. Their actions were also rather curious. Then, I got a glimpse of some glossy purple sheen. The blesbok herd! There was plenty of cover, so I managed to move laterally with them as I anticipated a small clearing they would reach. The wind was still in my face as I sat down in a tree shadow, looped up in my self-fashioned Ching sling, controlled my breathing, and snicked off the safety.

The large purple-bellied blesbok was obviously the ram, but I hadn't permission for him — only the ewes (which were quite a bit smaller, and without that stunning purple sheen, alas). This wasn't a huge disappointment as it was all about the hunting experience vs. an incidental trophy. The 125yd shooting gap to them was fairly narrow, and I had to wait until one of the ewes was completely clear of her friends as I knew that 200gr Barnes TSX would sail clear through such a small animal. Finally, I had a shot at one, slightly quartering toward me at target angle 300°. I set the Shepherd 310-P2 scope at 5x, focused the 100yd reticle circle just behind the shoulder for a clean lung shot, let out my last breath, and squeezed off 40 ounces of crisp Winchester trigger.

I called it a perfect shot, and the *Kugelschlag* confirmed a solid hit. As her herd scattered, she ran off behind some brush.

I knew she wouldn't go far. The blood trail was more like a bloody pulp trail from that 200gr TSX. I found her just 30yds away, stone dead — illustrating the superior value of exit wounds (vs. the bullet ending up "*under the hide of the far shoulder*"). I'd hit exactly where I'd aimed, and that 200gr TSX went straight through, taking lots of tissue with it. For .308 and .30-06, I am heartily sold on a 200gr bullet.

The blesbok ewe was a very nice animal, cleanly killed. I was very happy with the morning's hunt, though it was briefly marred by learning from Mark that *the entire herd were ewes.* What looked like their ram was only the largest and most colorful ewe! (He'd previously remarked in passing that his blesbok were "*all lesbians*" so he'd naturally thought that I'd gleaned no ram amongst the seven. For me, this again emphasized the importance of confirming the intel beforehand!) In time I could have shot that big purple ewe. I quickly got over the matter and soon we were laughing about it. As I said, hunting is about the experience not the trophy. That morning stalk was a fine one indeed, regardless of the smaller ewe. I felt that way then, and I still feel that way now.

impala (*Aepyceros melampus*)   rooibok   swalapala
120lbs, 195 day gestation, 1 young, 12yr lifespan

Ruark: "*coat like a new penny*"

Beautiful herd animals, and challenging to hunt a trophy ram. (As canny and unpredictable as whitetail deer.) Capable of leaping 30' from a standstill. Many predators prefer impala. Your PH will likely begin your hunt with one, to judge your fieldcraft and rifle work.

Impala liver, hams, and filets are especially delicious.

gnu (wildebeest)
wildebeest, blue
(*Connochaetes taurinus*)   blouwildebees   nymbu
550lbs, 260 day gestation, 1 young, 20yr lifespan

Theodore Roosevelt: "*queer, fiery, eccentric*"

Called the "clowns of the veld" with their noisy, inquisitive, and comical behavior. Highly gregarious, forming large herds. Excellent peripheral eyesight, and thus often herd with zebra (with great hearing) for mutual benefit. They prefer short grass because it's more nutritious, and provides less cover for predators. Unlike zebra, wildebeest drink muddy water. Their loping gait is faster and more efficient that a trot.

He was #3 on my Selous list after buff and zebra, and the only possible stalk I had on them was when they were mixed with a zebra. So, I had to choose, and the zebra "won."

In the Transvaal, I got a bull and a cow, both one-shot kills from my .308 Savage Scout with 180gr.

Rifle: at least .308, for these are renowned for their toughness. Using your buffalo rifle on them is not overkill.

wildebeest, black (*Connochaetes gnou*) **swartwildebees**
350lbs, 260 day gestation, 1 young, 20yr lifespan

Aggressive and unwary, they used to teem in great numbers with the (now extinct) quagga, but were nearly hunted out by Boer farmers. Less than 1,000 survived as recently as 1948. Private game ranches and preserves have allowed a modest comeback to 12,000+, and they can now be hunted.

Their forward-positioned horns are easily distinguishable from the blue wildebeest, and they have a white tail. Their name "gnu" comes from the Hottentot word derived from the animal's *ga-nu* snort.

hartebeest

Many varieties abound: Coke, Jackson, Kenyan, etc. The Hunter's hartebeest is nearly extinct, however. None are considered handsome, or with desirable horns, but they are still good to hunt and eat.

Lichtenstein (*Signoceros lichtensteinii*) **kongoni**
300lbs, 40mph, 240 day gestation, 1 young, 13yr lifespan

A fairly large, inquisitive antelope. They are essentially grazers, but browse occasionally. Most common in East Africa, and rare elsewhere. Mature bulls are territorial.

Why this ubiquitous and homely guy fetched $558 vs. $480 for the uncommon and handsome Nyasa wildebeest I cannot fathom. Was only #4 on my Selous list, but the first shootable animal I encountered so I'd little choice but to take him. We spotted a herd of does and stopped so I could position myself for a shot if a bull appeared. Within a minute he bounded down the hill with a *Now just what the hell is going on here?!* attitude. His demeanor was all male, and made him easy to sex. He turned straight on toward me, exposing that very narrow chest at 96yds. From the shooting sticks, I pulled the shot slightly to the left into his shoulder, but he was damaged enough to run just 25yds and then lay down for a follow-up shot.

They really are a more handsome animal than pictures indicate, with very thin backskin stripes. Their almond eyes are similar to a goat. Though their legs are rather skinny, they are fleet (42mph in short bursts) and have a nice lope. They make a very unique sound, a short sneeze-snort (very similar to the sable). My bull was good sized with nice markings, and I was grateful for him.

Rifle: same remarks as the wildebeest, though hartebeest aren't *quite* as tough. A .308 will do nicely.

Red (*Alcelaphus buselaphus*)   rooihartebees

By 1875, they were nearly extinct, but they were saved in time. My Transvaal game ranch was teeming with them, but I'd other animals way ahead on my list. Besides, the price for one was nearly that of a wildebeest.

misc. antelopes
steenbok (*Raphicerus campestris*)   dondoro

The only antelope which buries its urine and dung. Quite diminutive, with impala-like coloring. They flush only at the last moment, dash away, but often stop briefly to look back (there's your chance). Very delicious!

In 2007 I got a decent ram from an 80yd offhand shot with my Shepherd zoomed up to 10x (in order to verify horns, since I'd no permission for a ewe). It was the only shot whence I used Cooper's "compressed break" of trigger. The .30-06 Barnes 200gr TSX soared through from left shoulder to right ham, damaging little meat.

duiker, grey (*Sylvicapra grammia*)   gyrs duiker   naya

"Diver" in Afrikaans, for their propensity to dart into heavy undergrowth and hide. There are many species, and often they are hunted by shotgun. Very wary and nervous, and difficult to hunt. They dress out at under 20lbs, but are delicious.

pig
warthog (*Phachoerus aetheopicus*) vlakvark ngiri
Capstick: "*His warts were as big as Irish potatoes.*"
As a favored prey of all hunters, it is a happy thing that warthogs are plentiful. Big boars can weigh up to 250lbs. All have tusks and warts, but only the males have a smaller second pair of warts just above the tusks. Diurnal and free wandering, they are great fun to hunt! They are the easiest to poach (smoked out of their holes and then speared), and the most sensitive to drought (they need daily water).

Only two were seen in the Selous, and those at a great distance running flat out with their tails antennae-straight (so that others can follow in the tall grass).

In the Transvaal, however, I had great success with a big tusker shot just after breakfast from atop the lodge's *kopje*. A 100yd shot as he walked slowly, and nicely captured on film. The next year I shot a big sow for camp meat.
Rifle: A .308 is plenty.

bushpig (*Potamochoerus porcus*) bosvark nguruwe
They travel in sounders of 20-50 head, and can be *very* aggressive. They feed on ag crops (sugarcane, maize, potatoes) and thus farmers consider them pests. Also hunted in riverbeds and forests. Very challenging.

It is a favorite prey of leopard, spotted hyena, and natives. Bushpig ribs and smoked ham are too delicious for words.

In 2007 I swatted a monster boar in the tall grass with my Marlin .45-70, but just two inches high (having underestimated its size). He ran off like a locomotive, even though that 300gr TSX left a gaping exit wound. We tracked the 100kg beast nearly all day, but lost him after he returned to the riverbed, strong as ever and his wound closed up.
Rifle: .308 and larger.

misc. mammals
baboon, olive nyani
Though only a $132 trophy fee, they are 21-day Selous hunt critters. Weird. We saw them about every other day. They are very active creatures dripping with personality that makes chimpanzees look comatose. It was fun to scope them for

a dryfire. Small, fast, and unpredictable, they would be very challenging to hunt. (A .308 Scout rifle would be ideal!) Because of their inaccessible roosts, sentinels, and guards, only leopards have much success (and even then, a big male baboon can kill a leopard).

Their social structure is complex and fascinating. I once heard a great story: a hunter had snuck in past a sentinel and got a successful shot. Short afterwards, he witnessed the troop severely thrashing the baboon who allowed it on his watch!

baboon, chacma (*Papio ursinus*)   kaapse bobbejaan

This southern Africa variety is larger than the eastern olive baboon. Troop size is 38 on average. Their distinctive booming cry of *WA-hoo!* you'll never forget. Considered pests, they are often culled by farmers (though this is somewhat frowned upon by officials). I've an invitation to a large farm to clean out some baboon and bushpig, and can't imagine a more enjoyable time behind a hunting rifle.

zebra, Burchell's (*Equus burchelli*) bontkwagga   quaaga
650+lbs, 375 day gestation, 1 young, 20yr lifespan

Is this a
dream,
a child of the snooze?
What's captured in
scope,
seen only
in
zoos.

Also called Plains zebra. The northern varieties have not the tan "shadow stripes" of the southern African zebras.

They are of the *equus* family, but are different from any horses you're familiar with. Highly sociable, and one of the few African animals which really learns from experience. Very intelligent, and quite a challenge to hunt if they've caught your wind. (They can be domesticated and ridden, but spook too easily at scent of lion to be useful in the *veld*.) Their lush "butterfat" condition is because they drink water every day, and can graze short grass by using their front teeth (vs. other herbivores which tongue-push grass into the mouth).

They are active in the cool of mornings and late afternoons, and don't stray far from clean water. They can be difficult to sex, but the male's behavior will be a strong clue (such as taking the lead when approaching waterholes).

I saw them nearly every day in the Selous, but they were usually running in herds 200yds away. In the Limpopo game ranch they are plentiful and good hunting. Zebra are very wary and intelligent, and easily spooked by your scent. Good fighters, they are no easy prey.

They don't make any sounds like a horse, but thrice emit a very odd high-pitched warbling *KWA-ha!* bark during contact with other zebra. They have five other calls: a two-syllable alarm, a loud snort when entering potentially dangerous areas, a long snort of contentment, a short and high squeal when hurt, and a foal's long wail of distress.

They generally graze, but will browse for nutrition. Their stripes are surprisingly effective camouflage, and help individual animals become indistinct in herds (which confuses predators). They also help conceal the animals at twilight (especially in thin cover). They herd with wildebeest because lions prefer the latter (and the wildebeest haven't caught on).

It was an odd sensation for me to hunt zebra, their being obviously a horse. I may hunt a southern variety (with its "shadow stripes"), and then call it quits.

The quagga was a dark-rumped zebra hunted to extinction south of the Orange River by 1878 by European settlers for grain bags and water carriers. It's slowly being bred back through the residual genetics of the Cape Mountain zebra.

Grevy's zebra are as big as horses, but cannot be hunted in their native Kenya.

Rifle: Zebras are *amazingly* tough (can often fight off a lion attack), so the .308/.30-06 is absolute minimum. You're not overgunned with a .375 or even .416. One-shot kills are uncommon, and even though I perfectly placed a .416/400gr behind the shoulder for a high heart/lung shot at just 80yds, my stallion did not drop "*as if poleaxed.*" Rather, he reared up and spun around, kicking for several seconds. (Hamlet took longer to expire.) From a .416 Rem Mag!

Since their hides take longer to prepare, try to take your zebra early on. Your skinners will appreciate this.

giraffe (*Giraffa camelopardalis*)   kameelperd   twiga
From the Arabic *xirapha* ("one who walks swiftly"). The Latin *camelopardalis* means shape/size of a camel, but with leopard spots. They walk by swinging both same-side legs forward at the same time. (A trait shared only by three others: okapi, gerenuk, and camel.) They have 7 cervical vertebrae like other mammals. (They also have a larynx, contrary to myth.) Males don't bend their necks while feeding. They never lie flat on the ground, and rarely sleep. Up to 8 subspecies exist, such as Reticulated, Kenyan, Southern, Baringo, etc.

Since the brain is 10-12' from the pump, a giraffe heart is quite the device: 25lbs, two feet long, with walls as thick as 3". The pressure equalization apparatus is unique: a spongy complex of small arteries (the "wonder net") prevents overpressure from harming the brain, and blood returning to the heart is allowed to pass through the jugular vein via a series of one-way valves. Engineering. Pure *engineering*. (Macro evolution my rump!)

"*Say, Ted, why do you keep blacking out?*"
"*Well, it's because my 'wonder net' and one-way valved jugular never evolved like yours did.*"
"*Bummer, Ted!*"

Rifle: none, I would hope. Giraffe are so docile that there is no hunting involved, just *killing*. My Transvaal PH had fourteen, and I walked to within 50yds of them routinely. Mere killing is wrong, especially something as beautiful and unique as giraffe. Their cantering is simply poetic.

porcupine (*Hystrix spp.*)   ystervark   nunguri
African porcies have much fatter quills than ours, and they are often seen dislodged along their trails. I never hunted one, given our old admonition of *Never shoot a porcupine*, though they are *superb* eating. Nocturnal and rarely seen.

rock hyrax (*Procavia capensis*)   dassie   pimbi
Diurnal 5-10lb critters, usually seen basking on rocks. Their footpads have sticky secretions for climbing, and their very tough skins are preferred for rugs (*kaross*). They are said to be the only animals able to stare at the sun. The natives find them very good eating.

birds

ostrich (*Strutho camelus*)   volstrius

Capstick: *"thoroughly sporting . . . they will kick your gonads through the top of your hat any time, given the chance"*

Sharp-eyed, wary, and 8' tall. There is no sneaking up on an ostrich, and there's no outrunning one, either. Animals such as wildebeest use ostriches as an early warning system. Boddington describes them as good anti-poaching patrol on fencelines.

Females do the courting, and males can roar like a lion. Eggs are the size of cantelope, equivalent to 20 chicken eggs.

I had the rare fun of stalking up within 20 yards of three ostriches, but they were all hens and I wanted a male. They were pecking for food like chickens, to my amazement. When the wind shifted they hiked up their skirts and ran a full 400yds before even looking back. A half hour later they again saw me at a distance, and this time they ran a half mile. Very challenging to hunt, and their leather is of excellent quality.

Rifle: .308 and up. Use a fast, explosive soft, and aim for center of body.

crowned guinea fowl   taretaal

Large, highly nervous birds, with a strong-tasting meat.

francolin   fisant

An African partridge. Fun hunting and great eating.

Natal (orange legs)	kwali-KWALI-kwali
Swainson's (orange face)	krrraaak-krrraaak-krrraaak
Crested (black skullcap)	kwerri-kwetchi (*"beer and cognac"*)

hadeda ibis

Their insane *ha-ha-HA* chatter always cracked me up. I do a good hadeda impression, so ask me if we ever meet.

grey lourie (*Corythaixoides concolor*)   "go-away bird"

The bane of hunters. They are infamous for following your stalk from treetop to treetop with their raucous *Kweh!* I've seen them ruin several approaches of mine. It will happen to you. If you blast one with your rifle, your PH will understand. A slingshot might be just the medicine for them.

When you can stalk with such stealth that not even go-away birds notice you, you're getting pretty good.

ox-pecker (*Buphagus erythrorhynchus*) *"tick-bird"*
These birds drop suddenly upon a herd of animals (often buffalo) for a symbiotic snack. Thus, they can pinpoint your prey's location. Listen for their *ksssss-ksssss* sound.

venomous bushveld snakes

None move faster than 13mph, so any athletic person can outrun them. The puff adder accounts for most snake bites. Venoms vary: cytotoxic (destroys local tissue), hemotoxic (a blood poison), and neurotoxic (paralyzes nerves).

	length	shy?/excitable?	poison
Puff adder	5'	slow	cytotoxic
Black mamba	10'	excitable	neurotoxic
Snouted cobra	5'	slow	cytotoxic
Mozambique spitting cobra	4'	slow	cytotoxic
Rinkhals	3'	slow	cytotoxic
Boomslang	5'	shy	hemotoxic
Vine snake	4'	shy	no antivenom!

In my 50 some odd days in Africa, I saw only *one* snake: a nonvenomous rock python (constrictor). In short, I wouldn't really worry about snakes. Your PH will advise when entering any snake-risk area. You can wear snake-resistant gaitors, but you'll be the only one on your block (unless hunting with Europens, who are terrified of snakes).

❖ 13

CAMP LIFE

I am always amazed when I think of how much living can be compressed into a tent settlement . . . . It takes fifty minutes to set it all up, and the next day it bears the earmarks of a thriving city. Somehow it suddenly becomes logical to go to the john in a canvas cell and to wash your dirty body in a canvas coffin, in water full of living things, and to sleep soundly with hyenas tripping over the tent ropes.
— Robert C. Ruark, *Horn of the Hunter* (1954), p. 52

Since Cornwallis Harris first made the analogy in 1839, hunters have observed that a safari is like a ship going to sea, self-contained and surrounded by an ocean of nature.
— Bartle Bull, *Safari: A Chronicle of Adventure* (1988), p. 128

SOUTH AFRICAN GAME RANCH

Jagplase vary considerably in size and luxury; all sell game meat commercially. Some have large suites, with many staff members. I prefer a more basic environment, which seems more in tune with hunting.

My outfitter was a fairly modest family affair which could accommodate only a few hunters at a time. During my stay, I was the only client. Mark guides just 20 hunts/season, and remains booked a year in advance. A family ranch since just after WWI, when his grandfather bought it. They originally raised cattle, but transformed it into a game ranch not long ago (as have many other cattle ranchers).

They have a connected side business using their ranch as an ecological camp for UK students (most of them quite liberal).

After a few weeks, these kids understand that hunting is a valid and honorable part of Life and Death, and that modern conversation of wildlife depends mostly upon hunting.

The property had a main lodge building (with an upstairs bedroom), a swimming pool (closed in August, a paradox for a Northern Hemispherean), a separate family home, and processing buildings. My *rondavel* efficiency had a kitchenette, bathroom, and three beds. It was no more fancy than any decent motel room, but that's all I needed. (Prince William was once a guest there in 2001 for wingshooting.)

Mark and Lisa have two young daughters, and I brought some toys and trinkets over for them. After a few days, it felt as though I was hunting with a family vs. a commercial outfitter. (They all struck a proper balance since I *was* the client, and never were informality and friendship excuse for sloppiness.)

The meals were informal, but always excellent. I especially enjoyed the backyard BBQ (*"braai"*). The daily rate included reasonable quantities of beer and wine (which I never exceeded), and I was often treated to a cocktail or shot of Scotch. Regarding biltong, I probably skirted close to gluttony, but I *had* warned them about that in advance! (I easily ate a pound of it a day. Just the thing to snack on in the field, especially when it's your own wildebeest.)

The hunting was fairly easy (compared to the Selous), although we did walk 8 hours per day (7-11AM and 2-6PM). The scenery could have been central Arizona, and while it was not *quite* as evocative of Africa (as was the Selous with hyenas and wild elephants and tented camps and charter flights), the ranch was always pleasant to hunt. Temperatures were a perfect 80° or so, and without any mosquitoes.

owner/PH

I fortunately had the chance to meet him six months before, when he was in the USA for SCI. A relaxed and cheerful fellow, I liked him at once, and basically committed to a 10-14 day safari. Arrangements with him were simple and straightforward, and he delivered exactly what he promised. I enjoyed the experience so much that I returned the next year, staying for a month as a hybrid client/staff member.

Mark's fieldcraft and knowledge were exemplary. (His Shangaan tribal nickname is "*the hunter*.") He knew his game stock quite well, and had a real sense for where a particular animal could be found. Hardy as a goat, and always cheerful, he made every day seem a boy's adventure.

A real bonus to my hunt were his working dogs and wingshooting at day's end. I'd bought a Japanese copy of the fine Winchester 101 O/U 12 gauge, but had yet to take it afield. I hadn't done much bird hunting, and my high-school days of skeet shooting were long past, but it all came back to me. Also, this was the first time I'd ever worked with pointers, and now I can understand the addiction! Some outfitters charge $1/bird, but Mark's quail, francolin, and guinea fowl were on the house.

The only friction we ever had was early on, when we were still learning each other's styles. We'd come on several bull kudu in thick cover, and snuck up within 10yds of them. Mark pointed out the proper bull for me to shoot, praising its size. It walked about 20' behind some trees and emerged. Mark then commented on it again, but in a way which led me to believe that it was a *different* kudu, causing me to delay my shot until I reconfirmed. They ran off by the time I was back on the trigger. In fairness to Mark, I was also rather tense during my first crack at kudu, when a quick snapshot would have settled matters. Close up, these elk-size antelope and their 50+" horns can instill "kudu fever" in most hunters. And we were about as close to kudu as you can get without touching them. (Later, when I took 100yd and 150yd shots at a very large 52½" bull, it was *kudu vudu* all over again!)

We discussed it walking back to the Rover, and I explained that what I needed from a PH is a *very* clear series of *brief* communications, in which the correct animal was indisputably identified to me (ignoring all others). Once he knew that I was on the same animal and had given me a green light to fire, I preferred no more communication unless some reason for cease fire. With a bit of practice, we developed a system, almost fighter pilot-like in its precision and brevity, which is what I needed in order to enter and remain in my "bubble" while taking a shot.

Mark is a renowned expert on grasses, and lectures annually at an American university. Knowing the local botany will give you, the hunter, an edge on where game will likely be, what brush can be more reliably shot through, etc.

Mark's wife, Lisa

Between homeschooling and running the camp, this was a very busy lady! She had two African gals to help, but the three of them took care of all camp needs. Lisa is an excellent game cook, and her menu was always a pleasure. Though not a hunter herself, she had a fine tracking eye for blood spoor, which I regrettably had to employ one early morning.

head tracker

Herbert was a great fellow with a brilliant sense of humor. Always cheerful and hard-working, he really proved himself when we had to follow-up from 7AM to 2PM my botched kudu. He had a phenomenal game eye, and superb hunting instincts. A very solid team member with whom I daily looked forward to being afield. Except for the certification, he's practically a PH.

skinners

A Wyoming friend of mine with a lot of hunting experience saw my safari photos and remarked at the quality of skinning my animals showed. I agree. John was quite expert, and took pride in his fine work.

PH's nephew, Nigel

Nigel was the 15 y/o son of Mark's brother, recently emigrated from the failing Zimbabwe to the (also failing) UK. He annually spends six weeks at his uncle's game ranch, to hunt and lend a hand. He filmed many of my shots, and having a dedicated cameraman is a real treat (unless you're shooting like crap). A great kid and an accomplished hunter with bow and .308. (He beat me out on baboon and bushpig, *argh*.) Nigel was a great asset to my hunt, and is clearly PH material. There's nothing more he loves than to be in the field. Maybe in a few years he'll be guiding his *own* clients.

the girls, Carissa and Daniella

These two little clowns always brightened the day. Their sweet and innocent nature confirmed that country life is the only way to properly bring up quality children. Carissa recently caught her own fish, shot her first impala, and loves the *veld*. Dani seems destined for a comedy career with her astonishing wit and imagination. (*"Dani, I never said that!"* exclaimed Carissa. 5 y/o Dani replied, *"No, but you were thinking it!"*) Quite a pair, those two.

TANZANIAN TENT CAMP

> *The longest journey you will make is from the cessation of shooting light until you arrive in camp, where a hot bath, a hot fire, a cold martini, a hot dinner and a warm bed await you.* (161)
> — Robert Ruark's *Africa*

They will vary in quality, though generally not as luxurious as the South African fixed camps in private ranches. To me, a tented camp *means* a true safari.

My camp in the Selous exceeded all expectations. I'd have been perfectly fine with dirt floors and outhouses, but the dining room and tents had *concrete* floors. Behind each tent (there were three) was a private outdoor shower and *flush* toilet. An 8' thatched wall gave ample privacy. Each tent had a pair of single beds with nightstand tables.

Such camps take 20 men two weeks to construct, and would last for at least 2 seasons. My camp was built next to a stream for its ample water (20gal hot showers!), but was quite far from our hunting areas (which took 30-90min of driving). PH Craig had in mind a more central location for the next camp, and I hope to see that happen.

Each morning would begin at 5AM with the start-up of the 8kW Honda generator, which would crank up the overhead lightbulb I had fallen asleep to the night before without turning it off. A couple of minutes later, a camp boy would come by with a pitcher of hot shaving water and a "*Good morning.*"

An ample breakfast of sausage and eggs was served at 5:30AM, with plenty of coffee, juice, fruit, and second helpings. Then, back to the tent briefly for any last-minute personal business before we drove out at 6:15 or so. The camp staff assembled to see us off with best wishes for a successful hunt.

We usually had a packed lunch in the field from noon to about 2PM, except for when I'd twice taken my animals nearby and in the mornings. Those times we headed back to camp to drop off the animal, and stayed for lunch. It was odd to see the place in the daylight as we normally left and returned at dark.

After the day of hunting we'd get back between 8 and 10PM. We would shower (prepared in minutes), then have drinks and snacks around the campfire before dinner. (This was my favorite time, and it was always too short.) There we'd recount the day and bask by the warm fire in clean clothes with a delicious drink. (I taught our head waiter, Alberto, a new drink, called the *Colaschoppa*, a sort of shandy made 50:50 from cola and beer. Quite a thirst-quencher I learned of in Germany years ago. Use a good ale, as the lagers don't work as well.)

Dinner always began with some delicious soup. Our chef had been well-trained, so I expect every one of their camps serve fine meals. Our chef, Vitarus, commanded quite a field kitchen with an astonishing collection of utensils, spices, and other gear. He was an absolute magician. In the Land Rover back to camp each night I'd be licking our chops over what scrumptious meal would be waiting for us. I ate some of all of my game, and the zebra was a knockout winner.

Then, I'd shuffle off to bed — tired, fed, clean, and blissful. Though I tried to read a bit every night, the most I got through was about 3 pages before I was out. There was no time to keep a journal or do much of anything else but hunt.

Camp service was *splendid*. I rarely had to ask for a thing as all needs were well-anticipated. One evening it began to drizzle (rare for early September), and getting back to my tent I was pleased to see that somebody had meanwhile thought to bring in all my shower things from outside. During the days, tents were swept, beds made, water bottles replaced, and the laundry was done. I had brought only one bandana (which I used daily), so they kindly washed and pressed it every evening during dinner. And every day during our absence there were a few guys guarding the tents from random marauders.

In summary, I was quite stunned with the quality of experience at camp. If it could have been more pleasant, comfortable, or memorable, we don't know *how*. Camp manager Jackson and his crew were simply top-notch. And they were, to a man, *genuinely* friendly and kind.

PH

Craig was a young and hardy South African with a good sense of humor, and fine fieldcraft. He never tired at answering questions. Months later, back home, I was embarrassed that my hunting partner "friend" claimed Craig's elephant. (I've done what I can to rectify that.)

driver

James was a Toyota Landcruiser man, and had little experience with a diesel Land Rover. Every time he overrevved it, Craig would mutter *"There goes another 0.3mm of metal!"* By hunt's end, he began to acquire the touch and impress even Craig with his gentle shifting.

head tracker

Ebony seemed a bit sullen at first, but warmed up later. He had a *phenomenal* eye for spotting game from the Rover, and a gift for tracking them. Only once was he (and the rest of us) fooled by an old *dugga* boy who had doubled back on his tracks, thus wasting an hour of our afternoon. I found his weakness for lemon drops, the only time I saw him smile.

Our PH had a fine game eye, but Ebony was better still. Be sure your crew has an *exceptional* native tracker. He will make all the difference on those difficult hunts.

junior tracker

Still green and prone to dead-end meanderings, he redeemed himself on the last day by spotting a herd 250yds off in the bush that none of us had seen. We made sure to praise him well. Not a great tracker, but he was helpful in other ways and always cheerful. Well dressed — *dapper*, even. With his bandana worn as a sort of ascot, we called him "007." When he goofed, we'd subtract a few points and he'd then be "004." (Once, he became "-001", but got back into the positives later.)

game scout

In Tanzania a game scout must accompany each hunt. I didn't expect much daily help from such a guy in brush clearing, tracking, etc., but our fellow pitched in regularly.

Green and somewhat a stickler for the regs, he carried a really beat Mauser 98 ("Safari DeLuxe" mfg. unknown) in .375 with about the worst bore I'd ever seen. (Once, a twig got lodged in the muzzle and somebody whispered that the bore was *so* bad, things were now *growing* out of it! This was during an intense stalk, and it was all we could do to not crack up.) An issue rifle from the game department, but some previous hunter had left him with a box of Federal solids. Africa is all about the contrasts.

OTHER PHs & RANCHES

In 2007 I had the great opportunity to help out on that Limpopo game ranch and get in some hunting of my own when time allowed. I joined many hunting parties to track spoor, glass for game, form a beater line, find wounded game, arrange trophies for photos, drive the Rover, and skin animals. We had all types of hunters: American, European, and South African. Novices and pros, young and old. It was a most enlightening experience.

Some Americans made me proud, while a boorish clan from Omaha were an embarrassment. The Europeans were generally OK, except for a tape measure trophy-maniac from Spain. The South African biltong hunters were pretty competent, and the most fun.

We hunted also on two other game ranches:

game ranch #2

After spending a day on this grossly overpopulated and overgrazed 1000 acre property, I am forever down on hunting from towers. The ranch was a small rectangle just 800yds wide, with elevated watchtower blinds every 300yds down the 2500yd middle. The overnumerous wildebeest, impala, blesbok, and eland would be sent from one end of the property to the other in a continuous panic. The "hunters" up in 30' high towers would blast away at whatever ran within range, like Whitman in the U.T. Tower in 1966. They wounded and lost nearly as many as they killed, and what they killed was generally poorly done. (All this was excused as a "culling" operation, by the way.)

My PH was there to assist, and his wealthy European client took a shot at a previously wounded wildebeest as the herd passed by. He then opened up on a *second* wilde, taking four shots over 10 minutes to finally kill it. At each shot it would go crashing down, only to weakly get up a minute later. (180gr .30-06 Nosler Partitions are *not* up to Africa. Very poor performance.) It was utterly heartwrenching to watch, and toward the end I very nearly finished it off myself from 300yds away but it had finally leaked out. I walked up to it, finding a puddled sieve of a wildebeest, which rose my disgust to a new level. Out of respect for my PH friend, I said nothing to his client, but my face and body language spoke volumes.

Meanwhile, the first wounded wildebeest had limped off. It took eight of us several hours to find it again. During the follow-up I once raised my rifle at it since it was a multi-hunter wounded animal, and thus fair game for the camp to finish off as quickly as possible. The client tried to block my shot thinking that he had sole right to the poor creature.

What really angered me was the partying afterwards by all these "hunters" who were totally oblivious to the obscene carnage and gross lack of sportsmanship. Many animals had been wounded by multiple shooters. (From then on I called that ranch "Slaughterhouse Five." I will never be a part of anything like it again.)

game ranch #3

This was for a nyala hunt, with my PH friend again guiding "Mr. Wildebeest." This ranch was neither overpopulated nor overgrazed, and the client began to understand what true *hunting* was all about. (No more rapid fire from elevated towers.) Due to his lack of experience from improvised field positions, he missed two nyala bulls over two days. (The gods of the hunt do have a memory, it seems.)

It was a treat to see nyala for the first time!

TAKE YOUR RIFLE *EVERYWHERE!*

Do not be fooled by your camp's artificial oasis of comfort and civilization. You're in the middle of the African wilderness. Wilderness means *wild*. Critters large and small are prone to pass through, often quite unexpectedly. So:

> When in the bathroom, lean your rifle in the corner.
> When dining, rest your rifle in the rack.
> At the evening campfire, have your rifle within arm's reach.
> When retiring for the night, lay your rifle just under your bed.
> **Your rifle goes where you go, 24/7!**

Unless you are actually in the field in Condition One (loaded mag and chamber, safety engaged), everywhere else your rifle should be in Condition Three (empty chamber/loaded magazine). Your PH may insist on an opened bolt in camp, at least until he feels comfortable with your safe gunhandling.

YOU & THE CAMP STAFF

You are the client, thus you are the boss. Be cordial, but not buddy-buddy. There is an undeniable hierarchy, and that arrangement works. It's what they expect, and if you compromise it with some inflamed sense of friendliness or egalitarianism, you will confuse them. They will also lose respect for you. You're the client; you're the boss. Act with benevolent and calm authority, and the natural order of things will prevail just as it should.

Conversely, don't abuse your position. They are skilled and experienced at what they do, and you are fortunate to have them at camp. Be polite and give them their due. Pay compliments where due, and publicly.

There is a chain of command to recognize, and you're the general. If you've a complaint, tell your PH. He is your colonel and will pass it on down to his captain, the camp manager. These two men are your liaisons, your cultural intermediaries. The African has his own rules, rules which you will not learn in just a week or two. Your PH will handle the situation most effectively for you, yet allowing the staff to save face. He knows the intra-camp pecking order, you don't.

Be sure to find something in particular to praise *each* staff member. The game eyes of your tracker, the Rover handling of your driver, the stamina of your gunbearer, the finesse of your skinner, the soups of your cook, the bushcraft of your PH. This will mean more to them than gifts and tips.

securing your valuables

Cash, passport, and important papers I'd take with you in the Land Rover every morning, as you won't likely have your hard case with you (as at a lodge). Everything else you should leave in camp. We had an honest staff, and even though they were necessarily in and out of our tents all day long, nothing was ever taken or even misplaced.

Granted, people are people and bad eggs are everywhere, but we had a strong feeling of confidence in our camp staff and were never disappointed. Consult with your PH about this. Most camps have had to deal with petty theft in the past, as thievery is *rampant* in Africa.

EATING WHAT YOU KILL

[This first time hunter from America] *was a daily delight. Nobody else had ever been to Africa before. He discovered elephants and lions and leopards. He was the first living man to see a green plain dotted with a million antelope and gazelle. Nobody else had ever laid eyes on a buffalo.* (220)
— Robert Ruark's *Africa*

This is an unparalleled joy. Ox-tail soup and buffalo tongue from your Cape. Zebra filets. Bushpig ribs over *rooibos* coals. Eland *tournedos* wrapped in a strip of fat. Impala liver and kidneys. Wildebeest brisket. Kudu marrow on toast.

Study up on each animal's delicacies so that you are prepared to insist on them. Otherwise, the cook and camp staff might eat better than you will. Also, give advance notice about your food likes/dislikes/allergies. (Regular French's yellow mustard doesn't seem to exist in Africa, so bring your own else you'll be stuck with "mustard sauce.")

biltong (beef jerky African-style)

What a delicious treat. In Afrikaans *bil* means "buttocks" and *tong* means "strip." Simply made with just salt, pepper, vinegar, and coriander (for flavoring and to relieve flatulence), it takes about 4 days to cure. Insist on an early and very ample supply of several pounds for snacks. The Selous camp cook was to have prepared some buffalo biltong but regrettably failed to follow up on this. You've a right to as much of your own animals as you can eat, so don't be shy about insisting on lots of biltong.

Although the USDA prohibits its importation, whatever you don't consume in Africa you can give away before you leave. However, *do* take some for your flight home. They can't confiscate it from your stomach! I bought 13lbs of it for my two-week road trip, gorged on it throughout, gave some away, and was still chewing on the rest as my plane landed at Dulles.

DRINKING

I love liquor. It has been a good and constant friend for over twenty years. I have never used the bottle to hide in from fear or frustration, and I've never been on a protracted bat. I just like its taste and the way it feels and the wondrous atmosphere of celebration, of relaxation, of pure festivity it creates. Each drink in my book should be an adventure, neither a dull habit nor a screaming necessity.
— Robert C. Ruark, *Horn of the Hunter* (1954), p. 108

South Africa has some superb wines (both white and red), and beers (Windhoek and Urbock were my favorites). The Tanzanian lagers are quite good. Your camp will likely have a decent selection of spirits, which are often included (in moderation) in the daily rate. (The previous group of hunters drank like fishes over their 21 days, and early on drained the camp's ration. Comparatively, I was nearly abstemious.)

Beers were daily packed in the coolbox for the ride home each evening, a most welcome treat. (Be a hero and bring some blue ice packs to leave there!) When I arrived in camp, Alberto tended a full bar for campfire drinks. Sometimes I enjoyed a shot of whiskey, sometimes a shandy, and sometimes beer. With dinner we usually had a decent bottle of red wine.

Twice we had lunch in camp vs. the field, and although my PH would not have denied me a mealtime beer, it is better to not drink during the day. Yes, a grown man will metabolize a beer over lunchtime, but I think it advisable to wait. This is what I did, and it impressed my PH. I was there to *hunt*, not to drink.

THE SOUNDS OF AFRICA

The sounds become wonderfully important. There is a dove that sounds like a goosed schoolgirl. He says: "Oooh. Oooh! OOOHH!" The bush babies cry. The colobus monkeys snort like lions, except it does not carry the implied threat. At first it is hard to tell the baboons from the leopards when they curse each other in a series of guttural grunts. A hyena can roar like a lion. A lion mostly mutters with an asthmatic catch in his throat. The bugs are tumultuous. A well-situated jungle camp is not quiet. But the noise makes itself into a pattern which is soothing except when the hyenas start to giggle. A hyena's giggle is date night in the female ward of a madhouse.
— Robert C. Ruark, *Horn of the Hunter* (1954), p. 52

I'd read much about the sounds of the African bush, but you really must hear them yourself. Take a quality digital voice recorder (with USB port) and capture these sonic treasures forever. Every night I heard hyenas crunching on the bones of our day's kill. Several times I heard lions and leopards, and often baboons. Bloody marvelous stuff!

In the Selous we were treated to the rusty honk of the hartebeest, the hilarious banter of overhead hadeda, and the high-pitched yelp of the zebra (no, they don't whinny like a horse). Our first afternoon amongst a buffalo herd of 150 seared into memory their practically subsonically low grunting.

The sounds are unlike anything you've ever heard. I feel sorry for the natives who are inured to it all.

READING

For his nine-month safari, Theodore Roosevelt had made a customized portable library of *sixty* volumes, all bound in pigskin. Now, *there* was a man who savored reading! If you want to take part of the day off, a good way to spend it is with a good book on a *kopje* or in a blind. I take a couple of gripping novels and some books on African game or history. It's a fine way to either switch gears or plug in to the continent.

YOUR ATTITUDE

There is one thing to say: Go out there expecting to learn something, and to enjoy the heat with the cold, the bugs with the dust, the mud in the waterbag and the busted springs on the hunting car as part of the spectacle, and you will have a wonderful time. Go out as a wise guy and you'll hate Africa. I never knew a nice guy who had a bad time on safari. I never knew a sour apple who had a good time. Safari, like the sea, brings things out of man that he can camouflage in the city.

A man can always find what he looks for in Africa, even if it's only himself. (162)
— Robert Ruark's *Africa*

[My wife] *told me I was trying too hard, and I was.*

There were many dreams at stake on that trip, and a lot of scimping and saving and extra worth had gone into it. . . . You want

> [success] *so badly that you simply can't allow yourself the natural mistakes — the bad shots, the blown stalks and the screwups. But they're part of hunting, too . . . If you take the bad along with the good, then the good is all the more enjoyable. But if you can't accept the bad, chances are that you'll have more than your share of it.* (p.10)
> — Craig Boddington, *From Mt. Kenya to the Cape* (1987)

Your safari (especially the first one) will not likely be perfect, and probably due to at least one example of your own bad shooting. Anticipate this. Then, when it happens, try to quickly get past it so as not to bring down the entire hunting party.

I had a rough start during my first safari in 2005. My hunting partner (*i.e.,* the nonstop-talking kleptomaniac) was grating on me, and it wasn't until Day 4 (of 7) that I finally had my chance at an animal. I was way too keyed up, had no experience on shooting sticks, and after 10 minutes on/off the sticks on a 200yd hartebeest I missed him by a yard. We caught up to the small herd, I got on the sticks again at a tricky downward angle, and I missed him again. After reconfirming zero, I bitterly admitted, "*Well, guys, I just @#$* missed!* " I glowered quietly in the Rover all the way back to camp, passing up even the coolbox beer because I was so ticked off at myself.

A hot shower, cold drink, hot meal, and a night's sleep did wonders for resetting the mechanism. I awoke the next day with a much improved attitude. I practiced dry-firing off the sticks coupled with proper breathing. I got a nice hartebeest that morning, and a perfect one-shot zebra the day after. Even when I missed my dusk buffalo (more on that next chapter), I maintained a cheerful *That's the way it goes!* attitude, which stayed with me not only for the rest of that trip, but to this day. It is *your* choice how you feel about misfortune. Stay chipper. You're on an Africa *safari*, after all! How grand is *that?*

❖ **14**

HUNTING

One cannot hunt the African bush just once. When you have heard the call of the fish eagle by moonlight, only death will prevent your return.
 — Jeff Cooper, *Gargantuan Gunsite Gossip 2* (2001), p. 115

You know, there's an awful lot of God loose around here.
 — PH Harry Selby, to Robert Ruark in the 1950s

PRACTICING

Are you competent for Africa?

Just because you've occasionally hunted whitetail over the years doesn't automatically qualify you for impala. You should take Africa very seriously and increase your shooting skills before you go. Become as serious about it as the Germans:

> *The idea that just anyone can go hunting, as long as he buys a license, is foreign to the Germans.* **To them a hunter is a specially qualified person, wearing certain clothes, speaking an antique jargon, observing special customs, devoted to his hobby, and carefully examined before taking to the field.** *A man is either a Jager or he is not. It is not a casual thing. To earn a hunting license (Jagdschein), one must enroll in certified schools and learn all sorts of things from wildlife biology and game management to rifle marksmanship and the traditions of the chase.* **The curriculum is about as extensive as that of an American AA degree and normally takes a couple of years to complete**, *though "crash courses" are possible. The credential, once earned, is good for life. It establishes you as a qualified hunter.*
>
> *This system works, and provides excellent hunting together with an abundant supply of game.* . . . **It effectively eliminates the**

> ***"slob hunter,"*** **enemy of us all**, *and it removes the need for those iddiwa* red shirts... *German hunters wear green.*
> *Wild shooting poses no hazard to the farmer because there is no wild shooting. The man in green with the Tyroler hat and scoped rifle can be depended upon to use his weapon with care.*
> — Jeff Cooper, *Fireworks* (1998), pp. 84-85

a good test of shooting skill

In *African Hunter II* Craig Boddington wrote that you must be able to hit a 6" target at 100yds offhand, and the same target prone from 200yds. He further urges you to have fired at least 50rds in practice with your heavy. All great advice.

One Wyoming outfitter requires proof of prowess:

> *The outfitter wouldn't let you go hunting until you proved to him that you could shoot. You had to hit...a metal disk about the size of a basketball...from the top of the canyon and make the sucker ring with a 200-yard* [offhand] *shot. They wouldn't even let you get in the truck until you hit it.*
> — John Nosler, *John Nosler Going Ballistic* (2005), p. 212

A basketball diameter disk downhill at 200yds from offhand is a fine test of basic skill and challenging enough to weed out the unready. It's a shame that all outfitters don't demand this from their clients.

practicing

> *First of all, you need some practice ammunition. Second, you need a place to shoot in your own way. Third, you need to make the time to do it, not just once or twice before you leave, but a couple of times a week for several months prior to boarding the plane. Most important, you need a practice regime that is fun. Not an ordeal, not painful, not forced, but fun to the point of being addictive.*
> *Assuming that you are already an accomplished hunter and familiar with rifles, you should plan to shoot a minimum of 300 rounds through your dangerous-game rifle before you leave. Of these, probably 50 should be full-power loads.*
> — Terry Wieland, *Dangerous Game Rifles* (2007), p. 317

Once zeroed from the bench, practice only from *field* positions! Offhand, from sticks, squatting, sitting, kneeling, and prone (rarely used). Dryfire daily (with second shot bolt work). I used color copies of animals and placed them all around the house. Train your eye and your body. Cast bullets are cheap practice ammo which save barrel and brass wear.

I highly recommend a Ching Sling, and remember to wrap it also around your support wrist.

shooting sticks (retail, or homemade)

Although I had much practiced with my .416 from offhand, sitting, and squat positions, I'd *no* experience with the shooting sticks so commonly used by PHs in Africa. They are three bamboo poles about 6'6" in length lashed together near the top to form an adjustable tripod to brace a standing shot. Sticks are widely used, and great for shooting over tall grass. Achieving NPOA (natural point of aim) can be challenging, and I was very unsteady left/right at first. Though I got better, I was never truly confident on them. I wish I'd instead taken two of my Selous shots from sitting. On my two South African hunts, I never used sticks for any of my 21 animals.

Neither of my two PHs spent any time with me on shooting sticks, and this is typical (because PHs are so used to them). Insist on some live fire with sticks at the zeroing range.

Moral: get your own (www.sportwc.com) and practice with them! Dryfire often on your PH's sticks. Wieland's *Dangerous Game Rifles* has great advice/photos on training.

> You can make your own and acquire invaluable practice before you go. Go to a home improvement store or garden department and buy five bamboo poles (6 foot long poles) along with two vacuum cleaner belts (Eureka F&G size). Your total cost should be well under $20.00. To make the tripod shooting sticks, put three poles together and wrap one of the belts around the poles three times. Roll the belt down about 6 inches from the top. Use the same procedure for the bipod set, just wrap the belt around the poles four times.
>
> You may want to wrap the top portion of the shooting sticks with something soft (leather, cloth, etc.) so as to protect your rifle. I have also seen tripod sticks where one of the poles (above the belt) has been cut off, so as to make it easier to support your rifle.
>
> — Terry Carr, www.accuratereloading.com forum

books and clinics

Jeff Cooper's *Art of the Rifle* (Paladin Press) is the best work on the subject. Concise with plenty of photos, it's a must.

Rich Wyatt of www.gunsmokeguns.com (303.456.4545) teaches a Jeff Cooper inspired/approved "Safari Prep" course. In 3 days you will be well trained with your heavy rifle, greatly adding to your hunting competence and safari enjoyment.

Another shooting clinic is www.flyingbranch.com.

You should have 200+rds of pre-hunt practice with your buffalo rifle, 500+rds from your plains game rifle, and thousands of dryfires, all from field positions. Your shoulder mounting, cheekweld, trigger press, and bolt work should be utterly automatic and natural.

The skill to acquire is flawless 100yd 6" accuracy from all *field* positions (*i.e.*, not the bench), and from 200yds prone.

If you cannot do this, then you are *not* yet ready for Africa!

In fact, you shouldn't even be hunting Texas whitetail deer. It is a moral crime to make game suffer from bad shooting, of which you had the *duty* to spare it by your own *competence*.

YOU'VE ARRIVED IN CAMP!

I was entranced with the notion that this was really happening. Events of this sort are anticipated, and then remembered, but there is a tendency at the time to overlook the fact that they are actually in progress. I told myself repeatedly that this was one of those experiences which I would be able to treasure and pass on, and that it was not happening in the past or in the future, but exactly now.
— Jeff Cooper, *Shotluck* (2006), p. 115

The first time, it was difficult for me to "plug in" to actually being in Africa. This surprised me, given that I've extensive travel experience, and to such countries as Mexico, India, Sri Lanka, and Nepal. Africa, however, truly is a world all its own, and everything about it is just different enough to affect your equilibrium. The smells are different, the grass is different, the sounds are different, the light is different, and the southern sky is certainly different. It's really all quite overwhelming.

When did it finally "click" that I was there? Not until I got back! No kidding. It wasn't until I burned a stack of photo CDs and saw that screen full of thumbnail jpgs that I could grasp where I went and what I did. There was simply so much to absorb while there that my mind could not keep up. Much of it felt like a dream or an out-of-body experience. I think it hampered my shooting a bit; it was difficult for me to focus at times when on the sticks. (Not having hunted in years contributed to feeling quite rusty, and it took me a few days to get connected.)

To help counteract this, it is vital that you are *well worn* in your boots, your clothes, your gear, and your rifle. There is so much in Africa to quickly become accustomed to that you'll have little mental reserves left for the stuff you brought over. Stay alert and focussed every minute. You are in the wildest place on earth. There's no 9-1-1, no OnStar, no do-overs.

The most disconcerting thing about living and hunting in remote African regions is the mathematical fact that you have to make so many right decisions to stay healthy, whereas it requires just one thin slice of bad luck or simple indiscretion to get yourself crippled or dead. In the long run the odds have an annoying way of winning out...
— Peter Hathaway Capstick, *Death In The Long Grass* (1977)

zeroing

This will be done soon upon your arrival, on a travel day not counting as one of your hunting days. You are verifying your rifle's zero after 10,000 miles of airlines. With today's superb hard cases, guns and scopes are rarely damaged, but the field is no time to discover that your zero has shifted. Africa is likely drier than home, and your wood stock will shrink. (Confirm over there that your action screws are still snug.)

Zero with exactly the same rounds you plan to hunt with, and with a *full* magazine (to test the floorplate catch).

Your PH is verifying that you can actually hit a piece of typing paper at 100yds. (If you cannot, he will be very, *very* nervous of your ability to kill cleanly.)

There are two scope zeros to consider: 100yd and 200yd. Below is the general trajectory for .375/300gr/2500fps, which is very similar to .416/400gr and .458/500gr at 2400fps:

muzzle	100yd	200yd	300yd
-1.5"	zero	-5.9"	-21.4"
-1.5"	+3.0"	zero	-12.4"

Capstick recommended a 100yd zero with DG rifles, having only to remember drops of 6" and 2 feet. (Rarely will DG be shot past 200yds, anyway.) This 100yd zero also makes better sense for <100yd shots since point of aim/impact never exceeds 2".

If using your DG rifle on plains game, then a 200yd zero is preferable, especially in Namibia (200-300yd shots common).

Your softs and solids should print sufficiently close to each other out the practical maximum range of your hunt.

If you have backup iron sights, zero them for 100yds.

If you zero with optics for 200yds (+3" at 100yds), you'll never be more than a 5" radius from your aiming point out to 225yds. Aim for the lungs and you'll make good hits.

Once satisfied from the bench, take a few shots off the shooting sticks as they do take some getting used to.

Finally, clean your bore thoroughly and then fire a single fouling shot. (This will replicate consistent bore conditions.) Always hunt with a single round having been fired through a clean bore. (A great tip from both Craig Boddington and John Nosler.) *Now,* your rifle is ready for the field.

ballistics

While most bushveld shots won't exceed 150yds (because you should stalk closer), you may have to reach out to 250yds. Get dope on your rifle from 25 to 300 in 25yd increments, and tape this data on your stock.

One hunter in the Selous wishes that he he'd done so. He overestimated bullet drop on his 130yd buff, held 8" too high (from his 100yd zero) and barely clipped one lung. The upper scapula shattered that old nonbonded core Hornady (which he shouldn't have been using) and two frags went into the spine, else we'd have chased that buffalo for miles.

Afterwards we thoroughly discussed bullet drop of the .416 400gr, and concluded that out to 250yds it was the same as a 300gr .375 H&H. .416s (and .458s) at 2400fps are decently flat, so don't imagine some .45-70 rainbow trajectory.

loaded cartridge rotation

The same rounds shouldn't stay at the magazine's bottom during much shooting, else recoil will compress bullet seating. After every shot (or string of shots), bring the bottom rounds up.

dryfiring on game

This is an easy and realistic way to gain experience. Many times on the way back to camp, I'd dryfire on some kudu (to help me get over *kudu vudu*). It really helped.

THE CRAFT OF HUNTING

> From a [professional] hunter's standpoint the ideal customer is a man who is scared enough to be cautious but brave enough to control his fear. He follows instructions, knows and is frank about his own limitations on stamina, and quits when he has had enough of mountains and swamps and dust and bumps for one day.
> — Robert C. Ruark, *Horn of the Hunter* (1954), p. 76

> As every election is a qualified disaster, every hunt is a qualified success.
> — Jeff Cooper, *Shotluck* (2006), p. 128

I am no expert hunter by any means, but I've done a fair amount of it. And I'm certainly no expert *African* hunter after just three safaris and two dozen animals. However, what I have to say about hunting has been complemented by many experts. Read books by Capstick, Boddington, etc. to absorb the finer points.

Jeff Cooper made a worthwhile point that one's first hunt should *not* be about buffalo:

> I say again, as forcefully as may be, that one should not go for buff on his first time out. On your first African excursion you should go for antelope, zebra and pigs, if you choose, but do not stake your whole experience on one critical objective.
>
> If you go to the right place you may indeed connect, but the buffalo experience may or may not be the Wagnerian climax that you expect. It is quite possible to deck a buffalo with no drama at all, and if you have saved and saved, and planned and planned, and sacrificed and sacrificed to get to a place where you get a buffalo, see him, fire one shot, and watch him drop in his tracks, you may well get the notion that you have spent your life hunting the wrong thing. Buffalo indeed can provide excitement, but a really dramatic buffalo kill is about as probable as a really good bullfight. If you do not work up to it, you may not even appreciate it if it happens.
>
> **The African experience should be enjoyed for its own sake and not for the sake of any specific objective.** The joy is in the hunt itself and not in the trophy. The buffalo is grand, but he is by no means the only reason to go to Africa.
>
> — Jeff Cooper, *Gargantuan Gunsite Gossip 2* (2001), p. 513

If this position seems too stringent for you, then at least be happy with any decent old bull (*i.e.*, 38"ish) and save the 40+" for another trip. *I.e.*, always leave something to look forward to.

seeing game

> Another difficulty in the first few days until you get used to it will be that of recognizing what you're looking at even though you see it. You will rarely see entire animals standing about as if on a pool table, waiting to get swatted, but you must learn to recognize mere parts of them. Try not to look for a complete outline but for more obvious things, such as legs beneath bush cover, the twitch of an ear or a tail tip. Motion, . . . is the big give-away.
> — Peter Capstick, *Safari: The Last Adventure* (1984), p. 153

Modern man has unlearned the use of his eyes (and ears) to an astonishing extent, as the first few days of your hunt will show. Constantly strive to improve your game eye by looking *through* the bush for critter shapes, colors, and movement.

hunting Cape buffalo

> To my mind there are two sorts of hunting — "buffalo" and "other." I delight in both but the pursuit of the buffalo is special. In other hunting there is a pursuer and a pursued, with the buff the hunt is less a chase than a confrontation. No matter what you use nor how good you are, the buff does not necessarily drop to the shot, and if he does not he will do his best to kill you — which is exactly as it should be. Irascible, determined, and unbelievably resistant to gunfire, nyati *is an adversary rather than a quarry.* Elephant, lion, tiger, rhino, and the great bears can kill you, but they almost never display the single-minded, unswerving vindictiveness of the wounded buffalo.
> — Jeff Cooper, *Shotluck* (2006), p. 114

You are hunting bachelors 10+ years old. They will usually be alone, but sometimes hang out with a buddy or two. They're called *dugga* ("mud" in Shona) boys because their last few years are spent rolling in the muck. These old guys have usually seen quite a bit of fighting, and may be even carrying a bullet or two from hunts past. Known for short tempers, aggressiveness, and bravery, *dugga* boys are the quintessential dangerous game.

Old bulls are sometimes found in herds, but not often enough. Sure, herds are much easier to track but you'll end up wasting a lot of time getting up close only to learn that they're full of cows. My PH greatly preferred tracking *dugga* boys.

tracking buffalo

The drier the climate, the more migratory buffalo will be. You will drive to known buffalo locales, looking for tracks in the road on the way. About 20% of the time you'll see fresh sign that way. If not, then you'll dismount from the Rover and begin a long hike. It's walk, walk, walk, and then stalk, stalk, stalk. Animals lie up during midday, and you will too from 1-3PM. Then it's an afternoon of walking and stalking. Within an hour before dusk is generally when you'll encounter buffalo.

Once you're on fresh spoor you'll be looking for fresh dung. (What irony that you're spending $700/day only to search for a pile of steaming dung, but that's hunting!) Good trackers can time-estimate dung within a half hour.

Once you're on a *really* fresh track, move more quietly and smoothly. *No talking!* Be ready at any moment to suddenly see them just a few yards away.

hunting plains game

Generally, you will begin with the least expensive critter on your list, to test yourself and gear. Thereafter, you and your PH will usually discuss the day at hand over breakfast and settle on what to go for during each morning's hunt. If successful, then over lunch you'll discuss the goal for your afternoon. Since you'll never be able to anticipate what you'll run across, it is vital that your rifle/scope/ammo be worthy for *any* animal on your list, regardless of range within sporting distances. You will generally have but a few seconds to make a clean shot, especially in close cover bushveld country.

stalking

> The Bushman tracker] *would keep an almost non-stop running commentary. He would tell us all about the sex of the animal, its age, whether it was in a hurry trying to get somewhere or was at ease with the world, or whether it was beginning to thirst, or whether it was perhaps looking for some part of its diet that was not available in this section of the country and various other information. When the animal stopped, he would try and assess whether its purpose was to look back and see if anything happened to be following it or whether it was just tiring and looking for some shade.*
> — Geoff Broom, *A Life On Safari* (2004), p. 51

You've walked and walked, and have found the spoor of very close game. Now it's time for stalk and stalk.

> *Msasi haogopi mwiba.* (A hunter is not afraid of thorns.)
> — Terry Carr, www.accuratereloading.com forum

carry your rifle with you, *always!*

> More than any other, Africa is the land of the rifle — the queen of weapons. The rifle, plus the skill to use it well, places the individual man in command of the Jovian thunderbolt, with his power to destroy or spare at whim. This is an almost eerie sensation, and explains why it is unseemly, to the point of sacrilege, for the wanderer to venture forth unarmed, especially so when he is theoretically "protected" by some hired hand who may or may not know how to handle the problem.
> — Jeff Cooper, *C Stories* (2004), p. 136

work the wind

Your PH may have an ashbag and will use it constantly. (Others simply kick up some dirt.) Staying downwind of your prey is the single most important factor in getting into position. I lost more game through suddenly unfavorable wind than due to any other factor. Or, as I say, *"Wind is Murphy's wife."*

stay as low as you reasonably can

I duck-walked many a hundred yards in order to get close in. Make sure that you're in physical shape to stay low, if not belly-crawl! Much of your final movement and shot positioning will be done through crawling. Often I had to belly-crawl to glass a herd and once took a wildebeest after a 100yd crawl in what was one of my most gratifying shots.

From Rich Lucibella is a great method of staying low which I used to get within 30yds of a large eland herd:

> [A] *technique that I learned from Danie Van Graan in Tanzania. We sat in single file, feet forward, with our rifles across our laps. To move forward, you simply stretch your legs, dig your heels in, and, palms to the ground a your sides, you lift your butt from the ground and move it forward. This allows you to cover a fair distance quickly, without dragging and scraping. It also allows you to shoot* [from sitting position], *if necessary...*

Practice this and leopard-crawls (with field clothes and gear) *before* Africa. String up some wires or bars to measure your lessening height. Get some rhythm and smoothness going for yourself before the hunt. Lose your gut. It will greatly pay off.

stay quiet — *no talking!*

Or, as Capstick wrote, *"eyes open — mouth disengaged."* The human voice travels farther than you think and naturally alarms game, which could be just behind the next bush. Whisper or use hand signals. Learn to walk silently in the bush, especially during the final stalk. (Some hunters slip into leather moccasins or go bareboot.) "Cornflake" dry leaves cannot be trod on quietly, so brush them aside before each step.

Walking over ashen ground raises a fine dust which cannot but tickle your throat. I anticipated this and brought plenty of cough drops with me into the Selous. They really help.

use your ears

My PH often cupped his ears to pick up the *kssss-kssss* of oxpecker birds which often accompany a buffalo herd. It works.

do not stare at your quarry while stalking

Many PHs have come to believe that animals have a "sixth sense" when they are being stalked. Intermittent glances, only.

if buffalo spook and run off

Don't worry; buffalo are not like elk. They don't like to run far, and will slow down/stop within 500yds. Many times herds would catch our wind and spook, but they'd settle down within 10 minutes, and then we'd circle into the wind and try again.

Plains game, however, tends to run off farther.

the final stalk

Once you've decided on an animal and are about to make your final stalk to get as close as you can (*i.e.*, between 20 and 120yds), it pays to check yourself and your gear one last time.

 Is your rifle loaded and a round chambered?
 Is your muzzle clear of all debris?
 Is your safety still engaged?
 Is your scope still tightly mounted?
 Leaf sight on correct yardage?
 Have you plenty of spare ammo?
 Is any of your gear making noise?
 Do you need a cough drop, just in case?
 Should you leave behind any gear, such as your Camelbak?
 Will the rest of your hunting party remain behind, low, and quiet?

target angles (be *choosy*)

I've taken game at all angles, and I'll use arrows to signify position; imagine the arrowhead as the animal's head:

  ↓ 0° ↙ 45° ← 90° ↖ 135°
  ↑ 180° ↗ 225° → 270° ↘ 315°

broadside (left at 90° and right at 270°)

Except for eland (because of its thick shoulders), the ideal shot is full broadside (90° if facing left, and 270° if facing right). If you're patient, you will likely be presented with such. Here you have the "magic triangle" of shoulder, heart, and lungs.

For a heart shot, aim above the leg, a third up from the breastbone. Any shot placed there is a killer, though not necessarily a one-shot drop. (Our deer and elk live in colder climates, and thus have higher hearts: 8" in elk. Heart positions in African game are lower than what you're used to.)

If you are slightly unsteady, then go for the lungs. A double lung hit is a killer, though he may run 50-200yds. Aim just behind the shoulder, about mid-line of body. I like lung shots because they waste very little meat. I brought in a kudu cow for camp meat this way with a 350gr Swift A-Frame from my Marlin .45-70. It was very tidy affair, and not even a half-pound of meat was damaged.

Shoulder shots are rarely quick killers, but they do usually anchor an animal well. However:

> **There's no good reason to shoot to** [merely] **disable. If you can't thread a bullet to the vitals, best wait until you can....** Shoulder shots have their advocates,.... Smashing it keeps the animal from going far, and the bullet is likely to damage the vitals between the shoulders. **...But because a shoulder shot often requires a follow-up, and because it ruins a lot of meat, I seldom use it.**
>
> — Wayne van Zwoll,
> *The Hunter's Guide to Accurate Shooting* (2004), p. 290

My 90° gemsbok bull was a 40yd snapshot, totally busting up his left shoulder and greatly damaging his right. He could only clump around, giving me plenty of time and safety (wounded gemsbok are dangerous) to finish him off. In retrospect, I'd have preferred to find him dead after 100yds from a lung shot.

With a 200gr Swift A-Frame my .30-06 swatted a warthog square in the front shoulder at 225°, exiting the left shoulder.

I have learned through experience to *avoid spine shots*. It is far too easy to miss a ½" diameter spinal chord, especially during your early safaris. I wounded a very large (100kg/220lb) bushpig because I misjudged his size through the tall grass. Although the 300gr TSX from my Marlin .45-70 perfectly did its job (creating a large exit wound), I'd aimed 1½-2" too high as I thought him smaller than he was. (Unless you are *very* familiar with game sizes, do not shoot at significantly obscured animals.) He ran off like a locomotive, and we tracked him in dense riverbed for hours. By afternoon, his wound had congealed and we lost blood spoor. This was the only animal of 2007 that I lost. It convinced me to avoid spine shots altogether.

quartering away (135° and 225°)

My next favorite is a quartering shot if I've still got a clear line of sight to the vitals. (This is the best angle on eland.) If quartering *away*, go for the far shoulder. My zebra was at 225° and I slipped in a 400gr soft just behind his right shoulder. (Some buff, zebra, and wildebeest have stomachs too fat for severely quartering away shots. Your PH will advise.)

I've had one extreme angle kill, and that was an escaped waterbuck cow at 225yds. The 300gr TSX went from right rear gut all the way to left neck, which I considered excellent penetration from an 1800fps MV bullet at that distance.

quartering toward (45° and 315°)

Not a bad angle, but not one of my favorites. If you go for the near shoulder, you'll likely also get the far lung and maybe also the top of the heart. These are often messy shots.

While hunting impala, a nice steenbok ram showed himself at 80yds/45°. My .30-06 sent a 200gr TSX into his left shoulder, exiting through the right ham with a perfect, straight line track. This proved the value of nonfragmenting heavy bullets for even small game, as little meat was wasted.

facing straight on (0°)

This offers the heart (and the neck, if his head is up). You've little windage room for error, however. This was my first hit on a hartebeest, and I center punched the pump of a bull wildebeest. (Heart sizes and positions differ per animal, so do your homework! Know game anatomy like a surgeon.) Heart shots are rarely instant stoppers as animals can often run quite a distance on residual hydraulic pressure.

I used this shot angle on a 25yd impala ram with a 350gr A-Frame (.45-70), hoping to keep the bullet inside. He dropped like a sandbag. The bullet exited through the ham.

from dead astern (180°)

The *worst* position. It's messy and too rarely drops the animal. (Cooper called it *"rude."*) I had to follow-up my hartebeest this way, and spined him at the base of the tail.

Although a neck shot may be presented here, it's usually too fine to make reliably and it unnecessarily wounds.

if you've a poor angle or there is too much brush, wait

Often, brush is in the way, and don't be tempted to shoot through it. The animal will move, so wait. If he doesn't, then you will have to. *Don't be impatient!* There will be *other* angles and *other* animals and *other* safaris. Proper ethics are to hunt cleanly, or not to take the shot.

on game walking through a small clearing

Often you can anticipate an animal's path and be ready to fire as he passes through a gap in the brush. With a bit of practice, this can be done with acceptable reliability. Lead him smoothly and keep the rifle moving as/after you fire.

a hunter is better known for the shots he *passed* on

Anybody can lob a 250gr .338 artillery shell at a 400yd wildebeest. Anybody can throw sufficient lead at an animal to finally kill it, but hunting is about *hunting* (art and science, governed by ethics), not killing.

Whenever I hear of long-range bragging, I know that for every animal killed there were several others missed and wounded. You've a right to brag only if you stalked within a sporting range of 300yds, and preferably within 150. You have an obligation to reduce risk of wounding to a minimum, thus you must get as close and as steady as possible, and then shoot only if you're at least 90% sure of your shot.

If you have gotten as *close* as possible and as *steady* as possible, yet still are not 90% sure of your shot, *then pass it up.* **This is the mark of a true sportsman.** There will be *other* game, but a poor shot burns forever. **Do it *right*, or not at all.**

when a shot is absurdely *easy*...

Luckily driving into a docile herd is *not* hunting. You may as well shoot animals at the zoo. A worthy kill involves a bit of effort, sweat, skill, and anxiety. When things go *too* right, you are cheated from some of the safari experience.

My first warthog was a very close call in this respect. I'd just had breakfast, and Herbert spotted a nice warthog from the *kopje* behind the lodge. I quickly finished dressing, grabbed my rifle, and clambered up. The tusker was 100yds off at target angle 90°, slowly walking at 20° declination, totally unaware of our presence. I led him three inches, fired, put it right in his shoulder, racked the bolt instantly during the recoil, and gave him an insurance shot after he kicked. (Because of my bolt work speed, they called me *"Belt-fed"*.) Upon reflection, the kill was more of an assassination than hunting. While I don't quite regret it (because I shot him so well — see photo), I *almost* do because it was so easy. It was as easy a kill as I ever want.

In 2007, I had another very easy shot when a grey duiker failed to see me behind cover. I was rifle glassing some waterbuck about 40° away and my peripheral vision picked up a little ram walking toward me. *Slowly* shifting my rifle on him took about 20 seconds, but once I'd done that it was about impossible to miss him at 20yds. A 200gr TSX at 2600fps on such a small critter at such close range is devastating, which added to my impression that the affair was not as challenging as I'd have liked. (Also, it got me sentimental about not hunting the very little antelope. I may have shot my last duiker and steenbok, and could never press trigger on a klipspringer.)

Obviously, I'm not advising you to get carried away with such purist notions, but if you ever are presented early on with a shot *so* easy that it feels like mere killing vs. hunting (and you'll know it when it happens), you may want to pass on it.

"Should I take this animal, or wait?"

The important thing about the African hunt is to enjoy it, and to do this you must free yourself from the nagging feeling that every day that does not bring a prime trophy is a waste of money. In my view, it is a good idea to set up a particular objective, such as a special size of a particular animal, and then to surround it with whatever else the countryside affords. **Wide experience has convinced me that it is unsound to pass anything up.**
— Jeff Cooper, *C Stories* (2004), p. 149

This is fine advice indeed. I went to Tanzania with the goal of hunting a Cape buffalo and a zebra, with a third animal as optional (mostly depending on my finances). The first animal I had the opportunity to shoot was my *last* choice, a Lichtenstein hartebeest. I was not very keen on this homely critter and his long donkey face, but it was Day 4 and we'd not seen anything for days. It was a $558 trophy fee animal, too.

So, I had to make a quick decision, especially since I was allowed *two* buffs on that hunt and I wouldn't have the money for that hartebeest *and* a second buff. But since I'd yet to shoot my *first* buffalo, I took the risk and took the hartebeest. In retrospect, I'm glad I did. It got me squarely in the game; I had hunted in Africa and could relax a bit. (There was no guarantee that I'd see any other shootable animals, and I'd rather have "merely" a hartebeest than nothing at all.)

shooting through brush (*i.e.*, don't!)

> Any shot that requires a "brush-busting" bullet is best left alone. That's because there are no brush-busting bullets. In tests, I've sent a variety of bullet through sagebrush screens into paper targets and found that branches small enough to snap between your fingers can turn even heavy bullets. Husky 250-grain .35s entered the paper sideways several inches from center — though the paper was mere feet behind the brush.
>
> — Wayne van Zwoll,
> *The Hunter's Guide to Accurate Shooting* (2004), p. 297

Boddington wrote of a sapling in front of his buffalo deflecting a .470 solid — a "brush-busting" bullet if there ever was one! That 500gr solid was deflected *three feet* in just 30yds!

beware of exiting bullets and other game

Most bullets (especially well constructed caliber-heavy ones) will exit, so make sure the background is clear of other animals. For example, every one of my 200gr TSX and A-Frame .30-06 bullets sailed completely through. Not one was recovered. Great blood spoor, yes, but watch your backdrop.

do not shoot *tough* game in late afternoon

Buffalo, zebra, oryx, eland, and wildebeest are very hardy, and if you botch a shot, you probably won't be able to catch up to one before dusk. Save such game for the morning if possible.

a quick word about trophymania

> Can you imagine the odds, given the extent of your visibility in bush country and how many millions of miles you'd have to walk with perfect intercept timing to come across a number one record animal of any species? What, for that matter, are the chances of you and the animal even being alive in the same time period, let alone crossing paths when you were armed, ready and shooting properly?

> *Obviously, trophy hunting is largely luck, coupled with field skills and plenty of time on safari.*
> — Peter Capstick, *Safari: The Last Adventure* (1984), p. 236

> *In my view the trophy is the memorial evidence of a profound experience....Pursuing the task is an end in itself, with or without objective success.*
> **Hunt for the experience, rather than for the outcome.**
> — Jeff Cooper, *Shotluck* (2006), pp. 84, 87

There's no reason why your dinner kudu cannot have big horns, or that you cannot eat your Rowland Ward gemsbok. But don't let the tape measure control your experience. I saw a tape measure hunter in 2007 after a 54+" kudu. He was placed on the sticks *three* times, only to ask, "*Is it Rowland Ward?*" When he finally took a chance on a very large bull, he was later greatly disappointed that it was "*only*" 51". His chain-smoking ingratitude soured the whole camp on him, and when he later phoned to book another kudu hunt he was politely rebuffed.

Sure, a 54" kudu is preferable to a 51" but since hunting is mostly a matter of *luck,* how much pride can one truly claim over having walked into a monster bull? What *should* matter more than horn length is the quality of the stalk and the precision of your shot. **Hunting is properly an inner-directed joy**, not one enslaved to the record books. There should be more satisfaction in a 48" kudu taken after a long and challenging stalk vs. a placid 58" standing by the road.

Besides, you will not likely equal or exceed the record book animals, anyway. Those days are gone. That a middle-class guy can even hunt Africa in the 21st century is a miracle, so don't get caught up in lengths of horn.

A Texas A&M student understood this well, and would have been completely satisfied with that Spaniard's 51" kudu. Instead, the gods of the hunt shined on him for his correct attitude and he took a beautiful 55" after a thrilling barefoot stalk within 20yds. Derek kept shaking his head in awe over the experience, glowing all the way back to camp (and beyond).

Your main trophy is being able to enjoy a safari at all! That capacity will be found only in your grateful heart. If you haven't a grateful heart, your African hunting experience will largely be wasted on you.

taking aim
are you as close as you can reasonably get?
Ruark urged to get as close as you can, and then 10 feet closer. Duck-walk, scoot, and crawl.

from eye to scope
> One of the major problems I have had with my clients' shooting has been the common failure to use a scope properly when game is located and it has been decided to try for a shot. I can't emphasize this point strongly enough. The most common fault occurs when the shooter raises his rifle to sight through scope and loses the target. The reason for this among even fairly experienced hunters is that they tend to look at the scope rather than simply fitting it between their eye and the target while not taking their focus off the animal. The big trick is to keep both eyes open, never varying the point of focus of the eye from the target....
>
> Once you've located the target, don't take your eye off it, simply raise the rifle and fit the scope between the eye and the animal. The rest will come naturally.

— Peter Capstick, *Safari: The Last Adventure* (1984), p. 104

This is the whole point of a Scout scope, and with lots of practice you can begin to bust clays, it's *that* natural. For hunting within 300yds, you don't need a 3-9x scoped magnum. A simple .308 or .30-06 with Scout scope is the ticket.

Regardless of scope, practice rifle presentation to make your stockweld and cheekweld *automatic*. Keep both eyes open, focus on a kudu photo across the room, shoulder smoothly, dry-fire, and immediately cycle the bolt.

the shot
> You should, from the time you raise your rifle to fire, be able to either decide not to shoot or get the shot away in fewer than five seconds. ...In fact, an experienced game shot would be dragging his feet if it took him three seconds.

— Peter Capstick, *Safari: The Last Adventure* (1984), p. 104

> Aim small, miss small.

— *The Patriot*

Before you commit to a shot, *absolutely verify* with your PH *which* animal he means. Use something obvious as a reference point, such as *"OK, do you mean to the left of that stump, the kudu facing right with his head down?"* In thick brush you may not be able to see what your PH sees; a bit of angular difference can obscure an animal to the hunter.

Also, I *strongly* recommend identifying animals by *position* (*e.g.*, third animal on the left) vs. sex, as some bulls and cows (such as buffalo, wildebeest, oryx, and zebra) to the novice hunter are difficult to distinguish. Keep it simple and unambiguous so that "*bull or cow?*" judgment is not a factor. Even for PHs, some animals are notoriously difficult to sex, especially zebra. The PH may need time to be sure, but be *ready* (with proper natural-point-of-aim) to shoot *quickly*.

When in shooting position, don't forget to disengage the safety. You may even want to chamber check one last time, if such can be done quietly.

Then, take the shot by the numbers: BRASS

Breath, **R**elax, **A**im, **S**queeze, **S**hoot

Take a few breaths, and (depending on your preference) let out half/all of your last one, then really focus on your front sight.

> *I was watching, freezing myself deliberately inside, stopping the excitement as you close a valve, going in to that impersonal state you shoot from.*
> — Ernest Hemingway, *Green Hills of Africa* (1935), p. 76

Say "BRASS" to yourself, pick the proper kill zone, and then pick the smallest distinguishable spot within that zone. **You are not shooting at shapes, but at *spots*.** (Such spots are much easier to see on a zebra or leopard than on a gray buffalo.)

> *I . . . saw the bull through the aperture, marvelling at how big he looked and then, **remembering not to have it matter, that it was the same as any shot**,...*
> — Ernest Hemingway, *Green Hills of Africa* (1935), p. 230

If you are trying for the *heart* (especially on a frontal shot), aim *so* low that you begin to feel *uncomfortable*. (This was great advice from Mark on my 0° wildebeest bull, and I utterly center-punched the pump. That *Kugelschlag* I'll never forget! He was dead on his feet, but still ran 50yds on hydraulic pressure.)

If you are not at least 90% sure of your shot, pause, rebreathe, and try again. If you have more than 10% doubt because of the target angle, shooting position, brush in the way, nerves, etc. *then stay off the trigger* until conditions improve.

Once you've chosen the smallest spot available, say "BRASS" to yourself again, focus your front sight or reticle on it as you press out the trigger. **Front sight—press—front sight!** You must focus and press, else the pressure to simply get your shot over with will interfere with an accurate shot. Remember to see your front sight (or reticle) before and *after* the shot.

You've fired thousands of times; *this is just another shot* with all the same required basics. Do not concern yourself with the recoil or muzzle report. If you are properly concentrating, you will scarcely discern either. Nothing else matters but front sight—press—front sight.

Remember *not to have it matter*, as Hemingway advised.

Without having rushed the shot, *quickly* work your bolt! Do not move your feet from that spot until you have rechambered! (I was pleased that my dryfire practice had really paid off, and was often seen to have rechambered my second round while the first shot was still echoing.) *Reload!* The hunt is not over until you've actually touched his dead unseeing eyes.

shots on running game

Unless following up on a *clearly* wounded animal, I recommend strongly against running shots. Not only is your judge of distance more important (because your bullet's time of flight now matters), you have to judge the animal's speed as well. This is very difficult to do accurately.

5mph = 7.3fps   15mph = 22fps   30mph = 44fps

A .308 of 180gr at 2600fps MV has the below times of flight (assuming perpendicularity with the hunter's bullet):

animal's distance	bullet's time of flight	(you must lead animal by:)		
		5mph	15mph	30mph
50yds	.059 seconds	5"	15"	30" (2.5 feet)
100yds	.120 seconds	11"	33"	66" (5.5 feet)
150yds	.180 seconds	16"	48"	96" (8 feet)
200yds	.249 seconds	22"	66"	132" (11 feet)
250yds	.319 seconds	28"	84"	168" (14 feet)
300yds	.391 seconds	34"	103 "	206" (17.2 feet)

A trotting 15mph kudu at 100yds needs a *three-foot* lead. A running 30mph kudu at only 150yds needs an *eight-foot* lead. Only *18 inches* of error will result either in a clean miss or a gut shot. What if he's 170yds and 24mph, and running away from

you at 115° vs. right to left at 90°? Are you *that* good? I'm not, and likely neither are you.
Do *not* make first shots on running game.

the animal's reaction
[T]he mechanical action of firing a shot at game can have three possible results. First, you kill cleanly. Next, you miss cleanly. The last possibility is that you wound the animal to one degree or another.
— Peter Capstick, *Safari: The Last Adventure* (1984), p. 154

One shot, meat. Two shots, maybe. Three shots, heap shit.
— Ernest Hemingway, *Green Hills of Africa* (1935), p. 172

If you've hunted a bit, you'll be able to tell by the animal's reaction if you hit him, and how well. (Your PH will definitely know.) Usually the bullet's impact (*Kugelschlag* in German) will be heard by all. It sounds like a baseball bat smacking a wet sandbag. No *Kugelschlag*, probably no impact.

immediately after your first shot
You may kill [a buffalo] easily with one bullet, but if you don't, the next fourteen .470s serve mostly as an irritant.
— Robert C. Ruark, *Horn of the Hunter* (1954), p. 288

Do not watch for the animal's reaction, *reload* and get a bead on him again. With all game, keep hitting him until he is down and dead. This is vital with DG. Staggering? Hit him until he's down. Down? Hit him until he stops moving. Not moving? Wait him out and allow blood loss and tissue damage to take their inevitable toll.

Important! ***Never* start yelling or whooping for joy just because your animal is down.** Very often he never saw you before you fired, and doesn't understand what happened to him. His herd will usually mill around after a shot. (This happened with my hartebeest and zebra. Buffalo and wildebeest herds, however, explode in stampede.) If you keep your voice down, he cannot identify his assailant. Remain quiet until your PH decides to approach.

Remember to retrieve your spent cases. They are fine momentos, and you avoid littering.

wounding an animal

> But it was excited shooting, all of it, and I was not proud of it. I had gotten excited and shot at the whole animal instead of the right place and I was ashamed;... (p. 259)
> ...I had a shot **and shot at the whole animal instead of calling the shot.** It was my own lousy fault. I was a son of a bitch for having gut shot him. It came from over-confidence in being able to do a thing and then omitting one of the steps in how it is done.
> — Ernest Hemingway, *Green Hills of Africa* (1935), p. 272

> Every ethical hunter abhors the loss of a wounded animal. For me, the experience is like a festering wound on my own body that never heals. It may fade from daily memory, but never really goes away, nor can it be atoned for.
> — Richard Conrad, *Safari Guide* (2001), p. 214

You are morally and legally obliged to spend every reasonable effort to track it down. That means all day, and even the next, if necessary. Loose scope, bad round, bad shot — whatever happened, *you* wounded it — you go find it.

I've had to do this twice, and it is a *thorough* bummer. Get as close as you possibly can, then get as *steady* as you possibly can, and *only then* take a 90+% certain shot. I made a 100yd kudu shot I suspected to be insufficiently steady, and thus made *everybody* pay for my mistake with a 7-hour follow-up. In thanks (and in penance) for the crew's effort, I took the entire camp out to dinner. **Moral:** it is *so* much easier to shoot well than clean up after a sloppy shot you shouldn't have taken.

if you are charged

> Living dangerously is twice blessed — it blesses the moment with elation; it blesses the after-day with warm memories. If a man has trodden unknown trails and landed on lost beaches, when age comes the domestic hearth is a campfire where old dramas are relived.
> — P.J. Pretorius, *Jungle Man*

When it comes to DG, do *not* turn your back. Do *not* run, which is the fastest way to get killed. Be prepared to dive out of the way, but stand your ground and very carefully shoot him in the face. **This is your *only* way to possibly survive.** Rule 4 applies here, so be careful not to shoot any of your hunting party. This is your last chance to maintain your calm and *do it right*, so make the most of it! How long you live depends on how well you solve your problem. Stand your ground and brain him!

I'll quote now from a PH who likely has more experience with surviving DG charges than any man currently living:

> I believe, whenever possible, dangerous game should be given the choice of how it is to die. I do not believe the beast should be shot into oblivion from 50 yards away, when, with a bit more care, the professional hunter and client can walk up and let him decide how he is to die. (at xiv)
>
> I don't know another professional hunter ever doing the same. But what is safari about? Is safari just about killing? Is it just about going home with trophies? What is a trophy without risk? What is life without risk? ...Is there no creativity left? Doesn't anyone want to take a chance? Am I that alone?
>
> A real charge is the last 30 feet. Further (sic) than that, it is only positioning. Let me explain. What danger is there in a buffalo 60 yards away? Answer: none. At that distance he has many choices including changing his mind and running away. Distance equals time, and at that distance you have all day to kill him. However, once he has committed himself and crosses that 30 foot threshold, he will not stop. He cannot be turned. He cannot be driven away. One of you must die. (at 23)
>
> The secret to executing the shot, I believe, lies in never, never, never, never thinking about the consequences. You must take the charge willingly and with great anticipation so that a negative thought cannot enter your mind. Nothing can distract you. You cannot think about dying. You cannot think about your wife, your children, your business. All these things are distractions and irrelevant at this moment. You cannot think about missing. You cannot think about being gored. You must be single-minded in purpose and resolve. You must set your mind to believing that YOU ARE TOUGHER THAN THE BUFFALO and that he cannot reach you. You must be totally committed in your resolve and in your determination. This is, after all, a life and death situation. Either you kill him or he kills you. It is that simple. Once he crosses that 30 foot barrier, there is not turning back for either of you. **I have often said that a professional hunter who hunts dangerous game is only as good as as the last 30 feet.** I truly believe this. I do not care if a P.H. can call the length of an impala's horns to a 16th of an inch at 200 yards. What really matters is the last 30 feet. (at 26)
>
> **Shooting early means YOU DO NOT HAVE THE CONFIDENCE in your ability to stop him.** It is that simple.... Absolutely, positively do not shoot early. You must hold your shot to the very last, like the Minutemen on Bunker Hill. Shooting early only conditions yourself into believing that you have an "option" in case you do not stop him. (at 28)

— Mark Sullivan, *Death and Double Rifles* (2000)

To say that Sullivan's bravado is, *uh,* "controversial" amongst PHs would be grossly understating matters. That aside — as long as the animal is not goaded into a charge — his philosophy of letting DG decide how it is to die strikes me as honorable and manly. Personally, I'd like to try it with buffalo.

follow-up shots
> *I reserve follow-up shots for animals I can positively identify as the initial target — animals that have been in sight all the time or that are so distinct as to be unmistakable.*
> — The Hunter's Guide to Accurate Shooting (2004), p. 307

Some animals (*e.g.*, buffalo, zebra, wildebeest) will usually require at least one follow-up shot. (Any animal hit only poor-fair will need a second shot.) A heart/lung shot is likely the best follow-up, unless you are *sure* of the spine (which is usually tricky, and has never worked well for me). Know your animal's anatomy and ask your PH what he recommends.

I had to follow-up my hartebeest with an offhand snapshot at his spine just above the tail. He crumpled immediately. Because I'd so much practiced offhand, that shot was a better one than the one from the shooting sticks.

immediate follow-up shots by the PH?
> *[A]sk your professional to back you up if you don't kill cleanly. Far from being unsportsmanlike, it is cheaper, safer and unquestionably more humane.*
> — Peter Capstick, *Safari: The Last Adventure* (1984), p. 160

It, however, is far better to be able to kill cleanly. If you cannot, then why are you hunting at all, especially in Africa?

Some PHs, in order to avoid long follow-ups, are a bit *too* eager to provide dubious insurance shots on their client's game. You should strongly discourage this in advance, except for DG.

approaching your animal
Have your rifle ready (*i.e.*, shouldered and off safety) for a quick follow-up shot. Do not leave it behind, and do not even sling it. Be prepared to shoot, *instantly*. Animals are often stunned by spinal concussion and wake up without warning. (No twitching often means he's merely spine-shocked. *Beware.*)

Many PHs will insist on an "insurance" shot, and this is good doctrine. *"It's the dead ones which kill you."* (John

"Pondoro" Taylor had his buffalos hamstrung with a razor-sharp hunting knife. Even if they were merely stunned, they were immobilized by two quick slashes from the tracker.)

My late grandfather taught me to always touch their eye to verify death. I think of him after every animal.

the kill

> *I looked at* [the kudu bull], *big, long-legged, a smooth gray with the white stripes and the great, curling, sweeping horns, brown as walnut meats, and ivory pointed, at the big ears and the great, lovely heavy-maned neck, the white chevron between his eyes and the white of his muzzle and I stooped over and touched him to try to believe it. He was lying on the side where the bullet had gone in and there was not a mark on him and he smelled sweet and lovely like the breath of cattle and the odor of thyme after the rain.*
> — Ernest Hemingway, *Green Hills of Africa* (1935), p. 231

> *Already I was beginning to fall into the African way of thinking: that if you properly respect what you are after, and shoot it cleanly and on the animal's terrain, if you imprison in your mind all the wonder for the day from sky to smell to breeze to flowers—then you have not merely killed an animal. You have lent immortality to a beast you have killed because you loved him and wanted him forever so that you could always recapture the day.*
> — Robert C. Ruark, *Horn of the Hunter* (1954), p. 102

> *One kills in order to have hunted; one does not hunt in order to kill.*
> — José Ortega y Gasset, *Meditations on Hunting*

There is a sense of sadness after any kill, as I do not take the killing of animals lightly. Thus, whooping, hollering, joking, and backslapping seems disrespectful and tacky. Joy is normal, but show dignity in expressing it.

Sometimes you may want to test a bullet in a fallen animal. Understand that meat will be sacrificed for this, and the black tracker simply will not understand (causing your stock value to plummet in his eyes).

photographing your animal

> *[R]espect your quarry and your surroundings. I cannot recall how many photographs display inappropriate behaviour, such as hunters sitting on animals, standing with a foot on the head, or in anyway degrading the animal with unnatural antics.*
> — *Nyati* by African Hunter (2003), p. 362

> *I believe that if an animal is worth shooting, it is worth respecting.*
> *The concept of respect for your prey will come clearly through the pictures you take by the implied relationship.... Don't sit astride a fallen trophy as if it were a side of beef. After all, it's a special animal that you have come a long way to hunt and kill under a strict code of ethics. You have taken its life to treasure it and the memory of conquering it on its own ground by ultimately mounting it as a trophy in your home. To have yourself photographed with your foot on the animal's body . . . isn't done in polite — or responsible — hunting circles today.*
> — Peter Capstick, *Safari: The Last Adventure* (1984), p. 263

Before any staged photos, take some photos of how/where the animal was found, and perhaps a view of the shot.

Very carefully prepare and stage the other photos by repositioning the animal for best light, removing all foreground grass and brush, brushing him off, etc. (Both of my PHs were painstaking in their photos.) In books, I've seen dozens of trophy photos ruined by sheer laziness in the field.

Tuck in your shirt and straighten your cap.

Fill the whole frame with your animal. Take many, many digital pictures from all angles, solemn and smiling, looking at the camera and 45° away, hat on and off, fill flash and not, with and without any shot/blood evidence. Use the sunset if you can.

Be sure to take some photos of your party with you and your animal, and offer to send them a copy. (Here is where a Polaroid camera is most useful. Or, if space allows, take a small photo printer for your digital camera. This can be run directly off the camp generator's 110V AC.)

A final piece of advice: **never allow *anybody* to pose *alone* with your animal** (which they could later claim as their *own*). That is *your* right as the hunter. (If my nutcase hunting partner had a photo of himself alone with Craig's elephant, he'd have no doubt shown it far and wide as "proof" of his story.)

to "appreciate" vs. being "appreciative"

To appreciate (a private emotion) is not the same as being *appreciative* (a social grace). Be *absolutely certain* to individually thank all members of the hunting party. They are the "shaft" of your "spear" and all hunts are a *team* success. They will rightly be proud of their contribution to your kill. Treat yourself, your hunting partner, and your PH to some small commemorative cigars. Some sweets for the rest.

GPS the location

Your PH will likely use his GPS to log the location, and I like to have the coordinates of each animal. (Curiously, I took my Selous zebra within 100yds of my hartebeest, two days later, within a 3500 mile^2 hunting block! Needless to say, we kept returning there. Never change a winning game.)

missing entirely

> *Every damned thing is your own fault if you're any good.*
> — Ernest Hemingway, *Green Hills of Africa* (1935), p. 281

This will be difficult to swallow, but missing is occasionally part of hunting. *Everyone* misses, though not everybody *admits* it.

My PH has a wise policy of charging 10% of trophy fee for any misses because one in ten misses are actually woundings (usually gutshot).

In 2005, I missed during the very last minutes of light on the very last day. We'd not seen any bulls since Day 1. By Day 7 we'd only tracked herds of cows, or a pair of immature bulls. Less than an hour before sunset we see a herd of 25 just 100yds from the road. There are a couple of bulls. We stop, dismount, and begin to work our way to them. The wind is finally cooperating. The entire stalk takes about 45 minutes, and I am on the sticks a total of *11* times during 4 internal stalks.

Twice I was on the trigger before the bull moved, and once I had a half pound of trigger pressure to go before my PH paused me. By the time I at last had a shot, we were anxious to beat the light (there wasn't time for even another 2 minutes of stalking and repositioning), and nearly incredulous that I actually, finally, had a shot at what was basically a dark silhouette of a buffalo at target angle 90°. I didn't think that I rushed it, and called it good, but there was no *Kugelschlag*.

We followed-up a bit that night, and again the next morning before flying out, but never found even a drop of blood. Somehow, I'd missed him clean. (It likely went high, as we found no lateral or below-animal evidence of the bullet.) It could have been from an inadvertent final breath as I squeezed the trigger, or perhaps the shot was good but struck an unseen twig and deflected.

At the time, I chalked it up to the pressure of the stalk. My PH with 10 years of experience remarked that he *"nearly pissed"* himself because of the drama, and that the stalk had been one of the top three most intense of his career.

If your hunting party and PH did their part in getting you to a viable shot, and yet you still missed, it is gracious to apologize to them for not making a kill. Remember, the hunt is not all about you, and they will also be disappointed. Keep your bitching and moaning to a respectable minimum, discuss with your PH what happened and how to improve. You missed, so vow to become better for next time. In summary, it is dispiriting to miss an animal, but it is far worse to wound an animal you never manage to find, yet must still pay for.

An interesting epilogue to my missed buff presented itself several months later, when I first confronted my nutcase hunting partner about his lies and thefts. Not owning up to them in the least, he counter-accused me of being too suspicious of people. Then he blurted out, *"You don't think I messed with your scope, do you?"* Realizing that he meant my buffalo, I replied, *"No, that thought had never occurred to me before."*

Later I recalled that, at his offer, he'd cleaned our rifles before *and* afterwards. He could have altered/reset my zero, and I wouldn't have been the wiser. While I've no proof of this, his pathological envy of others (and a post-hunt $10,000 theft he pulled on me) makes such sabotage possible, if not probable.

I emailed PH Craig Lang who had "seen the elephant" before we arrived, only to have that memory sullied by nutcase claiming the shot for himself. I mentioned the *"You don't think I messed with your scope, do you?"* remark. Craig replied:

> *I have also wondered about that missed shot on the buffalo. It was pretty dark, but you seemed pretty sure of your shot, and you had a good scope and a pretty solid rest. Very odd.*
>
> *I guess you'll never know.*

SKINNING

Some (though very few) hunters take no trophies whatever. *I shot him. He knows it, and I know it.* That kind of thing. Well, it does save $600-1000 in dipping/packing/crating fees, as well as the shipment home and taxidermy. Unless money is so incredibly tight, plan on taking home trophies, at least for your very first hunt. You'll regret it if you don't.

You will have to quickly decide how you plan to display your animal. There are two basic mounts: European and shoulder. *European* is just the skull/horns (plus the flatskin if you wish); *shoulder* means with head, fur, eyes, etc (plus you can keep the backskin). While full body mounts are possible, they are quite expensive and rarely ordered. Personally, I go European unless the animal is unusually special in some way.

help out with the skinning

While you've no obligation to do this, I consider it an important part of the hunting experience. Take a good skinning knife and sharpening stone with you, and get involved. These are marvelous animals, beautifully designed. Demonstrate some interest in the skinning, and in the morphology of your shots (which will show how well your bullets performed).

request that your bullets be found and saved for you

You'll want to know how your bullets did, and the track of your shots. Bullets can be difficult to locate, hence the small metal detector I urge you to bring. Many bullets end up in the stomach, and skinners usually aren't too enthusiastic about finding them.

identifying your game

About the only foolproof way I can think of is to use an engraving pencil to etch your name on each horn, skull, and tusk, and to use a permanent marker on the underside of the capes and hides. Take a DETAILED inventory of the items that belong in your shipment, get the PH to sign off on it PRIOR to leaving camp. Then, when you receive notice that your trophies are at the taxidermist (in Africa), FAX them a copy of the list so they can verify everything is there and properly tagged. Confirm this again when the taxidermist notifies you that your trophies are ready for shipment. Once the trophies arrive in the U.S., check the contents of the crate against your list. If correct, make sure you repeat the process with your local taxidermist. Then, provide him with some field photos so he can further assure himself that he is working on the correct trophy.

— good advice, from the internet

In the Chapter *Trophy Costs* I'll discuss the big bucks it takes to have your trophies flown home and cleared through Customs.

African taxidermy

This option can save you considerable time and money, if you've confirmed the quality/speed of work beforehand. The savings can be as high as 50%, though you will pay a bit more to ship/enter finished mounts than unfinished trophies. You should certainly query your safari outfitter, but since he will likely receive a kickback from the taxidermist, it's almost a case of asking the barber if you need a haircut.

Try to get references from previous hunters in addition to the outfitter's opinion. The further in the past the hunt, the better, as you want to know how the taxidermist's work has held up over time.

FINAL WORD ON THE BUSH

This remains one of his greatest pleasures, the fresh forest coolness of the morning, the lowering shafts of sunlight in the late afternoon; and the variousness beneath one's steps, pine needles, fallen oak leaves, ferns, dry grass, wet marshland; the smell earth, dogs, cordite; and the camaraderie, the excitement, and the kill itself with the hunting horns lifting an ancient chorus over the slain beast, a sound unchanged for a millennium; and the long trek back from the heart of nature, the sense of achievement and bodily exertion, the glowing satisfied beating of the heart's blood.
— Ella Leffland, *The Knight, Death, and the Devil*, p. 647

When you begin hunting you go through three stages. You start by thinking you know everything, but of course you know nothing. The second is when you realize you don't know anything at all. And the third stage is when you have learned a bit, but realize you will never know it all!
— Syd Downey

We had some good luck and some bad luck. Nobody got sick and nobody got hurt. Parts of it were rough, and parts easy. But it worked a sea-change on both of us that will never rub off. It is entirely true that Africa does strange things to a man. It grabs hold of a piece of his heart, and never quite lets go.
— Robert Ruark, "I've Got To Go Back" (1953)

You will have, at worst, a good time. At best, the utter time of your life. The only sad part is contemplating having to go home:

Back to the world of fraud and pretense.
— Pop Eastman, 1926

❖ 15

TIPPING

TIPPING YOUR CAMP STAFF

If you have quality people (which is likely), then departing them after only 7 days will feel like leaving a family. I know it did for *me*. They took fine care of me: delicious, ample meals, good drinks, perfect hot showers, tidy tents, the best laundry service I'd ever had, and always a waiting campfire.

Your entire comfort, safety, and well-being is in their hands, and they truly *care* if you have a successful hunt. It is not merely *you* who hunts, but the entire *camp*. You are just the point of the spear. Everyone else is the shaft behind the point. You couldn't easily do it without them, if at all. Your PH will be in the bush for months on end, away from his home and family and civilization. His every waking moment is spent thinking of your needs, which are more considerable than you realize. If he manages more than 6 hours of sleep each night, he's lucky.

Tip these people *well!*

They bust their butts for their clients, and they survive only on good tips. Do not be stingy! (I heard of one hunter tipping $5 for a 7-day hunt!) 5% of the daily rate is absolute minimum, 10% a good average, and 15% lavish. You'll discuss the camp tips with your PH, and hand them out on your last morning before your charter flight out. Remember to use the envelopes you brought.

camp staff (excepting vehicle staff and PH)

My Selous PH Craig explained that $100/day (that's total, not per hunter) was about right (if we enjoyed their service). He and the camp manager handled the allocation between the staff (*i.e.*, cook, skinners, head waiter, camp boys).

So, for our 7-day hunt, $700 for the camp staff was appropriate. They did a fantastic job and anticipated nearly every need. Since our camp manager Jackson was so superb, we decided to give the staff (excepting him) $600, and Jackson $150. (We later learned that he had never been tipped more than $100, and was completely bowled over by our generosity.)

vehicle staff (excepting PH)

There were four people: the driver, two trackers, and the game warden. Based on our PH's guidelines, we paid the following daily tips:

head tracker	$15
driver	$12
2nd tracker	$10
game warden	$ 7

So, between camp and vehicle staff, we tipped out $1060 total.

PH

Between $50 and $100 per day is appropriate, depending on service. We easily agreed on $100/day, as Craig surely earned it. He was most attentive to our needs, tirelessly answered a hundred questions, and worked mightily to find us shootable game in that sparse concession. A young man of 33 with a wife (also a PH) and two small children back in South Africa, Craig took fine care of us. A $700 tip seemed right. (I also gave him a pair of Motorola TalkAbout radios.)

If you calculate your PH's tip as a multiple of trophies (which is often done), then it's only fair to include any of your misses since it's not *his* fault that you missed.

tips for my 2006 South Africa hunt

Mark figured $400 for the field and camp staff, which was about 15% of the daily rate. Sounded fair to me. To Nigel I gave a Free State Wyoming silver coin (only a thousand minted), and later sent him a *Boston's Gun Bible* and a CamelBak. For Lisa I'd brought over a jug of 100% maple syrup (which is expensive there) and some presents for the girls. For Mark, cash was inappropriate to the owner, so I spent a morning back home and wrote up a detailed FAQ page, which he gratefully added to his revamped site.

❖ 16
HOTELS & SHOPPING

HOTELS

I stayed in only two Tanzania hotels, so I'm no travel guide, but my lodgings were nice.

Dar-es-Salaam (Msasani Peninsula)

Most outfitters have a relationship with one particular hotel. Zuka Safaris uses the very nice Sea Cliff, and has a small office next door in Sea Cliff Village (where they stored my rifle for me while I enjoyed Zanzibar the weekend before the hunt). $150/night provided all the modern amenities, and an excellent breakfast buffet. Nice pool, good staff (especially Nadine, the VP), and next door dining and shopping (including a *very* nice little supermarket). An excellent choice for first-timers who don't need any hassle or frayed edges. The Msasani Peninsula is an upscale part of Dar, without the hustle-bustle of downtown.

room phone calls

Oh, be very, *very* careful here! Any room calls will be quite expensive ($2/minute local numbers), and calls back to the USA will be exorbitant.

True story: I asked the desk clerk for the number to be connected with an American operator so that we could use our calling cards. He obliged. I then made several calls back home for my 3¢/minute, gloating all the while. Well, until I checked out and saw my phone charges. *$265!* (That was more than my room!) That desk clerk had misunderstood my question, and I had dialed *direct*. They wanted to charge me $30/minute. The safari owner called the hotel president, who kindly instructed

his VP to reduce the charges to cost (which was less than 10% of retail). A $22 mistake was much easier to bear than $265.
From your room, *receive* calls only.

Zanzibar
First, decide what you generally want to do, beach or town. (Base from one and enjoy the other.) I chose a good hybrid, the Mtoni Marine Centre (mtoni@zanzibar.cc), just 10min from Stone Town. Its beach is small, but clean with nice sand. It has one of the best restaurants in town, and the island's only sushi bar. Several levels of rooms are offered, from $30 to $100+. It has a good bar, and even Internet. Nice staff, too.

Alton House in Johannesburg
This is an upscale B&B near the airport which caters to hunters. Craig Boddington stays there often and highly recommends it. A good idea is to overnight there before you fly home, instead of risking the domestic connection the same day. (Mine was canceled and merged with a later one, giving me less than an hour to process my rifles and change terminals. I made it, but it was a pretty hairy experience.)

SHOPPING

shopping in Dar
Except for the ebony, I thought better stuff was available in Zanzibar, but I admit to not completely scouring Dar.

ask your safari company driver for prices
Since he is not the seller (though he might possibly know of some), he doesn't have a vested interest in keeping prices high. He knows what locals pay for stuff, and can thus advise you on a seller's bottom line. 1100 Shilling = $1 in 2006.

get a good Tanzania map
The two most detailed are the Macmillan (blue cover) and the BP (British Petroleum). Both are about Tsh6,000 *if* you haggle. The BP map is more detailed, but is north/south back to front, so you'd need to buy two maps and splice them together.

Any of the lively downtown streets in Dar with sidewalk vendors will have them. Ask your driver.

I also bought a couple of very nice laminated maps of the country from a stoplight vendor. (Everything is sold by these guys, from car tools to clothing.)

Tanganyika Arms

I visited Dar's only gun store, which actually had a decent selection of firearms (be thankful of our prices here!). Glocks, Berettas, and CZs were available (at twice our gun show prices). And they had a box of .416 Rigby (Federal Premiums, 400gr Woodleigh softs). One hunter inquired of the price (even though he had already hunted and still had ammo left). The armory manager tapped out a furious session on his calculator and then announced Tsh19,000 ($17). But not for the box.

Yep. $17 per *round*. That's *3-4x* what it would cost back home. I'm sure you can get anything you need in Africa, but *hoo-boy* will you pay for it. Nonetheless, if a hunter's bag was lost by the airline, he could still buy 10rds of .416 Rigby for $170 and still hunt with his own rifle. Kept in that perspective, $17/rd is a pretty good deal.

leather and fur goods

I expected quite a bit more than what is sold. Fabrics and wood abound, but very little leather or fur. I couldn't even find a zebraskin hatband in all of Dar.

ebony artifacts (Slipway, Mwenge carvers' market)

Very nice are the so-called "family trees" which are lengths of one-piece ebony limbs and trunks with very intricately carved figures. How they carve with such detail on the *inside* of the piece is quite impressive.

Pieces are $20 and up. Selection and prices are merely fair at Slipway, so go directly to Mwenge carvers' market.

One such piece was 4' in diameter and nearly 7' tall! It must have weighed near a ton, and was just magnificent. Asking price was Tsh80,000 (about $7,300). It no doubt could have been had for $6,000 tops (and then there's the matter of crating, transportation, and customs duty), but would fetch at least *10x* that in some Aspen boutique. Truly an incredible piece of art. It may still be there for you to see.

fabrics

Tanzania offers many beautiful shirts and wraps which make for great gifts back home. The vibrant patterns are quite unique, and scream *Africa!*

souvenirs

I very much like the green Tsh500 note because of its Cape buffalo. Sometimes you will receive consecutively numbered bills. Only 45¢, and a great trinket for friends back home. (I mean, who doesn't like receiving *money*?)

jewelry

Oh, is there ever nice stuff there! I bought my girlfriend several necklaces (including a Masai purple beaded one) to her delight. Beautiful, yet very affordable goods.

The semiprecious blue stone Tanzanite is $500/carat, and prices are rapidly rising. Arusha is the best source.

postcards (airmail postage is Tsh600)

Be sure to send a card to the nice Dutch customs officials who processed your rifle transit permit.

the world's best hot sauce

There is a steak house called Shooters. They make their own red hot sauce, and a 750ml bottle goes for $5. Oh, my! It has a very unique sweet mixed taste, and is great on spaghetti.

shopping in Zanzibar

Zanzibar has many more street touts (*papasi*, or ticks) than Dar, and repeated firm responses are required. Never act scared (you're not in any danger), and do not trust them.

One of them had a nice elephant hair bracelet and was asking $9. One hunter quickly haggled him down to $2 (which I thought oddly low). Through some street vendors later on we learned that he had bought a *grass* bracelet which had been cleverly died with black shoe polish. (FYI, "Hakeem" is tall and skinny, with very bad teeth he insists showing with frequent unctuous smiles, if you meet him on Shangani Street near Tembo House Hotel. *Caveat emptor.*)

Stone Town

My day of snorkeling ended at 2PM, so I had plenty of time to walk about. Stone Town is the oldest and most colorful part of Zanzibar. The Arabic influence can be seen in every building.

A perfect way to spend some time is on the rooftop bar of the Chavda Hotel on Baghani St., enjoying cold Kilimanjaro beers and tasty snacks with a beautiful overlook of the twin-spired St. Joseph's Cathedral and Indian Ocean. (Chavda Hotel would be a fine place to stay for those not opting for beach accommodations.)

The evening's highlight was Forodhani Gardens, an outdoor market across from the Old Fort which comes alive at dusk. (This alone for me was worth the trip to Zanzibar.) Rows of fresh, steaming food (everything from octopus to goat to fresh bread), and dozens of artifact vendors. All the locals hang out there, and some European tourists (including skanky French women who go to Zanzibar for their own purposes).

HAGGLING WITH THE LOCALS

Haggling is not rude, it is the expected behavior. (Watch Monty Python's *Life Of Brian* for a great scene on this very thing.) Jettison your sensitive American mores and take a cue from the locals.

how to haggle

Never, ever be the first to offer a price, and never, ever pay his initial asking price! With Americans, he is used to starting out 5-10x over what he normally sells to locals. If he begins with $15, snort in polite disgust and counter with $1. He's insulted you — return the favor. If you counter with $12, you have decided an absurdedly narrow range of negotiation (and to your detriment). Keep that first range as wide as possible. He comes down to $11, then you increase to $2. Once you've gotten pretty close (*e.g.*, you are at $5 and he at $8), begin to walk away. Don't agree to $7 or $6, or even $5.50. Remember, he is in competition for your money — you are not competing for his goods (which can be bought from many others, most of whom just several feet away in the same market). Just when he realizes that you will walk away and buy elsewhere, he will agree to your $5. (This failed only twice in over a dozen hagglings.) Never increase your offer in succession, only in alternation to his decrease.

And, as I suggested in my *Boston's Gun Bible*, show him the money! I once haggled for a very nice copper bracelet, and the vendor got down to $4. $2 was all I wanted to pay, as I'd seen several other vendors with the same bracelet. He remained firm at $4, so I pulled out $2, laid it on the table and said, *"I can walk away with the bracelet, or the money —your choice."* His colleagues began to snicker at the seller's predicament. He still held firm on $4, so I began to reach for my $2. He crumpled and stopped my hand. I took my bracelet and put it on with the grinning approval of his friends. The seller just stood there, stunned.

When that happens, you *know* you got a great price!

The closer the sellers are to a nice hotel, the higher the prices and the less willing they will be to haggle (because they've learned Westerners don't haggle well, if at all). In Dar, there is a nice upscale market called the Slipway. It's a calm, quality selection — and you will pay for it.

So, go to the local market. In Dar there is the fantastic Mwenge carver's market which specializes in the most amazing ebony pieces. I'd teamed up with a guy who could haggle unsuspecting sellers down to local prices. We were something of a sensation there, and they were stunned at our bargaining prowess. (Our driver, upon learning that he'd bought an authentic Masai panga for just $9, after an initial asking price of $40, just shook his head and said, *"Not even I can buy for such a price!"*) Seller after seller were left awash in his wake, shaking their heads in grudging respect.

I quickly had the idea to let him be my buyer, with great effect. **By dividing the issue, we conquered.** I was disengaged from the price; he was uninterested in the goods. Thus, the sellers had no leverage whatever on either of us. They couldn't appeal to me on the haggling, and they couldn't appeal to him on how nice were their goods. If you've a buddy who is an accomplished haggler, try this technique. I am a pretty good haggler when I *care* to be, but often don't want to spend the time or hassle to reach the absolute lowest price.

The more *time* you force the seller to invest in your deal, the more *leverage* you have. This, of course, works in the reverse, so you must portray an image of having the entire day to haggle on some $8 purchase. You have the advantage because he is there to sell more things than you are there to buy, so he will eventually give in.

Final thing: don't be concerned that you are skinning the locals by haggling to a low price. No seller will ever sell below cost or even below his necessary profit margin. Their self-interest will always prevail! *It is a buyer's market, you have the money and leverage and choice —use it!*

♦ 17
TROPHY COSTS

OK, here is the painful part. The safari price quote given by outfitters will *not* include transportation home of your trophies. They can't know *what* you will harvest, much less *how* (sea vs. air) such will be sent home to you, and what brokerage and customs fees remain to be paid. (Even if they could accurately calculate this in advance, the total amount would likely scare off much of their business!)

Before my safari I read many books, and none of them offered any clue to the costs involved. While game fees and daily rates were often mentioned, *nada* about repatriating your trophies. Although I can't generate exact price quotes for *you*, I can give you a heads-up based on what I had to pay.

While you are making a budget for your hunt and deciding just what you can afford to ❶ hunt, and ❷ bring home, I urge you to contact local importers and taxidermists for quotes. I was pretty stunned at the myriad of additional fees that got tacked on (see the next page for an itemized list).

Those on an extremely tight budget may consider not bringing home *any* trophies. (I'm told that this is fairly common amongst European clients.) For a buffalo and zebra hunt, this will shave $4,000+ from a safari's total cost! (That kind of money could make or break one's decision to hunt at all.) This is an extremely harsh measure, and one which you may indeed regret years later, so think it over very carefully. Happily, it's something you can decide not only after the hunt, but after you return home since it will be weeks or months until the trophies leave camp for the home office in Africa to be packed. Perhaps by then you'll have saved up enough funds.

DIPPING, PACKING, CRATING

Even if you don't have the taxidermy done in Africa, your trophies must be carefully prepared before shipping to the USA. This must be done in a veterinary-approved facility before export permit can be issued. Then they are packed, and then they are crated. (This is often included in your safari cost, but clarify such before you sign the contract.)

If no taxidermy is being done in Africa, then you could save time and money by having the dipping/packing done by somebody like Dip Pack (www.dippack.com), as taxidermists usually don't consider this work as lucrative.

Swine must be separately packed, and primates must have CDC clearance. Both must be re-dipped in the USA.

Be *sure* to get a photocopy (or take a digital picture) of your PH's hunting register of your animals, and that he has included such with your trophies to the shipper or taxidermist.

GETTING YOUR TROPHIES HOME

Here is what four trophies (one Cape buffalo, two zebras, and one hartebeest) cost in 2005 to send by air freight, clear, and deliver to the taxidermist (*i.e.*, his fees are separate).

importer/bonding agent:

import air freight	$1830
entry & customs release	$115
cash disbursement	$ 90
storage charge - carrier	$ 50
airline import svc. charge	$ 30
cartage & services	$ 45
U.S. Fish & Wildlife services	$ 50
messenger services	$ 35

clearing agent:

inspection/processing	$900
TOTAL	**$3145**

Ouch! That's $786.25 per animal (two of which were heads and hides, the rest merely hides), and before taxidermy. (I've yet to import my trophies from 2006 and 2007, though the taxidermy has been paid. Please tell your friends to buy my book so that I can afford to bring home my past two years of game!) Trophies are expensive, so plan your budget wisely before you commit in the field to saving everything you shot.

November to February is perishable season in Africa and cargo flights are quite full, so plan accordingly.

Hunters are no longer (thanks to CBP) able to commingle their trophies in a common shipping crate/manifest. (One conceivable way around this is to list all trophies on the register in one hunter's name, though your PH may balk at such.)

Get a good licences customs broker to handle this for you. A reputable one is www.coppersmith.com, which has an extensive website FAQ that I highly recommend you study in lieu of my reproducing such information here.

TAXIDERMY

If you can prepare and mount your own trophies, dandy. If not, then you'll have to contract the services of a taxidermist. Local recommendations from friends is the best way to find a good one who will deliver within a year (and that's *after* the six months it takes to even get them to the USA!).

in the USA

I was fortunate that a friend knew of a fine local taxidermist who was semi-retired. His prices were only half of what the large shops charged.

Cape buffalo hide tanning (no backing)	$200
zebra hide tanning (no backing)	$200
hartebeest cape mount	$450
hartebeest backskin tanning	$ 80

Had I wanted a rug mount backing for the hide, I'd have paid another $200.

how long will he take?

Figure at least three months for mere hides, and longer for cape and full body mounts.

taxidermy in South Africa
Assuming quality service, this will likely be the better choice. My finished trophies from 2006 and 2007 will be sent in one crate to save on shipping and clearing costs.

make sure he is a member of TASA
Taxidermists Association of South Africa. While membership doesn't guarantee a perfect experience, it goes a long way in weeding out the crooks and incompetents.

how long will he take?
Figure on about a year to take delivery, so be patient. In the meantime, you can go on safari again, right?

taxidermists in other African countries
Your chances of disappointment and loss are *far* greater. Have your trophies flown into South Africa for local work. Leaving them in Zim is begging for heartache.

DISPLAYING YOUR TROPHIES

For an impressive collection of displays, visit the Safari Club at the Thermopolis, Wyoming, Holiday Inn. It will also give you a good idea of what you may want for yourself. (Jonas Brothers outside Denver also has a fine showroom.)

Unless you're wealthy enough to afford a trophy room, you'll likely have to resort to hanging up your mounts in the living room or den. Depending on your home and/or spouse, this will work out with varying degrees of success. Sure, you could always just put your trophies in storage in the meantime, but that borders on dishonoring the animals.

My hartebeest shoulder mount went on loan at a friend's gun store until I'd made other arrangements. Such a Win-Win deal may also work for you.

I recommend that you decide in advance where and how they will be displayed *before* your hunt. (This is a helpful bit of reality planning that will help curb any *"Make them all shoulder mounts!"* trophy fever.) If you don't have the wall space, then tanned flatskins or felted rugs are your only realistic choice.

❖ 18
PLANNING TIMELINE

For your first safari, you should give yourself *plenty* of time to learn what you need and arrange all the details. Nine-12 months is not at all unreasonable, although I've packed it all into 60 days after a lifetime of foreign travel experience.

Anything requiring the cooperation of bureaucracy or Africa should be activated ASAP. (However, what can be done by credit card is more efficient, so there's not as much pressure.)

One major factor depends totally on you: getting into good physical shape. If you are not able to hike 10 miles/day by the time you arrive in Africa, then you're just not serious enough. The quality of your hunt greatly depends upon your fitness.

9-12 months out
- read and daydream about your safari
- buy used copy of Ortega ý Gasset's *Meditations on Hunting*
- begin to research what you'd like to see and do and hunt
- read *Safari Dreams: A Practical Guide To Your Hunt In Africa*
- create a file for all your safari information
- scour the Internet; post questions on forums
- establish a relationship with a travel agent (*e.g.*, Gracy's Travel)
- create a budget and a way to meet it
- begin selling off anything necessary to make your budget
- choose your country and contact outfitters for quotes
- check outfitter/PH references by phone conversation
- plan before/after hunt excursions/tours (Kruger Park, Zanzibar)
- start getting into African 10 mile/day shape (with gear and rifle)
- arrange vacation time from work
- share this list with any hunting/travel partner and coordinate

6-9 months out

- ☐ attend Safari Club International in Reno (January)
- ☐ send 50% deposit for hunt if written contract is acceptable
- ☐ make flight reservations
- ☐ book side trips and excursions
- ☐ buy travel and medical insurance
- ☐ apply for passport, or renew if expiring w/i six months of return
- ☐ decide on your firearm(s), and purchase as necessary
- ☐ travel documents needed? (visas, gun permits, health, etc.)
- ☐ get Forms 4457 for your guns, camera, laptop, binos, etc.
- ☐ have your PH send invitation letter to RSA gun permit liaison
- ☐ leave rifle for any gunsmithing
- ☐ create packing list and begin to acquire items
- ☐ decide on taxidermist (either RSA or USA)
- ☐ can you hike 2-4 miles a day with gear/rifle?

3-6 months out

- ☐ send Dutch firearm transit form if flying through Amsterdam
- ☐ send by U.S. Global Mail your SAPS 520 gun permit form
- ☐ arrange for African cell phone (perhaps from gun permit folks?)
- ☐ buy premium bullets (*e.g.,* Barnes, Swift, A-Square)
- ☐ develop handloads
- ☐ mount scope and zero with <2MOA loads
- ☐ make your own shooting sticks
- ☐ begin practicing with your rifle from all field positions and sticks
- ☐ book appointment for vaccinations and prescriptions
- ☐ research malaria risk in your area, and best precautions
- ☐ book eye and dental checkup appointment
- ☐ can you hike 4-6 miles a day with gear/rifle?

1-3 months out

- ☐ choose and purchase high quality binoculars
- ☐ buy and wear boots/clothing/gear in your training
- ☐ compose or revise your will
- ☐ renew credit cards if expiring during safari
- ☐ confirm receipt of SAPS 520 gun permit (DHL its replacement)
- ☐ confirm receipt of new passport
- ☐ purchase your rifle case (*e.g.*, Pelican, Hardigg, TuffPak)
- ☐ arrange 2-3 home contacts for emergency (general briefing)
- ☐ get eye and dental checkup
- ☐ can you hike 6-8 miles a day with gear/rifle?

4 weeks out
- ☐ arrange for petsitting or boarding
- ☐ arrange for housesitting
- ☐ directly confirm flights, hotel, rental car
- ☐ confirm that hunting boots are worn-in
- ☐ buy Africa guidebooks
- ☐ can you hike 8-10 miles a day with gear/rifle?

3 weeks out
- ☐ confirm arrival of tickets, reservations, etc.
- ☐ confirm issuance of your South African gun permit
- ☐ get your vaccinations and prescriptions
- ☐ create travel document folder

2 weeks out
- ☐ detailed travel briefing of friends and relatives
- ☐ purchase travelers' checks
- ☐ arrange for ride to airport, or long-term parking
- ☐ pay credit cards in order to have sufficient traveling balance
- ☐ has Dutch firearm transit form arrived by fax?
- ☐ finalize packing list acquisitions
- ☐ test pack your bags and rifle case, checking weight and size
- ☐ final info to home area emergency contacts
- ☐ email African outfitter your home area emergency contact info
- ☐ get International Drivers' License from local AAA
- ☐ can you hike 10 miles a day with gear/rifle?

3-7 days out
- ☐ suspend newspaper and mail delivery
- ☐ confirm your outbound flights with airlines
- ☐ start taking malaria meds as directed (watch for any reactions)
- ☐ board pets
- ☐ notify credit card company of your upcoming African usage
- ☐ compose auto-notify for your email accounts
- ☐ begin to close down house (don't forget food in fridge)
- ☐ acquire what cash you plan on taking
- ☐ laptop: remove/encrypt any sensitive data; install TrueCrypt
- ☐ wash/dry-clean clothes, treat with Permethrin, store in the dark

2 days before your flight
- [ ] carefully look over packing/planning list
- [ ] confirm unloaded status of firearms as packed for last time
- [ ] confirm presence of: passport, tickets, 4457s, safari folder, $
- [ ] print out all emails from outfitter, hotel, travel agent for folder
- [ ] do any last-minute shopping
- [ ] complete *all* packing, leaving tomorrow for rest and calm
- [ ] place your packed bags by the front door; travel clothes on chair
- [ ] have a farewell dinner with family and friends
- [ ] confirm that 2-3 people will phone you a wake-up call
- [ ] change answering machine/cell phone outgoing messages

the day before your flight
- [ ] set more than one alarm clock (one of them *not* on 110VAC)
- [ ] **have utterly *nothing* left to pack or do before your trip**
- [ ] spend the day in the most relaxing way possible
- [ ] go to bed early enough for at least 7 hours of sleep

the day you leave
- [ ] confirm first thing by phone your flight's status
- [ ] leave early enough to arrive (even in worst traffic) 3 hours <flight
- [ ] relax enroute because you've done everything right and on time
- [ ] **arrive cheerful and excited as your adventure now begins!**

I consider it *vital* that the day before your flight be one of no duties or errands. Spend it reading, relaxing, hiking, watching movies, visiting friends, etc. Thus, you will not feel rushed, and you'll sleep much better.

ONCE YOU'RE IN AFRICA

upon arrival at Johannesburg airport
- ☐ exit Firearms Office with rifle case
- ☐ collect local cell phone from friend or commercial greeter
- ☐ call your PH, and family
- ☐ exchange $100 into local currency *before* domestic check-in
- ☐ check-in for domestic flight, *and stay by your gate*

ONCE YOU RETURN HOME

You're going to naturally be in quite abuzz once you land, and being back home will seem a little odd. (Africa is a powerfully disorienting experience, even when wholly positive.)

Life will readjust pretty easily, but don't be yet another self-absorbed American who forgets all about his new African friends once back home. There is courtesy to maintain and likely promises to keep.

- ☐ inspect your checked bags for any airport staff pilfering
- ☐ pick up your pets
- ☐ change your voice mail outgoing messages
- ☐ don't forget to take the rest of your malaria pills
- ☐ take a day or two off in order to ease back into home life
- ☐ phone/email your outfitter that you arrived home safely
- ☐ notify credit card company of your return, taxidermy $, etc.
- ☐ make sure your rifles are clean
- ☐ wash out your CamelBak water bladder
- ☐ compose a group note of your travel recap
- ☐ add new African friends to your address book, and email them
- ☐ begin to *immediately* follow-up on any promises made there
- ☐ photos: develop, or arrange digital photo folder (w/captions)
- ☐ take out to dinner your fine friends and family
- ☐ distribute all the gift and trinkets you brought back
- ☐ start looking into a broker for your trophies coming in next year
- ☐ be grateful for your trip to Africa, but that you live in America!
- ☐ begin to save money for going back!

Safari Dreams

Kenneth Royce

❖ 19
PACKING CHECKLIST

on your person
neck pouch
- ☐ passport
- ☐ International DL
- ☐ credit card
- ☐ travelers' checks
- ☐ $1000 cash (w/small bills)
- ☐ outbound airline ticket
- ☐ rifle Form 4457

ankle wallet
- ☐ travelers' checks receipts
- ☐ spare credit card
- ☐ copy: passport, DL, 4457

travel vest
- ☐ return airline tickets
- ☐ small notepad and pen
- ☐ digital camera
- ☐ GMRS radio pair half
- ☐ travel folder (see pg. 5/10)
- ☐ digital camera
- ☐ digital voice recorder
- ☐ SureFire flashlight
- ☐ batteries: AA, 3V lithium
- ☐ cell or sat phone
- ☐ bandana
- ☐ 6 energy bars
- ☐ sunglasses

belt pack
- ☐ toothbrush
- ☐ small tube of toothpaste
- ☐ earplugs in a 35mm film
- ☐ inflatable neck pillow
- ☐ blindfold (for sleeping)
- ☐ safety razor
- ☐ shaving cream
- ☐ Bandaids
- ☐ unscented baby wipes
- ☐ eyedrops
- ☐ coughdrops
- ☐ Ziploc with latex gloves
- ☐ hand disinfectant
- ☐ clear spray bottle mister
- ☐ malaria tablets
- ☐ dysentery pills
- ☐ nasal spray
- ☐ *Healthy Travel — Africa*
- ☐ energy bars

small Ziploc with:
- Immodium
- aspirin
- Bandaids
- Neosporin
- antihistamine
- cortisone cream
- moleskin
- toilet paper
- handcleaner
- unscented baby wipes
- eye drops
- GSW bloodclot
- burn gauze

3000in² carry-on pack
- 8x42mm binoculars
- underwear, shirt, socks
- collapsible water jug
- windproof jacket
- hat
- GPS
- S/W radio and earphones
- this copy of *Safari Dreams*
- books (reference, novel)
- 12 energy bars
- mylar Space blanket
- rain poncho

(NOTE: What is on your person and in your carry-on may be *all* you end up with, hence the many survival items listed. Africa is *always* changing, so pack like you're going to a possible war zone.)

hard rifle case
- ☐ rifle(s) in soft case/sleeve
- ☐ ammo in MTM boxes
- ☐ belt knife
- ☐ spare scope (in rings)
- ☐ copies: passport/contact #
- ☐ handheld metal detector
- ☐ Leica rangefinder
- ☐ paper targets
- ☐ spare locks for airport staff

8000in² checked bag
footwear
- ☐ hunting boots
- ☐ sandals/Crocs
- ☐ 4 pair field socks
- ☐ 3 pair town socks
- ☐ gaitors?

clothes
- ☐ 2-3 pairs field pants
- ☐ 2-3 field shirts
- ☐ 6 pair underwear
- ☐ safari hat
- ☐ wool watch cap
- ☐ head net?
- ☐ 2 OD/camo bandanas
- ☐ sweater?
- ☐ fleece or sweat pants
- ☐ gloves (thin/warm/tactile)
- ☐ town clothes
- ☐ tie and blazer (South Africa)
- ☐ swimsuit

misc
- ☐ ammo (if required by airline)
- ☐ gifts for native children
- ☐ gifts for hosts, camp staff
- ☐ camera belt pouch
- ☐ 4oz flask?
- ☐ Frisbee?

hunting belt pouch
- ☐ toilet paper (from MREs)
- ☐ scentless wet wipes
- ☐ stubby driver/bits for rifle
- ☐ Loctite (blue)
- ☐ Boresnake in Ziploc bag
- ☐ bore solvent
- ☐ tiny bottle of gun lube XF7
- ☐ broken shell extractor
- ☐ latex gloves
- ☐ lemon and cough drops
- ☐ tweezer/magnifying glass
- ☐ cigarette lighter
- ☐ compass
- ☐ cigar cutter
- ☐ spare sling swivels

CamelBak M.U.L.E.
- [ ] multitool
- [ ] lots of spare batteries
- [ ] signal mirror
- [ ] orange whistle
- [ ] many energy bars
- [ ] extra ammo
- [ ] Leica rangefinder
- [ ] pen, small notepad
- [ ] antibacterial soap
- [ ] water tablets
- [ ] mini *Perfect Shot* book
- [ ] lens pen
- [ ] takedown cleaning rod
- [ ] broken case extractor
- [ ] roll of electrical tape
- [ ] matches and lighter
- [ ] cable saw
- [ ] length of paracord
- [ ] zip/cable ties
- [ ] Goldbond foot powder
- [ ] AA, AAA, 3V lithium
- [ ] sunglasses and case
- [ ] Ace bandage
- [ ] GMRS radio
- [ ] latex gloves
- [ ] sharpening stone/steel
- [ ] cloth tape measure
- [ ] black Sharpie pen
- [ ] Fisher Space pen
- [ ] pencil
- [ ] waxed dental floss
- [ ] cigars
- [ ] spare sling
- [ ] sunscreen
- [ ] DEET
- [ ] chapstick with sunblock
- [ ] moisturizing cream

❖ 20

FOR WOMEN ONLY

Last, and certainly not least, are some thoughts and info for you huntresses out there (God bless you!). I saved your chapter for last to encapsulate much of *Safari Dreams* for you. I will hit the highlights of rifles, gear, etc.

While safari hunting is predominantly a man's sport, women are quickly discovering what Paleolithic hunters have known and enjoyed for millennia.

CLOTHING

Sure, you could dress in men's camo, but you'd look like a sort of dumpy boy, and there's no joy in that for anybody!

Resist the temptation to dress too ornately; keep it as simple as possible. You want good fitting, fairly loose, but rugged clothes. (Forsake the gun side earring as it can interfere with a good cheekweld.)

Safari apparel for women has exploded since 2000, and you've many sources for stylish, rugged clothing. These companies should have what you'll need to look good and hunt well. (If not, then create your *own* line. Others have!)

www.shehunts.com
www.highmaintenancecamo.com
www.foxyhunters.com
www.shesafari.com

CALIBERS & RIFLES

You'll be pleased that I will spare you the repetition of 80 pages previously written. Your choices are fewer and simpler.

plains game calibers

Most ladies should be able to comfortably shoot a 180gr .308, if not a 200gr .30-06. This will be sufficient for any plains game (even eland at 75-100yds). If the .308/.30-06 seems to recoil too much, have some reduced handloads made for you (but keep muzzle velocity at least 2200fps with a 200gr bullet, and stalk within 100yds).

If a reduced load .308/.30-06 is still too much gun, then try a 7-08 or 7x57. That's the lightest caliber I can in good conscience recommend for Africa plains game such as kudu and gemsbok. Truly, you should work yourself up to handling at least a .308 with comfort and confidence.

Whatever your caliber choice, use either Barnes TSX or Swift A-Frame bullets and you can't go wrong. (Northfork and A-Square are also fine, but less commonly available. Skip everything else, for simplicity's sake.) Load the heaviest common weight for your caliber, such as 175gr for 7mm and 200gr for .308/.30-06.

plains game rifles

You will want to "resonate" with your gun, regardless. While I don't care for Rem 700s, Ruger M77s, and Browning A-Bolts... *you* might, and there's nothing wrong with that.

If I could recommend one rifle to you, it would be a Winchester Model 70 Classic. (The "Classic" means a modern reincarnation of the "pre-1964" version which was prized for its quality and reliability since the 1930s.) Try an M70 at the range. If you like it, *stop there* and forget about the myriad of other rifle choices, as you won't be missing anything better.

Your M70 can be perfectly customized to your body and tastes with a variety of different stocks, scope bases, slings, etc. Avoid a stainless rifle unless you will have it coated to eliminate the shiny glare.

plains game scope

You just can't go wrong with **Leupold VX-III**. A 3-9x variable is the *most* you'll need, and probably not even that much, as a 2-7x is lighter (and 7x is plenty). Even a 1¾-6x will do just fine.

If you're a good shot and fancy longer distances, then seriously consider a **Shepherd 310-P2** scope. Such is very nice on a .30-06 for anything on the planet short of bear and DG. It's my ideal for a general-purpose light rifle.

buffalo calibers

Regarding a buffalo rifle, you probably will find the .375 H&H all the gun you want to carry/shoot. It is adequate for buffalo, but only adequate, so shoot it well. To do that, you must have practiced with it for at least 100 rounds, if not 200-300. Make sure that the stock length is not excessive, and that the rifle feels "right" in your hands.

Again, regarding, bullets: caliber-heavy Barnes TSX or Swift A-Frame. All other discussion is just guy-talk academics.

buffalo rifles

For the money, get a Winchester Model 70 Classic (or a pre-64 in .375 H&H). Just *trust* me on this. Yes, a CZ 550 is less money, and Rugers may be more common. But just trust me that Winchester is the way to go.

Have a quality stock (laminated wood or fiberglass) custom fitted for you, with a generously thick recoil pad.

buffalo rifle scope

Pick a scope with *lots* of eye relief (at least 4"), so that you won't get "bit" by the ocular lens ring easily. Leupold is known for long eye relief (and superb quality), and I strongly recommend their VX-III 1¾-6x32mm in *matte* finish.

Use Talley (or Leupold) rings and bases.

bolt manipulation

The more "one" you are with your rifle, the better you will hunt because your bolt work will already be natural.

It's vital that you be *totally unafraid* of your DG rifle. Neither its weight, balance, or recoil must bother you, else you'll tend to shoot it poorly.

MISC. GEAR

binoculars
The less experienced your game eye, the better your binos must be. Don't skimp on quality; spend at least $500 for something *very* nice. Such seems like a lot of money, but quality binos are precision optical instruments which will last a lifetime. Think of them as *heirloom* goods, like custom furniture.

laser rangefinder
Any model from Leica is a jewel, especially their newest compact 1200 yard version.

MISC. CONSIDERATIONS

meet your outfitter and PH at SCI!
Women are naturally more attune to nuance and character than most men, and thus you'll want to *meet* the people who are so directly key to your safari experience.

Go to an SCI convention in Reno and talk to many prospects for your trip. When you encounter the right outfitter with the right PH for you, you'll know it.

training with your rifle
Most boyfriends and husbands cannot train their ladies well because the relationship is too personal. (Either he turns into your gruff dad, or you turn into his emotional daughter.)

So, *expect* that you'll likely have to find somebody else for shooting and field lessons. An uncle or grandfather could be ideal, if not your own father.

Barring a relative, just *pay* for quality training from www.gunsite.com and their two rifle courses (270 General Rifle and Hunter Prep). Those 8 days of training cost about $2900 (about as much as your total airfare to South Africa), but your hunting and marksmanship skill will be very solid.

High Country Adventures
This is a recommended conduit for women into African hunting, and they would be very helpful in arranging for your first safari. You can meet them at SCI in January.

❖ 21
RESOURCES

BOOKS & VIDEOS
books
Safari Press (www.safaripress.com)
    This is a great place to start for your African library. They offer many books not found elsewhere.

The Perfect Shot, Kevin Robertson
    A PH and veterinary, Robertson's color photo book is a classic. A must for every African hunter. While my PH and I believe some of his recommended shots are a tad too high, such is merely our own opinions.
    Also available in pocket-size.

Meditations on Hunting, Ortega ý Gasset
    The hunter's Old Testament Scripture; a beautiful work. Explains why men have always hunted, and always will. Out of print, but any big gun show will have bookseller with a $30-60 copy. (I paid $35 for a used *library* copy!) Do not go to Africa without reading this first!

Safari: A Chronicle of Adventure, Bartle Bull
    A beautifully written and pictured history of the African safari. Many bio chapters from Livingstone to Selous to TR to Robin Hurt. Great background reading!

Green Hills of Africa, Ernest Hemingway
    His only nonfiction book. Some useful insights.

The Short, Happy Life of Francis Macomber, Hemingway
Papa used PH Harry Selby (and others) as his composite.

African Game Trails, Theodore Roosevelt
"I speak of Africa and golden joys"; the joy of wandering through lonely lands; the joy of hunting the mighty and terrible lords of the wilderness, the cunning, the wary, and the grim.

In 1909 TR contracted with the Nairobi firm of Newland and Tarlton for a 9-*month* hunt all over British East Africa (what is now Kenya) with son Kermit. Meeting them in Mombasa was F.C. Selous himself (who would die from a German bullet eight years later in WWI). TR and Kermit took hundreds of game, many of which are now at the Smithsonian Institution Museums in Washington, D.C.

TR hunted with a 3-rifle battery: an M1903 .30-06 Springfield (now at the Springfield Armory Museum), a Winchester Model 1895 in .405 (now at the Cody, Wyoming museum), and a Holland & Holland .500/.450 Nitro Express double (now also in a museum).

I am privileged to own an original 1910 printing of this classic, a gift from my mother. Its 582 pages sag with photos and wonderful prose of a hunt impossible to duplicate today. Simply marvelous!

Horn of the Hunter, Robert Ruark
Hunting in northern Tanzania in the 1950s. Wonderful! Ruark is a great stylist and highly enjoyable to read.

Robert Ruark's Africa
A posthumous collection of many of Ruark's 1950s magazine articles. Most enjoyable.

The Hunter and the Go-Away Bird, Stephen J. Smith   Zimbi Books
The founder of PHASA, Smith was one of the PH greats. Great reading and historical background to the safari industry.

Safari Hunter, Elmer Keith
Out of print and rare, but a must for any safari library by one of the greatest riflemen of American history.

The Politically Incorrect Guide to Hunting, Frank Miniter
Written for American hunters, it's chock-full of great info.

White Hunters, Brian Herne
   A superb book covering East African safari history and PHs since the 1930s. Abounds with many great tales. Written by an experienced PH. A must.

African Hunter II, Craig Boddington, Peter Flack   (Safari Press)
   This is a sequel to the 1975 *African Hunter* by James Mellon. A luxurious color coffee-table book covering every hunting country in Africa. Beautifully done, with excellent photos, details, and stories. Not cheap at $135, but a real treasure. I'd splurge on this if I were you. This is the book that clinched my going to Africa as early as I did.

Gargantuan Gunsite Gossip (2 vols.), Jeff Cooper   (Gunsite Press)
   While not an African safari book, much on the subject is randomly contained therein. These two books helped to whet my appetite for big game.
   Although his favorite .460 G&A has been totally eclipsed by the .458 Lott, he was ballistically correct in his 500gr/.458/2300fps values. I've fired his custom CZ 602 ("Baby") after it was repatriated from the RSA in 2006. Quite the rifle.
   The *GGG*s are chock-full of tidbits on life and living, shooting, history, etc. A feast of reading enjoyment by a unique man who contributed much to my thinking. His several other books all contain tidbits on Africa, and are well worth reading for their own sakes.

Safari: The Last Adventure, Peter Hathaway Capstick
   Dated (1984), but rife with great advice and tips. His unique sling position (weak side, muzzle up, rifle to front) I've never seen elsewhere. Out of print, but very helpful.

African Lives, Denis Boyles

Safari Guide, Richard Conrad   (Safari Press)
   A bit fat on personal anecdotes which, though generally interesting, are of little help as a guide. Still, it's a worthwhile book for the first-timer. Prices are outdated.

Solo Safari, Terrance Cacek   (Safari Press)
   Not that newbies should hunt buff in Zimbabwe without a PH, it can be done when you're experienced. Worth reading to

more appreciate your PH and camp staff! They *well* earn their daily rate and tips.

Horned Death, John Burger
    Considered the bible on hunting buffalo. Outdated, but the great stories are well worth the price.

African Rifles and Cartridges, John Taylor   (Safari Press)
    The classic. "Pondoro" set the elephant minimum as .458/500gr at 2400fps and to him anything less is a compromise.

Buffalo!, Craig Boddington   (Safari Press)
    A must for any buffalo hunter by a most experienced man. Lavishly color pictured, and very thorough.

Safari Rifles, Craig Boddington   (Safari Press)
    If I didn't write enough about rifles here, buy this book. Great information especially on doubles. Prices are dated.

Dangerous Game Rifles, Terry Wieland   www.countrysportpress.com
    Excellent recent (2006) book with a Foreword by renowned Tanzanian PH Robin Hurt. I learned a lot from this book, though disagree with Wieland's take on the .416s.

Any Shot You Want, A-Square   (available from Brownells)
    Reloading, hunting, bullet design, cartridge comparison, etc. A treasure trove for any rifleman, and one of the most useful books I own! Art Alphin is a true ballistics pioneer.

Safari Dreams: A Practical Guide To Your Hunt In Africa, Kenneth Royce
                                                www.javelinpress.com
    A unique compendium for the novice/intermediate safari hunter, collecting advice and wisdom from the masters, along with Royce's experiences over three trips to Africa. With this one book a quality outfitter and PH, you will have a great safari!

The Safari Companion: A Guide to Watching African Mammals,
            Richard D. Estes,   (Safari Press)
    This insight to behavior of game will enrich your hunt.

African Wildlife and Safari Guide, Eddie and Nicki Young
    An excellent reference work.

Tanzania, Mary Fitzpatrick (The Lonely Planet)
This guide was all I needed to assure myself of a fun trip in 2005. I found its info helpful and accurate. Buy a copy and plan your stay. The only beef I had with this book was its patent snubbing of hunting. To the author, safaris are cameras only. If you compare what hunters contribute (at $700+/day) to wildlife preservation, it is obvious that mere photographic tourism cannot come close. African game is protected by *hunting*, not by sappy liberals who take photos of quarter-tame critters from tour buses.

The Accurate Reloading Africa Book
6"x9", softcover, 174pp. (28 color plates), $30ppd.
California residents please include $1.88 for sales tax.
You can pay by credit card through PayPal to the account of dwbieber@earthlink.net
David Bieber
P.O. Box 1586
El Dorado, CA 95623

Profits go to the Cullman and Hurt Community Wildlife Project in Tanzania. The Cullman and Hurt Community Wildlife Project was originally founded by Professional Hunter Robin Hurt, and supports educational efforts to encourage local communities to take part in conserving their indigenous wildlife.

(Royce note: I've not yet read this book, but the forum of accuratereloading.com is an excellent one.)

book sources:
Randy Duckett Publications
www.redgunbooks.com
719.510.8919

www.ks-militaria.com
915.837.5053

videos

www.outdoorvisions.com

Out of Africa (Best Picture, 1985)
From a true story that took place in 1913-1920 Kenya. A bit sappy and overdone, but the cinemaphotography is lovely, especially the flying scenes and long shots. And rifles are correctly featured as part of daily life in the bush. Meryl Streep did a superb job, but Redford (as always) played Redford.

In The Blood (1986)
Great hunting film featuring Theodore Roosevelt's famous Holland & Holland .500/.450 Nitro Express and two of his descendents, TR-4 (a Manhattan investment banker) and TR-5 (his 8 y/o son). PH Robin Hurt (whom I met at SCI 2007, *"one of the good guys"* according to my PH) led the 21-day hunt. This film sparked my first interest in Africa years ago. A very good introduction to your friends/family who are squeamish or even anti-hunting.

Boddington on Buffalo (2004)   www.craigboddington.com
The renowned modern hunter travels to the Zambezi Valley with a Dakota .375 H&H to chronicle the hunting of Cape buffalo.

by Kenneth Royce (Boston T. Party)

You & The Police!   (revised for 2005)

The definitive guide to your rights and tactics during police confrontations. When can you *refuse* to answer questions or consent to searches? Don't lose your liberty through ignorance! This 2005 edition covers the *USA PATRIOT Act* and much more.
    168 pp. softcover (2005) $16 + $5 s&h (cash, please)

Bulletproof Privacy
How to Live Hidden, Happy, and Free!

Explains precisely how to lay low and be left alone by the snoops, government agents and bureaucrats. Boston shares many of his own unique methods. Now in its 10th printing!
    160 pp. softcover (1997) $16 + $5 s&h (cash, please)

Hologram of Liberty
The Constitution's Shocking Alliance with Big Government

The Convention of 1787 was the most brilliant and subtle *coup d'état* in history. The nationalist framers *designed* a strong government, guaranteed through purposely ambiguous verbiage. Many readers say this is Boston's best book. A jaw-dropper.
    262 pp. softcover (1997) $20 + $5 s&h (cash, please)

Boston on Surviving Y2K
And Other Lovely Disasters

Even though Y2K was Y2¿Qué? this title remains highly useful for preparedness planning. **Now on sale for 50% off!** (It's the same book as The Military Book Club's *Surviving Doomsday*.)
    352 pp. softcover (1998) only $11 + $5 s&h (cash, please)

Boston's Gun Bible   (new text for 2006)

A rousing how-to/*why*-to on our modern gun ownership. Firearms are *"liberty's teeth"* and it's time we remembered it. No other general gun book is more thorough or useful! Indispensable!
    848 pp. softcover (2002-2006) $33 + $6 s&h (cash, please)

Molôn Labé!   (a novel)

If you liked *Unintended Consequences* by John Ross and Ayn Rand's *Atlas Shrugged*, then Boston's novel will be a favorite. It dramatically outlines an innovative recipe for Liberty which could actually work! A thinking book for people of action; an action book for people of thought. It's getting people moving to Wyoming!
    454 pp. softcover (2004) $27 + $6 s&h (cash, please)
    limited edition hardcover $44 + $6 (while supplies last)

Safari Dreams   (new for 2008!)
A Practical Guide To Your Hunt In Africa

Possibly the most useful "one book" for making your first safari. Thoroughly covers: rifles, calibers, bullets, insurance, health, packing and planning, trip prep, airlines, choosing your PH, shot placement, and being in the bush. Don't go to Africa without it!
    352 pp. softcover, 100 color photos (Jan 2008) $30 + $5

www.javelinpress.com
www.freestatewyoming.org

www.javelinpress.com

NOTE: Javelin Press is enjoying rapid growth, which may affect our address or pricing. Please verify both from our website *before* you send your order!

Prices each copy:	Retail	<40%>	<44%>	<50%>
You & The Police! 5½"x8½" 168 pp. 2/2005	1-5 copies $16	6-37 $10	38-75 $8.80	case of 76 or more $8
Bulletproof Privacy 5½"x8½" 160 pp. 1/1997	1-5 copies $16	6-39 $10	40-79 $8.80	case of 80 or more $8
Hologram of Liberty 5½"x8½" 262 pp. 8/1997	1-5 copies $20	6-19 $12	20-39 $11	case of 40 or more $10
Boston on Surviving Y2K 5½"x8½" 352 pp. 11/1998	1-5 copies $11	6-17 $10	18-35 $9	case of 36 or more $8
Boston's Gun Bible 5½"x8½" 848 pp. 4/2002	1-2 copies $33	3-7 $19.80	8-15 $18.48	case 16 or more $17.50
Molôn Labé! 5½"x8½" 454 pp. 1/2004	1-5 copies $27	6-13 $16.20	14-27 $15.12	case 28 or more $13.50
Safari Dreams 5½"x8½" 352 pp. 1/2008	1-5 copies $30	(see website after Jan 2008 for discount details)		

Mix titles for *any* quantity discount. This is easiest done as ¼ case per title:
¼ case of: **Y&P!** 19 **BP** 20 **HoL** 10 **BoSY** 9 **BGB** 4 **ML!** 7

Shipping and Handling are *not* included! Add below:

non-case S&H for Boston's Gun Bible Molôn Labé! :
First Class (or UPS for less-than-case) add: $6 for first copy, $2 each additional copy.

non-case S&H within USA for other titles (*i.e., Y&P!, BP, HoL, BoSY, SD*):
First Class (or UPS for larger orders) add: $5 for first copy, $1 each additional copy.

CASE orders (straight or mixed) UPS Ground: $30 west of the Miss.; $40 east.

Overpayment will be refunded in cash with order. Underpayment will delay order! If you have questions on discounts or S&H, email us through our website.

These forms of payment *only:*

Cash (Preferred. Cash orders receive signed copies when available.)
payee blank M.O.s (Which makes them more easily negotiable.)
credit cards (Many of our distributors take them. See our website.)

Unless prior agreement has been made, *we do not accept and will return* checks, C.O.D.s, filled-in M.O.s, or any other form of tender. Prices and terms are subject to change without notice (check our website first). Please send paid orders to:

JAVELIN PRESS ● c/o P.O. Box 31 ● Ignacio, Colorado. (81137-0031)